IF THESE STONES COULD SPEAK

The
History and People
Of
The Old Salem Burying Point

❧

DANIEL FURY

Salem, Massachusetts

BLACK CAT TOURS PRESS
MMXXI

For my grandfather, Daniel Woods,
who taught me to appreciate quiet walks in a cemetery

"*This graveyard was the most ancient in the town... Here, the sods had covered the faces of men known to history, and reverenced when not a piece of distinguishable dust remained of them; personages whom tradition told about; and here, mixed up with successive crops of native-born Americans, had been ministers, captains, matrons, virgins, good and evil, tough and tender, turned up and battened down by the sexton's spade, over and over again; until every blade of grass had its relations with the human brotherhood of the old town.*"

- NATHANIEL HAWTHORNE

Table Of Contents

ACKNOWLEDGEMENTS

The author would be remiss not to acknowledge the contributions of the many individuals who have committed time, effort, assistance, and research that has helped facilitate the creation of this book.

Especially deserving of acknowledgment are Alex Ayube, Elizabeth DuPré, Maureen Fisher, Elizabeth Frost, Jennifer Hornsby, Jeffrey Horton, Patricia Kelleher, Thomas O'Brien Vallor, Jeff Page, Everett Philbrook, Jen Ratliff, and Ilene Simons, Salem City Clerk.

Gratitude to the people whose efforts both inspired and enabled the writing of this book, David & Paul Stickney, Rev. William Bentley, and the Maple Tree Fellowship.

To my parents, Sue and Don Swain, for their love and support in all my pursuits. To my other parents, Tom and Kristin Jay, for their love and help with this book and all of our crazy ideas.

A stupendously special thank you and acknowledgment to my editor, designer, and amazing wife, Lara Fury, whose dedication, passion, support, and diligence has helped to make this book the best it can be. Lara's work creating the Burial Index is a monumental contribution to Salem history. Without your help, this book would not be possible. Also, love to my constant feline writing companions, Ebi-chan, Muta, Rameses, and as of this revision, The Twins: Hikaru and Kaoru.

This 2022 edition also includes revisions to several entries requiring updates. Thank you to readers Renee O. and Rachel S. Due to the expansive nature of this work, we appreciate any updated information or corrections from readers.

HODIE MIHI CRAS TIBI

(Today me, tomorrow you)

CHRISTIAN WIFE

TO RICHARD MORE

AGED 60 YEARS

DEC^D MARCH y^e 18

1   6   7   6

INTRODUCTION

When I began my research into the history of the Old Salem Burying Point, I was surprised at how little had been written about this unique site. To the early inhabitants of Salem, it was a place to bury the dead and reflect on their own mortality. In later years, it became a place to build monuments to the deceased, decorated with images of beauty and words of sorrow. To modern residents, it is a silent relict, often forgotten until its dusty paths fill with Halloween tourists. It is not uncommon today to hear a visitor wonder aloud if the cemetery is even real.

The Old Salem Burying Point (also known as the Charter Street Cemetery) is a place shrouded in myth and mystery. To many, it must seem strange and otherworldly; a place frozen in time where you find yourself surrounded by remnants of the past. Cold, grey stones engraved with eyeless skulls sit amongst the gnarled trees, and an eerie quiet sits heavily in the air as you shiver at the thought of the skeletal remains beneath your feet. The epithets, more often than not, seek to warn that you yourself will someday share the fate of the person whose name is etched forever in slate.

However, these stones are not merely a marker of death, they commemorate the lives of people who walked these same Salem streets as us nearly four hundred years ago. Their stories are those of the everyday and the extraordinary, the mundane and the magnificent. This historic cemetery, dating back to 1637, has seen Salem's harsh early days, times of both peace and war with the Native Americans, the infamous Salem Witch Trials, the American Revolution, Salem's maritime trading boom, and the devastating Great Salem Fire of 1914. These stones have stood largely unchanged as the fields around them became farms, mills, houses, factories, shops, and museums. They stood by silently as the great South

River was filled in by human hands and replaced by Derby Street, named for one of those buried beneath the earth here.

As a Salem historian and tour guide, I have exhaustively researched this fascinating historical site. Much of what was written in previous centuries is lost or out of print, and even records are hard to come by, and often inaccurate. This book is the culmination of that research, and is something I had wished existed when I began to try and learn more about this unique cemetery and the many people whose lives are commemorated in the place where their bones are interred.

As Nathaniel Hawthorne, whose own ancestors are buried here, inferred, there may be only dust remaining of this old town's earliest inhabitants, but their memories come alive again in the telling of their stories. This book will help give you insight on death and life in Old Salem, and I hope that it will show you that an old cemetery such as this is as much a place of life and laughter as it is of death and sorrow. The complete history of Salem may be found here, in the lives of the men and women who are interred beneath the green grass. Just imagine the stories these stones could tell us.

THIS BROKEN TOMBSTONE FOR JOHN NOURSE SITS
BETWEEN THE CROMWELL AND WARD SECTIONS

CEMETERY PRESERVATION

As you might imagine, the tombstones in the Old Burying Point have suffered the effects of their environment. Age, lichen growth, vandalism, acid rain, and many other factors, have caused the loss of many tombstones in this cemetery. The reason why Salem has several well-maintained historic cemeteries today is through the preservation efforts of the City of Salem, and many groups of concerned residents, currently including the Friends of the Downtown Salem Historic Cemeteries, and the Friends of the Broad Street Cemetery. Preservation experts have worked to repair broken stones and table-tops, reset stones that have sunk, created frames for damaged historical stones, and made new bases for table-tops.

Most of the gravestones are much larger than they appear, and may sink into the ground just as far down as they appear from the top. When one of these gravestones break, a new, concrete base is created. If the stone has broken and the pieces can be found, the stone will be fastened together again, and an adhesive used to fuse the piece back in place. When cemetery conservation began in the 19th century, the methods available were not as advanced as they are today, and in some cases, modern preservationists need to upgrade the correction.

From the 17th century to the present, it has been the duty of visitors and residents to avoid causing damage while walking through these ancient grounds. For this and any historic cemetery, please bear in mind the following:

- Adhere to marked paths. The paths laid down through historic cemeteries have been set where they are for a reason and going outside of those paths may pose a risk to the site, and perhaps your own safety.

- Do not enter a historic cemetery after dark. Salem restricts entry for visitors to cemeteries from dusk until dawn. This protects both the cemetery and visitors from harm.

- Do not take gravestone rubbings or clay castings. Most historic cemeteries prohibit gravestone rubbings as it causes damage over time. These days, taking pictures with your smartphone will produce better results than any rubbing. It is much more common practice to use color-changing effects to clearly read the inscription on a stone, and this causes no damage to gravestones.

- Do not touch any of the tombstones or table-tops. The natural oil on your hands will actually damage the stones, and could eventually erase the names.
- Do not attempt to do any restoration work, cleaning, or use any chemicals on a stone, without the express permission of the cemetery.

- Do not bring your dog into a historic cemetery. It goes without saying that dogs do not care if a tombstone is an artifact of historical significance. If your dog marks a stone, it will cause damage, among other things.

- Do not bring food or snacks into a historic cemetery. A capped bottle of water is recommended. While picnics in cemeteries were common in the Victorian age, historic cemeteries discourage this practice with good reason. Littering will not only ruin a cemetery's aesthetic and make more work for the staff, it will also endanger local wildlife.

- Do not approach any animals in the cemetery. In the Old Burying Point, it is common to see squirrels, birds, skunks and other small animals.

Conservation efforts in the Old Burying Point are ongoing, and by respecting the cemetery rules and being careful not to expose the tombstones to risk, you will be participating in keeping this historic site preserved for future generations.

THE INSCRIPTION ON THIS MARBLE TOMBSTONE IS
COMPLETELY LOST, LARGELY DUE TO THE AFFECTS
OF ACID RAIN

2021 Cemetery Map

THE OLD BURYING POINT
~ Map Key ~

1 - Derby Tomb Section

2 - Charter Street Section

3- Grimshawe Section

4 - 1922 Map

5 - Gedney Tomb

6 - Shattock Section

7 - McIntire Section

8 - Lynde Tomb

9 - Bowditch Section

10 - Hathorne Section

11 - More Section

12 - Robert Peele Lot

13 - Pickman/Toppan Tomb

14 - Bradstreet Tomb

15 - Ropes Section

16 - Ward Section

17 - Cromwell Section and
Pierce Tombs

18 - Turner Tomb

19 - Hollingworth Section

20 - Gardner Section

LOCATIONS ARE
LABELLED ACCORDING TO
SECTIONS OF THE BOOK

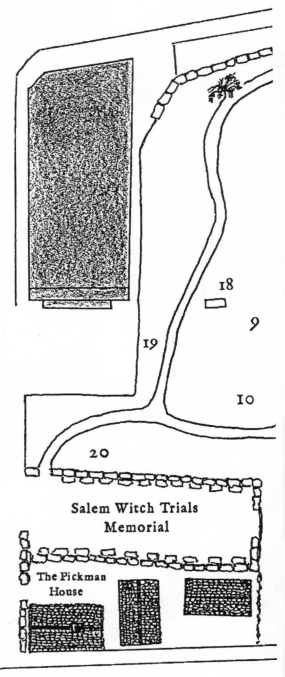

18

9

19

10

20

Salem Witch Trials
Memorial

The Pickman
House

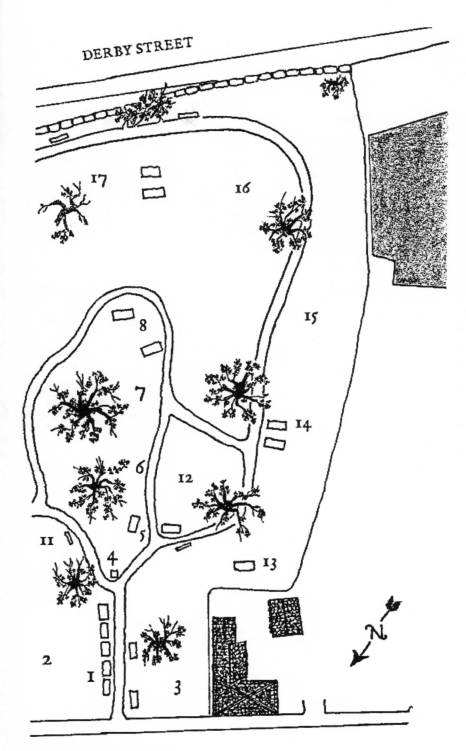

DERBY STREET

CHARTER STREET

MAP PROVIDED BY THOMAS AND KRISTIN JAY

Courtesy of the Phillips Library Collection

THE OLD BURYING POINT
CHARTER STREET GATE

CIRCA 1865-1914

WHEN USING THIS BOOK AS A GUIDE

This book will be written in such a way that Salem history lovers may use it as a guide through this ancient and fascinating cemetery. It will be laid out so that you may use it as a reference when entering the cemetery yourself, or if you are walking through its iron gates only in your own imagination. As there are no official names given to the sections of the cemetery and, as of yet, no names for the paths themselves; the areas will be identified by the names of prominent families or individuals interred in that section. For instance, the section titled "Hathorne" will have prominent members of the Hathorne family, however, not every person buried there is a Hathorne. Tombs serve as an excellent landmark and are easily identifiable, so the names of tombs will frequently be used to identify a specific area.

This journey through the Old Burying Point will begin at the Charter Street entrance. Starting at the 1922 large bronze map displaying graves of historical significance, we will first traverse the inner path which makes a small circle through the center of the cemetery. This path will bring us back to the map, where we will then take the second path which goes along the outer area of the cemetery and exits at the Witch Trials Memorial. The locations of the sections will be marked on the map provided in this book. Please note that this is currently the reverse of the entrance/exit that the Visitor's Center is utilizing, as this book was mostly complete prior to their announcement of intended use of the Memorial as the main entrance.

The majority of the photographs in this book were taken prior to the 2020 closure of the cemetery, some are even from over a century earlier. The landscape and the quality of the stones may have changed by the time of your visit. However, it is expected that all tombstones will remain in these locations unless removed for restoration.

Entries for persons buried in the cemetery will be written with the name bolded if they are a subject of the passage, along with the date of their birth, or baptism if the birth record is unknown, as baptismal records were usually more well-documented than births. Following the birth or baptism date will be the date of death or burial, whichever could be more definitively confirmed. If a birth, death, etc., date is uncertain, the closest possible month and/or year will be provided with an "abt." for "about." The format will look like this: **John Doe** (b. Jun 6, 1786, d. Apr 4, 1843). A married woman will have her maiden name listed in parentheses, such as **Jane (Jones) Doe** (b. abt. May, 1782, d. Jul 14, 1850). If a widow's maiden name is unknown, but her deceased husbands' is, the maiden name section will carry the prefix wd.

If you are interested in learning more about planning a trip to Salem's historic cemeteries, make sure to contact the Friends of the Downtown Salem Historic Cemeteries at www.salemcemeteries.org or email info@salemcemeteries.org. You may also view information and upcoming events for the new Charter Street Cemetery Welcome Center at www.charterstreetcemetery.com

THE
·BURYING·
POINT
1637

The Oldest Burying Ground In
The City Of Salem

Here Are Buried

Capt. Richard More
Mayflower Passenger

Justice John Hathorne
Of The Witchcraft Court

Samuel McIntire
Architect

Gov. Simon Bradstreet

Chief Justice Benjamin Lynde

• Rev. John Higginson •

Donated By: PEM

THIS HISTORIC SIGN, PROVIDED BY THE
PEABODY ESSEX MUSEUM, WAS REMOVED IN 2020
THERE ARE CURRENTLY NO PLANS TO RETURN IT
TO THE CEMETERY

THE OLD BURYING POINT
CHARTER STREET GATE 2021

History of The Old Salem Burying Point

The Old Salem Burying Point may well be America's oldest maintained European colonial cemetery. It was in 1637 that this plot of land was officially set aside for the burial of the dead, however, burials were likely taking place here more than a decade earlier. Originally, only the area closest to modern-day Derby Street would have been used for burials.

It was in 1630, or possibly earlier, that this quiet spot on the river was chosen to become the final resting place for the early English settlers of Salem. No date is recorded for the first interment, nor is any name given to the first person to be buried here. It may have been one of the early colonists who arrived with Roger Conant in 1626. Thomas Dudley, who arrived in Salem in 1630 with Governor John Winthrop, wrote, "We found the colony in a sad and unexpected condition, above eighty of them being dead the winter before, and many of those alive weak, and sick. All the corn and bread amongst them all, hardly sufficient to feed them a fortnight insomuch that the remainder of a hundred and eighty servants we had the two years before sent over, coming to us for victuals to sustain them, we found ourselves wholly unable to feed them."

It has long been supposed that the earliest burials here may have been members of the Winthrop fleet, such as Lady Arbella Johnson, for whom Winthrop's ship *Arbella* was named. Perhaps it was the "Minister of the Wilderness" Reverend Francis Higginson, who is credited with having named the town "Salem," after the Hebrew word *Shalom*, and also died shortly after the arrival in Salem. No stone or marker remains for these early interments. In those days, headstones were not common in colonial America. Instead, 'coffin rails' would likely have been placed over the burial site. These were essentially small wooden stumps placed at the head and foot of the grave with a wooden rail running between them.

In 1637, a small path to the burying point was cut along modern-day Central Street, down the western side of the Point along the river. In 1662, the selectmen allowed the land between the Burying Point and the South River to be sold. Fourteen men purchased the lots abutting the cemetery and there built wharves and shops. By 1668, Salem had grown significantly, and the land set aside for the Burying Point became too small to take on the deceased of the town. Additional land to the north of the original site was deeded from Henry Bartholemew in 1668, which started at the area of the Bradstreet tomb on the west, to the Bowditch section. Land to the east of the Point was donated by Edward Grove on August 29, 1669, which runs along Liberty Street from the Hathorne plot to up to the Derby Street wall. A small section to the northeast of the original site was deeded by Samuel Pickman on November 26, 1669, which became the Gardner section, and created a new entrance for the cemetery at Liberty Street.

As early as 1711, there was concern about the effects of erosion on the seaside cemetery. At a general meeting, the town selectmen (including Philip English, Stephen Sewall, Walter Price, and Joseph Orne) expressed concern that the cemetery was "daily washed away by high tides and storms." They proposed a "suitable highway for cart and horse to the south" of the burying place. A proposal was also made that the owners of the land between the cemetery and the river construct a wall high enough to prevent the water from reaching the graves. The situation grew more desperate in 1714, as a fence that had been constructed was torn down in a storm, and the selectmen offered the land for free to anyone who could wharf the area and build "a good stone wall to secure the bank from tumbling down." In 1718, the selectmen (now Price, Samuel Brown, Jonathan Ashby, and James Lindall) voted to divide the land up among themselves in order to complete the project.

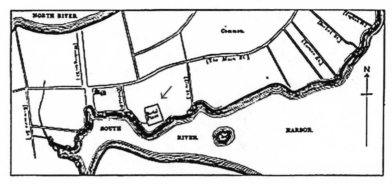

The illustration above shows where the Old Burying Point was located on the South River. Before the river was filled in, the burial point was a short distance from the edge of the water.

This map shows how the shore around the Old Burying Point was cut up into fourteen lots in the 1660s. These lots were owned by the Bartholemews, Gedneys, Brownes, Gardners, Hathornes, and other merchants, who built shops, wharves, and warehouses along the river. These illustrations are from Sidney Perley's The History of Salem, Massachusetts, Vol. 2

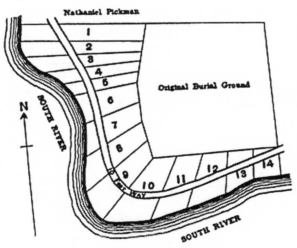

GRANTS AT BURYING POINT

The cemetery was further enlarged to the north on June 13, 1767, when land deeded from William Lander and Joseph Mottey was added, opening the area from the bronze map location down to Charter Street, connecting the cemetery with Charter Street, and creating a new entrance. By 1789, neighbors surrounding the Burying Point (including the Morongs and Ashbys) had built a number of encumbrances and encroachments onto the land, such as fences and "lintoes" (lean-tos). The selectmen voted to have these torn down, though they would later reconsider this action and tasked the abutters to assist in building a sea wall, showing the erosion problem was not yet solved. By 1811, the town committed to verify the true bounds of the cemetery to prevent any further encroachments.

In 1841, plans were made to build a large retaining wall along the west side of the cemetery. This wall may be seen to this day from the corner of Central Street and Derby Street, then continuing down Derby Street toward Liberty Street. This coincided with the decision to fill in this section of the South River and Mill Pond in order to develop the land for more homes and businesses, as Salem became a more industrialized city. By then, the days of the Burying Point being an active cemetery were coming to an end. There was very little space left in the cemetery, graves were being reused and caskets stacked on top of one another. By the late 1800s, special permission was required for burials, the majority of which were in reused tombs. The decision was made to cease burials, and newer cemeteries at Howard Street (1801), Green Lawn (1807), and Harmony Grove (1839) became the resting place of Salem's residents. The final burial in Charter Street seems to have taken place in October of 1882, which was Elizabeth Peele Ropes, and the last person entombed was likely William Bowditch, who was placed in the Turner tomb in May, 1896.

As Salem passed its bicentennial, there came a renewed interest in the city's unique history, specifically in the Salem Witch Trials of 1692. In 1892, the city embraced the growing interest in the witch hysteria and adopted the moniker of the "Witch City." The historic burial ground began to become a great point of interest to visitors. In 1894, restoration work began on the tombs and headstones. Three hundred gravestones were re-set and restored. Thousands of letters were re-cut into their stones, bringing the lost names and epithets to life once again. Table-top tombs were reset on top of new brick foundations. One year prior, the city filled in depressions in the cemetery grounds using street sweepings. In 1847, city funds had been used to plant deciduous trees, evergreens and shrubs throughout the cemetery. Maple trees would be planted in 1925.

In 1922, a large stone with a metal tablet was placed near the Charter Street entrance, marking the locations of graves of "Greatest Historical Interest." This tablet still exists today, though it contains several inaccuracies (see 1922 Map section). Another round of repairs to the tombstones occurred in 1949 and 1953, with stones being re-set and straightened. Repair work, restoration and preservative maintenance continues on these historic stones today, necessitating full closures of the cemetery to the public in 2016 and again from 2019 to 2021.

In the fall of 2020, the cemetery began its largest restoration since 1894. The old dirt paths were replaced by crushed stone walkways looping through the cemetery. Stairs were placed at the Charter Street entrance, and a handicapped-accessible ramp at the Witch Trials Memorial entrance. Lights were installed in several trees, making the cemetery visible at night for the first time. A large portion of the cemetery was re-seeded with grass, as much of the grass had been trampled down over the decades. The most recent phase of the restoration was completed in the spring of 2021. While the cemetery itself is municipal, the tombstones today are considered as belonging to the descendants. While this does not mean that family can claim and remove the tombstones of their ancestors, the descendants do have the option of paying for restoration and preservation work on the tombstones; many of which are in need of such care.

A portion of the proceeds for any sale of this book will be donated to the Charter Street Cemetery to help ensure that the preservation work continues for many years to come.

GLOSSARY OF TERMS

Much of the language found on the tombstones and records of the Old Burying Point is based in common terms used in the 17th and 18th centuries. This glossary is provided to assist with understanding these terms. Many of the people interred here made their lives on or by the sea, so maritime terms are included as well.

Æt: An abbreviation of the Latin word aetatis, meaning "age of."

Brig: A two-masted ship with an additional "gaff" sail off the main mast. They were favored for long voyages to pick up and drop off cargo, mostly due to their ability to handle rough weather.

Brigantine: A ship with two masts, square sails on the foremost mast and gaff sails on the second. These ships require a smaller crew than a brig, and were favored by merchants.

Carriage guns/carriages: Large guns mounted on a carriage, may sometimes be referred to as cannons on a ship.

Clipper: A ship with three masts, each one with a square sail.

Consort: An archaic term for "spouse," typically a wife.

Consumption: The archaic name for tuberculosis, or T.B., considered one of the deadliest diseases of the 17th and 18th century.

Cordwainer: A shoemaker, creating new leather shoes.

Dropsy: Edema, or fluid retention in soft tissues. When used as a cause of death, it could mean congestive heart failure, liver failure, or kidney failure.

Esquire: The 'esquire' honorific would signify the son of an influential and respected gentleman.

ſ: When transcribing the inscriptions on the graves and tombs for this book, we have attempted to keep them as true to the original carvings as possible. The use of "ſ" would be an "s" in modern typeface.

Goodman/Goodwife: The head of a household in Puritan society, "goodwife" for a woman, and "goodman" for a man. Sometimes shortened to "Goody" for women. Similar to the modern Mister and Missus.

Hectic: When used as "cause of death," refers to a recurring fever.

Indentured servant: someone who would be contracted to work for a family or individual for a set period of time and at an agreed upon fee, whether for actual payment in money or goods, or for trade in service, such as the cost of overseas passage

Intemperance: Usually refers to over-indulgence with alcohol.

Ketch: A two-masted sailboat whose main mast is taller than the aft-mast (or mizzen mast) 40 feet or larger. Primarily used by New Englanders in the 17th century, they would be replaced by schooners in the 18th century.

Merchant: When a person's occupation is listed as "merchant," it means they are engaged in the buying and selling of items. It was a very broad term, and merchants might trade in a specific item, or in many different types, depending on opportunity and demand. Some items that were popular for trade in 17th and 18th century Massachusetts were tobacco, fish, rum, molasses, pepper, sugar, salt, ropes, wooden planks, porcelain, and various spices.

Non compos mentis: Not having control of one's mind, an archaic term that generally meant temporary insanity

Relict: An archaic term for widow.

Schooner: A ship with at least two masts, the second mast being taller. Some schooners could have three or more masts, each one carrying gaff sails, which allow the ship to be more efficient in difficult weather.

Shipmaster or Master: The captain of a vessel.

Sloop: A vessel with one mast, a jib, and mainsail.

Snauw (or snow): A square rigged vessel with two primary masts and one "snow" mast (sometimes called a "try-sail") aft of the main mast. Similar to a brig.

Store: Usually refers to a warehouse.

FUNERALS IN OLD SALEM

Funerals in colonial New England were both somber and celebratory affairs. A death in town would usually put a hold to all work going on, as the community gathered to mourn. There would be no funeral service at the meeting house, but there might be a short ceremony at the deceased's home, which is where the casket would await the funeral procession. The bell would toll through the town square as the casket was carried from the deceased person's home to the burying place. The use of a carriage for a hearse was not common in the colonial days; a casket was carried from the home to the burial site by the bearers, and so the usage of the word 'hearse' meant the bier on which the casket was laid.

There would typically be two types of bearers of the coffin; the under-bearers, who would carry the actual casket, and the pallbearers, who stood at the corners of the casket and held the pall, which was the cloth spread over the casket. The under-bearers were usually strong young men, while the pallbearers were the elder family or colleagues of the deceased person. A burial site could be far away from the person's home, so there might be a second set of under-bearers waiting to take over the burden of carrying the casket from a halfway point.

A minister would be present at the cemetery, however there would be no religious service at the gravesite, and no words would be spoken over the grave. Few towns had an employed gravedigger, so often the deceased's friends would be the ones who had prepared the grave. Later an undertaker, such as David Boyce of Salem, would handle these arrangements. The duties of an undertaker would include digging a grave, preparing a tomb, shoveling snow, providing carriages, and, if requested, hiring a man to stand by a tomb the day following the interment as a precaution in case of untimely burial. If the burial was to be in a tomb, the bearers would carry the coffin down the narrow steps underground and lay it in a prepared space in the tomb. As time went by, the practice of a minister speaking over a grave and sometimes a round of pistol or musket fire being let off would be added to a colonial funeral.

A funeral in those days could be a very costly affair. Not only the burial itself, but the celebratory gathering that would be held the night before. The deceased person's family would be assisted by the women from other households in preparing food for the funeral. Wine, cider, gin, and rum would flow freely at these gatherings, and one of the greatest expenses of a funeral would be the bill for alcohol consumed. These gatherings had a cheerful atmosphere, contrary to what might be expected of the typically solemn Puritans. Nathaniel Hawthorne wrote, "They were the only class of scenes, so far as my investigation has taught me, in which our ancestors were wont to steep their tough old hearts in wine and strong drink and indulge in an outbreak of grisly jollity." The mourners would trade stories and jokes while drinking their fill from a table set with wine. Even a pauper's funeral would have wine provided by the town as charity. The debt for funeral alcohol might burden a family for years after the burial.

Another expense would come in the form of funerary rings, gloves, and scarves. These would be given by the family to relations, friends, and colleagues. Gloves were usually lambswool and could be quite costly. Mourning rings might have the name of the deceased fashioned into the inside of the ring, and could be adorned with a death's head or other morbid design. These rings were often made of gold, and ordering a large number could take up a good-sized percentage of a deceased person's estate. As time went by and funerals became more extravagant and costly, the governments were forced to step in. The tolling of the bells in Salem became so frequent as to be considered a public nuisance, and sextons were limited to only four tolls a minute. In 1741, the Massachusetts Provincial Enactment limited funerary scarves, gloves, and rings to only the bearers and ministers, both to curb the expense on the estates, and to tone down the ostentatiousness of the ceremonies.

A common sight at funerals would be hand-written or printed elegies made by the friends and colleagues of the deceased. These elegies could be somber, beautiful, or humorous, but almost always aimed to be poetic and clever. They would consist mostly of rhyming couplets about the virtues of the deceased person as well as praises to God and the occasional tongue-in-cheek comment. These papers might be passed around town, posted on walls, or even fastened to the hearse itself. Anyone could, and usually would, write an elegy, regardless of their education and writing experience. As one writer for the New England Courant wrote in November, 1722; "There is scarce a plough jogger or country cobbler that has read our Psalms and can make two lines jingle, who has not once in his life at least exercised his talent in this way." In another 1722 issue of the Courant, Benjamin Franklin, writing under his pen name of Silence Dogwood, wrote of the New Englander funeral elegy practice in a letter concerning the funeral elegy of one "Mehitable Kitel, Wife of Mr. John Kitel of Salem." There was a Mehitable Kittle of Beverly who passed away around that time. Franklin includes such lines from the elegy as:

> *Come let us mourn, for we have lost*
> *a Wife, a Daughter and a Sister*
> *Who has lately taken flight*
> *and greatly we have missed her*
> *She kist her Husband some little*
> *Time before she expir'd*
> *Then lean'd her Head the Pillow*
> *On Just out of Breath and tir'd*

Franklin's letter goes on to attempt to provide a recipe for funeral elegy writers by way of mocking the common content of elegies, suggesting they "season all with a Handful or two of Melancholy Expressions, such as, Dreadful, Deadly, cruel cold Death, unhappy Fate, weeping Eyes... prepare a sufficient Quantity of double Rhymes such as Power, Flower, Quiver, Shiver, Grieve us, Leave us... and if you can procure a scrap of Latin to put at the End, it will garnish it mightily."

THE CHILDREN OF THOMAS AND MARY MOULD
BROKEN SINCE BEFORE 1901

OF THOMAS & MARY MOULD

THOMAS MOULD
AGED 16 MONTHS
DYED Ye 1
OF AUGUST
1 6 8 1

ELIZABETH
MOULD AGED
16 MONTHS DYED
AUGUST Y^e 20
1 6 8 4

*(The Missing Inscription is for Elizabeth Mould
Died February 6, 1680. Aged 1 Year 9 Months)*

Tombstones and Symbols

The condition of the tombstones in the Old Burying Point are a testament to Salem's preservation efforts through the centuries. Family members are often grouped together, but this was by no means a requirement. Space in the old cemetery grew scarce, and while families usually tried to bury their loved ones close together, often a person would need to be interred in an entirely different spot in the cemetery from the rest of their family. The graves would typically be set facing east, so that on the Day of Resurrection, they would be facing the rising sun. It is believed that ministers would often have their graves facing west, so they would arise to face their congregation in the hereafter. Most gravestones in this cemetery are facing east, however, there are many stones which face west. This does not mean that the person buried there is not facing east, despite the direction of the stone, or could also mean that the stone was moved at some point. A burial for the dead facing east, towards the rising sun, was also a custom of many Native American tribes in New England.

Most of the tombstones in the Old Burying Point are slate. In 17th century England, the most popular slate for tombstones was imported from Wales. It has been theorized that this desire for Welsh slate carried over to the American colonies. However, historian Harriet M. Forbes' work documenting New England tombstones in the 1920s showed few, if any, records of tombstone shipments from Europe to the colonies. It is possible that English slate was used in the earliest gravestones, however, the abundance of local slate would have quickly dominated the market. Marble tombstones and marble table-tops for tombs, as well as sandstone table-tops, may be found throughout the cemetery. Marble tombstones, while beautiful at first, have not stood up well to the weathering by the elements and acid rain. Most marble tombstones from the 18th century are now illegible, their inscriptions lost to time.

The engraving and carving of the stones would have been performed by local artisans. In Salem, there may have been a mason or other artisan that carved stones, however, the majority of the tombstones in the earliest days were carved in Boston. One gentleman in particular seems to be the source of many tombstones in the Boston area in the 1600s, however, his name was never recorded. He may have been the only stone-carver in Boston, as receipts for payment on tombstones refer often to "the stone-carver at Boston." Thus, this mysterious artisan has become known as "the Stone Cutter of Boston." His work can be found in the Old Burying Point, most notably, the tombstone of Mary Cromwell.

The Stone Cutter was known to include Latin verses as well, so it is possible the tombstone of Christian (Hunt) More (*Introduction*) was also his work. It seems the Stone Cutter had a number of apprentices, all of whom were influenced by his style. Another notable stone-carver was William Mumford, a Quaker, who rose to popularity after the retirement or death of the Stone Cutter. Mumford built a Quaker Meeting House in Boston on Brattle Street; however, he seems to have had good relations with the Mathers, who were a family of staunch Puritan ministers. It is believed that the tombstone of Nathaniel Mather (featured on the cover of this book) is identifiable as his work. Eventually, Salem would begin to produce its own gravestone craftsmen, such as John Holliman in the early 1700s, and Benjamin Day in the 1800s, who worked in marble tombstones and table-tops.

As you walk through the historic Charter Street Cemetery, you may immediately notice the symbols placed at the top of the oldest gravestones. These are often adorned with the designs of a skull with wings, or other images that we may consider morbid, such as the cloaked figure of Death holding a scythe, an hourglass, or a skull with crossbones. In the modern age, such images are frightening, however in the time that these stones were erected, they had an incredibly significant meaning. *Memento mori* is a Latin phrase which translates to "remember you must die." The phrase has come to apply to something created as a remembrance of death, a warning to those who view it that they, too, must someday die. The tombstones of the Old Burying Point contain many different types of *memento mori*, even if the ominous phrase is not etched into them.

HERE LIETH BVRIED
y BODY OF M^{RS} MARY
CROMALL WIFE TO
MR PHILIP CROMALL

AGED 72 YEARES
DEPARTED THIS

LIFE THE 14 DAY
OF NOVEMBER

1 6 8 3

Death's Head

The most common symbol to see on a 17th century Puritan tombstone would be the ominous Death's Head figure. This foreboding image of the winged skull is carved into most of the gravestones of the Old Burying Point. It is believed this image represents the death and rebirth of the soul, or possibly a reminder to the living of their own mortality. Pictured is the tombstone of Abigail White in the Charter Street Section, which features crossbones over the death's head, another example of the imagery of mortality.

In memory of
ABIGAIL the Wife of
JOHN WHITE Junr

who Died the 2^d of August

1 7 7 6

Aged 50 years

Hourglasses

The Death's Head might be accompanied by an hourglass as a reminder of time running out, and the observers own mortality. The hourglass image may sometimes have wings, perhaps to illustrate just how quickly the time goes, or to imagine the flight of the soul. This tombstone for Patience Smith is in the Shattock Section.

HERE LYETH BURIED
y^e BODY OF PATIENCE
y^e WIFE OF JOHN
SMITH·&·DAUGHTER·TO
SAMUELL & HANNAH
SHATTOCK AGED 23
YEARS DECEASED y^e TH7
OF APRILL 1 6 9 0

Soul Effigy

In the eighteenth century, the grinning skull would be replaced by the cherubic faces called Soul Effigies. While the Puritans thought it blasphemous to create images of Christ or angels for their tombstones, the succeeding generations would add these angelic images. The meaning seems to have been the same as the death's head, symbolic of death and rebirth. Pictured is a Soul Effigy on the tombstone of Joshua Richardson in the Charter Street Section.

Here lies Buried
the Body of M^r
JOSHUA RICHARDSON
who departed this life
February 26th 1774
Aged 28 Years

Skull and Crossbones

Similar to the death's head, these reminders of human mortality adorn many of the tombstones in the Old Burying Point. There are misconceptions that these represent some sort of wrongdoing on the person's part, however, there is no validity to that theory. As with the skull and crossbones images on poison, or the pirates' Jolly Roger, this is meant to be a warning of death. This tombstone for Mary Masury is in the Gardner Section.

Here lyes buried
the Body of
Mrs MARY MASURY wife
to Mr WILLIAM MASURY
died May 17th 1748 in the
27th year of Her Age

Urns and Willow Trees

A number of stones from the 18th century begin to depict urns. Cremation was not popular during these times, however the symbolism of the urn in the Christian culture goes back to the days of Rome. Remains of Romans were most often cremated rather than buried, and the urn itself here becomes a memento mori. There was renewed interest in ancient Rome in the 18th century, as it became fashionable among the educated to embrace the classical arts. Tombstones of this period also tend to be much larger than the earlier stones. Willow trees were popular features of tombstones in the eighteenth and early nineteenth centuries, and are often associated with the gospel of Christ due to their perpetual nature and perseverance. A willow tree may be regrown from the planting of a single branch, creating a potent, natural symbol of the Resurrection.

The beauty of a willow tree's flowing branches may also evoke a melancholy sadness. Willow trees would often be planted by hospitals for the same imagery of healing. Many willow trees were planted at the Salem Willows to provide shade for a nearby infectious disease hospital, which burned down in 1848. Often combined with urns on the images of tombstones, willow trees represent the rebirth of the soul to everlasting life. Pictured is the urn and willow tree motif on the tombstone of Dr. Moses Little in the Ropes Section.

HERE LIES
THE BODY OF
MOSES LITTLE M.D.

WHO DIED 13. OCT. 1811;

AGED 45 YEARS.

PHTHISIS INSATIABILIS!
PATREM, MATREMQUE
DEVORASTI;
PARCE, O! PARCE
LIBERIS.

(Insatiable Consumption!
Father and Mother
Thou Has Devoured;
Spare, O! Spare
The Children.)

Footstones

Dr. Little's tombstone is accompanied by a footstone. Throughout the cemetery, you will notice many small tombstones that are parallel to the larger stones. These are known as 'footstones,' whereas the larger stones would be 'headstones.' As the name implies, the headstone is placed at the deceased's head, and the footstone at their feet. The footstone markers will contain less information than the headstone; usually only providing the name, or sometimes just the initials. They will also occasionally have the date of death. If there are any designs, they are likely to mirror the designs on the headstone.

M. LITTLE. M.D.

Rising Sun

A few of the gravestones in this cemetery depict a rising sun, which may represent the dawn of everlasting life. This tombstone, which has legibility issues due to lichen growth, is for three children of the Storey family, and may be found in the Hathorne Section.

Salley Storey died June 17th 1782

Aged 2 Years & 8 Months

Elinor Storey died Sept 13th 1794

Aged 2 Years

Alexander Storey, died Dec 31 1795

Aged 1 Year & 3 Months

Children of Capt. Alexander & Sally Storey
Lay still Sweet Babes and take your rest
We trust in heaven that you are blest

Tools

Oftentimes, a person's trade would be reflected on their tombstone. A ship might denote the occupation of mariner. These pair of oars indicate Mr. Samuel Comfort's profession: an oarmaker. This tombstone appears near the Bradstreet Tomb.

HERE LYES yᵉ BODY
OF SAMᴸᴸ COMFORT
AGED ABOUT 38 YE
ARS DIED MARCH
yᵉ 27 - 1704

IHS

Unique among the surviving gravestones in the Old Burying Point is this stone for John Camball of Meath, Ireland. The I.H.S. inscription is not seen on any other existing stone in the cemetery. Known as a 'christogram,' it represents the first three letters of Christ's name in Greek, and is commonly seen on Catholic graves in Ireland. This gravestone can be found in the Ward Section.

I.H.S.
In Memory of
Mr. JOHN CAMBALL
native of Ireland
County of Meath
who died
April 4, 1840
Aged 42

Father Time

Father Time appears on many tombstones of this time, typically with a bag over his shoulder, and a scythe in his hand. This tombstone for Timothy Lindall (*Peele Lot*) displays multiple figures, including a winged Father Time with an hourglass over his head, as well as a skeletal figure, and soul effigy. The date of death showing as 1698/9 is not uncommon on English tombstones during this time. England did not fully accept the new Gregorian calendar at first, so the English colonies recognized March 25th as the start of the new year. The previous year and the new year will often be marked this way (i.e., 1698/9) on the gravestones of people who died between January 1st and March 24th.

SANCTORUM MEMORIA SIT BEATA
(*Blessed Be the Memory of the Saints*)

HERE LYETH BURIED
y^e BODY OF
MR TIMOTHY LINDALL
AGED   56   YEARS
& 7 M^O. DECEASED
JANUARY y^e 6
1 6 9 8 /9

Multiple Tombstones

This triple-tombstone for the Lindall children (*Peele Lot*) shows a great deal of wear and lichen growth, however, the designs above each panel are still visible. A skeleton, an hourglass, and a winged Father Time appear above the names of Rachel Lindall, Veren Lindall, and an unnamed boy Lindall. These are the grandchildren of Timothy Lindall, and their gravestone symbols contain the same elements as his. The appearance of these carvings actually gives the impression that they were drawn by children, which may be intentional with the design.

THE CHILDREN OF Mr JAMES & Mrs MARY LINDALL

RACHEL BORN	VEREN BORNE	A SON BORNE
AUG'T Y^e 9th	MAY Y^e 14 1711	APRIL Y^e 25th
DIED SEPT Y^e	DIED APRIL Y^e	& DIED Y^e
6th 1714	29TH 1712	SAME DAY
		1 7 1 4

A TABLE-TOP TOMB, WITH LEGS AND BASE INTACT,
LOCATED IN THE BROAD STREET CEMETERY,
SALEM, MASSACHUSETTS

TABLETOP TOMBS

As you enter the cemetery from the Charter Street side, you will immediately see a row of table-top tombs on either side of the steps leading into the burying ground. This area was added to the cemetery in 1767. Beneath each of these boxes are the entrances to underground tombs. The table-tops that sit atop granite block bases often bear the names of the families or individuals buried within. There may be some names listed, or none if the family felt it unimportant or too costly.

Originally, many of these table-tops could have sat atop six removable legs, such as the table-top tomb pictured, which is at the Broad Street Cemetery in the McIntire District in Salem. The table-top would be lifted up, and the legs would be removed. The stone slab beneath could be lifted or slid off to reveal the steps leading into the crypt. Once the casket was carried down and placed in the tomb, the slab, legs, and table-top would be replaced. Over the centuries, the legs would disintegrate, or otherwise break down, and would need to be replaced with a sturdier base. These bases were often made with bricks or granite blocks. As time passed, the mortar of these stones would also break down, and stucco could be used to protect the bases.

There are seventeen such tombs in the Charter Street Cemetery that presently exist, though not all of them still have their tablets, nor are all of those that have tablets still legible. There are seven tombs lining the entrance to the cemetery. These tombs all belong to influential Salem merchants. None of the tombs have been opened since the 1800s, and in those days, they had already begun posing a health hazard to the pallbearers that took the caskets down into the crypt, due to the decaying stairs.

There is no way to enter any of these tombs today. When entering the cemetery through the gates on the Charter Street side, the first tomb that appears on the right is for William Orne, behind that on the right is the Forrester tomb. On the left from the entrance back are the tombs of Allen, Fisk, Gray, Mason, and Derby. Further into the cemetery are the Bartlett, Gedney, Pickman/Toppan, Bradstreet, Wainwright, Pierce, Turner, Lynde, and Browne tombs. Though these are all that exist today, it is certainly possible that some tombs have been lost to time and the elements.

It is important to remember that while the bases of these tombs seem very solid, the table-tops themselves are in many cases the originals, and are extremely fragile. When visiting, do not sit, lean, or place any items on these rare and historic structures.

THE BARTLETT TOMB IN 2020
SHOWING SANDSTONE TABLET
AND STUCCO BASE OVER BRICK
REPAIRED 2016

CHARTER STREET TOMBS

Derby Tomb

Leslie's Retreat & King Derby

Captain Richard Derby Sr (b. Sep 16, 1712, d. Nov 11, 1783) was the patriarch of what would become one of the most influential families in Salem's long history. Derby was a shipmaster by the age of twenty-five, sailing the sloop *Ranger* to Cadiz, Spain. Most vessels in those days were owned by a merchant, or collective of merchants, who hired experienced shipmasters to take their ships to the farthest ports of the world. Rarely would a ship's owner also serve as the captain. Capt. Derby was an exception to this rule, and served as master of several vessels that he owned, such as the schooners *Dolphin* and *Exeter*. By 1764, he was owner, or part-owner, of many vessels, including the *Volant*, the brig *Neptune*, the *Antelope*, the brigantine *Lydia and Betsy*, the brig *Ranger*, and the *Mary and Sally*. His ships would travel to Spain, England, and the West Indies, trading mostly in fish, molasses, and rum. He would lose several vessels to privateers during the Seven Years War.

Late in the 1760's, Richard Derby Sr purchased the land on which the Derby House (168 Derby Street) now sits, as well as the land across what is now Derby Street, to build Derby Wharf. In February 1775, British Colonel Alexander Leslie stormed Salem with two hundred and fifty redcoats, in search of hidden cannons he believed Derby to have in his possession. Captain Derby allegedly mocked the Colonel, telling him "Find them if you can, they will never be surrendered!" This event would come to be known as 'Leslie's Retreat,' for the Colonel left empty-handed, with the jeers of Salem's patriots following him out of town. Col. Leslie would be stripped of his rank for cowardice due to this event.

However, his rank would eventually be restored when it was realized that he had acted correctly. Minutemen from all over Essex County had been mobilized, and would have vastly outnumbered his troops if he had engaged them in combat. The cannons had been safely hidden, and would be transported to nearby Lexington and Concord, where the first shots of the American Revolutionary War would be fired.

On February 3. 1732, Richard married **Mary (Hodges) Derby** (b. Dec 21, 1713, d. Feb 27, 1770). Together they had six children, each of whom lived to adulthood and married into wealthy and influential families. Two of the daughters married well known shipmasters; Mary Derby was married to Capt. George Crowninshield, and Sarah Derby married Captain John Gardner. Capt. Richard Derby Jr married Lydia Gardner, who was descended from one of Salem's original settlers (see *Gardner section*). Elias Hasket Derby married Elizabeth Crowninshield (both profiled below). **Martha (Derby) Prince** (bapt. Apr 29, 1744, d. Jun 26, 1802) married a physician, Dr. John Prince, and Capt. John Derby was married to Elizabeth Cheever. John Derby would be remembered for carrying the news of the Battle of Lexington to the Lord Mayor of London, avoiding detection so that he could deliver the news ahead of General Gage, making sure that the American version of events was the first to be heard. He would return to Massachusetts and report to General George Washington. Ironically, on April 4, 1783, Capt John Derby was master of the ship *Astrea*, which brought back to the colonies the news of the Treaty of Paris, and the end of hostilities. His sister, Martha (Derby) Prince, and her Loyalist husband fled to Nova Scotia when the Revolutionary War erupted. She returned to Salem in 1802 and died shortly afterward, being interred in her father's tomb.

After Mary (Hodges) Derby died in 1770, Richard Sr would remarry to Sarah (Langlee) Derby, who survived him and died in Hingham, Massachusetts, in 1790. Sarah was the widow of Dr. Ezekiel Hersey, and would be known in Hingham as "Madam Derby," founding Derby Academy in 1784. Captain Richard Derby Sr's brick home is part of the National Maritime Historic site on Derby Wharf. Richard wanted his coffin to be made from a locust tree that grew near his front door, which was cut down and used for that purpose.

Elias Hasket Derby (b. Aug 16, 1739, d. Sep 8, 1799) was a son of Capt. Richard and Mary Derby. He was given the nickname "King Derby" in Nathaniel Hawthorne's, *The Scarlet Letter*, and perhaps rightfully so. Whereas his brothers excelled as shipmasters, Elias H. Derby had a mind for business. As Richard Sr began to separate himself from his businesses in his old age, he gave Elias control over his merchant ventures, leaving the sea to his other sons and sons-in-law. Keenly aware of the new opportunities that American independence offered, Elias turned his eye towards trade with India and China. Derby's ship, the *Grand Turk*, captained by Ebenezer West in 1784, was the first New England ship to travel to China and successfully conduct trade. Derby's venture helped to open up trade relationships with India, Sumatra, and other Asian communities and islands formerly only possible through the reach of the British Empire. Derby made a fortune of over one million dollars, becoming America's first millionaire. Adjusted for inflation, this amount would be equal to about $30 million today. Derby was still possessed of a fortune of $800,000 ($23 million today) at the time of his death in 1799. Derby was known for his shrewd mind for business as well as his quick temper. He is also said to have had the rare condition known as heterochromia; one of his eyes being blue and the other brown.

Elizabeth (Crowninshield) Derby (b. abt. 1735, d. Apr 19, 1799) was married to Elias Hasket Derby on April 23, 1761. She was the daughter of John and Anstiss Crowninshield (see *Missing Stones*), a family who became known for their mastery as captains of vessels. Her marriage to Elias helped to cement the business relationship between the Derbys and Crowninshields. It was commonly said during this time that few ships would be seen going around the Cape of Good Hope that were not owned by Derbys and captained by Crowninshields. For the first twenty years of their marriage, the couple lived in the brick home built by Richard Sr in 1762. As their fortunes increased, they began to build another mansion on the property, known today as the Hawkes House (174 Derby Street). However, partway through the construction, the Derbys decided instead to purchase the Essex Street home formerly owned by William Browne (32 Derby Square). The house was torn down, and a new elegant mansion was planned. This change seems to have come at Elizabeth's urging, and she was very much involved in reviewing the plans for the construction and decoration of the new home. Elias wrote the following instructions to his London agents in 1788, "Mrs. Derby wants something to complete her house; she will write you. It is a business I know nothing of. I have given her an order for £120; you will do as she may direct with it." The plans for the new mansion were drawn by Salem architect Samuel McIntire, and may have been originated by Charles Bulfinch of Boston, as Elizabeth wrote "Mr. Bulfinsh's" on the back of the plans. Despite the great amount of work Elizabeth put into the creation of the new mansion, she would die before it was fully completed.

Though they were greatly respected for their contributions to Salem's prosperity, the Derbys also had a reputation for brashness. The minister of the East Congregational Church, Reverend William Bentley, kept a daily diary of the goings-on in Salem from 1784 to 1819, and gives us a glimpse into the daily lives of Salem's wealthiest family, under the harshly critical eye of the minister. He mentions Elias Hasket Derby's "rigid temper," and chides Elizabeth Derby for "vanity which she exposed to constant and deserved ridicule." After the death of Elias Hasket Derby, it became clear that he had been the steady hand on the wheel of the Derby family's fortunes. Elias had purchased homes for all of his children, but kept the ownership in his own name in order to control the finances. After his unexpected death from dysentery, the family began a fall from grace. Rev. Bentley noted in his diary "the family has lost their influence in the loss of their father," and later wrote in 1805, "the names Derby and Pickman no longer stand preeminent in the business and navigation of the town."

Elizabeth (Derby) West (b. abt. 1762, bur. Mar 11, 1814) was the eldest daughter of Elias Haskett and Elizabeth Derby, and was said to have inherited both her father's temper, and her mother's vanity. She clashed frequently and publicly with her parents and siblings. On May 23, 1783, she eloped with Captain Nathaniel West, contrary to her father's wishes. By 1806, the couple were estranged, and living in separate estates; Elizabeth living on the family farm in Danvers, Oak Hill. Prior to this time, Massachusetts law held that a woman who divorced her husband would only be allowed to keep a third of the estate that she had brought into the marriage. In the West's case, Captain West's family was far from impoverished, however it could not compare to the wealth of the Derbys. The divorce laws in Massachusetts changed in 1806, allowing that if the cause of the divorce was the husband's infidelity, he would be owed nothing from his wife's estate. Elizabeth accused her husband of infidelity and, with the assistance of her brother, General Elias Hasket Derby Jr, went so far as to bring thirteen prostitutes from throughout Essex County and Boston to court to attest to Captain West's adultery, even presenting children whom they alleged to be his illegitimate offspring. Bentley decried how she had, "displayed in open court... all the sweepings of the brothels of Boston, and all the vile wretches of Salem, Marblehead, Cape Ann, etc."

Public opinion in town turned to pity for Capt. West, whom they felt was wrongfully slandered by his wife. Rev. Bentley's diary reflects the public sentiment of the time, as he harshly criticizes Mrs. West, writing "the woman became all that is execrable in women from vanity, caprice, folly, and malignity and after every quarrel with all her relatives she waged open war against her husband." Bentley wrote of the "unfeeling perseverance of her malignant brother," Gen. Elias H. Derby Jr, whom the judges dined with the day before delivering their verdict. The court found in favor of Elizabeth, and she retired to the farm in Danvers, for, as Bentley notes "she had rendered herself unwelcome to any private family or boarding house."

Elizabeth removed to Oak Hill and lived there the remainder of her days. She had strongly spoken against being buried in the family tomb; however, she appears to have reconsidered in her later years. The hearse carrying her body arrived on March 11, 1814, accompanied by a grand procession of seven horse-drawn coaches and two chaises. Bentley remarks on her funeral as being, "in a manner as different from our customs as she had lived" and notes, "none but the relatives attended excepting a Minister." The great Derby Mansion on Essex Street would be torn down the same year, as the last vestiges of the great family fell. However, the name of Derby will still be seen in downtown Salem at Derby Square, where the Old Town Hall was built on the former site of the mansion.

Ezekiel Hersey Derby (b. abt. 1772, d. Oct 31, 1852) was the third son of Elias H. and Elizabeth Derby. On September 19, 1794, he married **Hannah (Fitch) Derby** (b. May 5, 1777, d. Feb 7, 1862). Ezekiel was invested in bringing scientific advancement to farming and agriculture, such as using manure for fertilizer, and using deep ploughing, which improves the soil for root growth. From his father, he inherited a farm in Danvers, which became known as Ezekiel Hersey Derby Farm, a landscape of which was painted by artist Michele Felice Corne. A room in the Philadelphia Museum of Art, known as The Derby Room, is patterned after the design of his home, formerly at 206 Essex Street, designed by Charles Bulfinch, and decorated by Samuel McIntire (*McIntire Section*).

In 1805, Ezekiel put forth a proposal that would change downtown Salem forever. He proposed the construction of a bridge over the South River, which would connect Essex Street to an area he was developing, Lafayette Street. The proposed bridge would connect at about the area of Central Street. The creation of the bridge would essentially close the South River, which was already seeing a great decline as a shipping port, due to the increasing size of cargo vessels, which the river was not large enough to accommodate. After the construction of the bridge, a large portion of the South River would slowly be entirely filled, making more land available for homes and businesses, and creating New Derby Street. Also interred in this tomb are Ezekiel H. and Hannah Derby's son **Ezekiel Hersey Derby Jr** (bapt. Sep 21, 1800, d. Nov 16, 1839) and daughter **Caroline Derby** (b. Dec 24, 1805, d. Aug 27, 1878) as well as their nephew, **John Derby** (b. Nov 14, 1792, d. Jul 8, 1867).

On May 19, 1807, the remains of **Sarah Crowninshield** (b. abt. 1764, d. abt. 1779), daughter of Capt. George Sr and Mary (Derby) Crowninshield, were removed from the Derby tomb, and interred in the Crowninshield Tomb, which is in the Howard Street Cemetery. She had been interred in the Derby Tomb for twenty-eight years, and her removal may be a sign of the bad blood which was rising between the Derby and Crowninshield families during this time.

FORRESTER TOMB

The Richest Man in Salem & The Privateer's Daughter

Captain **Simon Healy Forrester** (b. abt. 1748, bur. July 6, 1817) was born in Killeenach, Cork County, Ireland. He was remembered in Cork as a hot-blooded, and rough-and-tumble young man. A graduate of Cloyne College, Forrester yearned for a life outside of Cork. It is said that one day while working in his father's field, he suddenly threw down his tools and headed straight to Liverpool, where he gained employment on the sloop *Salisbury* of Salem, under the command of shipmaster, Captain Daniel Hathorne. Captain Hathorne was impressed with young Forrester, and when the ship arrived back in Salem, took him in as a ward. Years later, Reverend Bentley would record in his diary that Forrester had been a servant in Hathorne's home. However, Hathorne's daughter Ruth insisted this was not so, writing, "(Simon) was not a man to work in any family," and had been treated as a son by Hathorne. Captain Hathorne and his wife were not pleased when their daughter, **Rachel (Hathorne) Forrester** (bapt. Jul 30, 1757, d. Jun 29, 1823) fell in love with Simon, however the two were married December 7, 1776.

As with many young American sailors, 1776 would be a turning point in Simon Forrester's life. He quickly gained a reputation as a fearless privateer and was given the command of many ships, capturing prize after prize at sea. He commanded the sloops *Rover* and *Centurion*, as well as the ships *Jason*, the *Patty*, the *Exchange* and many more. As captain of the *Break of Day*, he captured an English merchant ship and, upon reading the ships documents, he discovered it was owned by

Luke Shea of Cork County, a friend of his father's. Rather than plunder the prize, Forrester allowed the ship and crew to return home, on the condition that the captain convey his regards to Mr. Shea. The captain was true to his word, and Shea gratefully reached out to Simon's father with news of his kind and generous son. The father received this news with tears of joy, for the war had prevented Simon from returning home, and his father had thought him dead.

Forrester purchased several of his own vessels during the war; the sloop *Black Snake*, and the brigantines, *Vigilant* and *Good Hope*, though he seems not to have captained any of them. As the war ended, he spent less and less time at sea, and settled into the role of merchant. His vessels would travel across the world, as far as Russia. On February 2, 1791, Forrester purchased a home (188 Derby Street) overlooking Central Wharf. The store he owned, which fronted Central Wharf, was burned in the Great Salem Fire of 1914.

While his business ventures were successful, his family was wracked with tragedy and sorrow. Their son, John, died at age twenty-four in 1758. Their infant daughter, Elizabeth, born in May 1783, lived just over a week. Their eldest daughter, Mary, succumbed to fever in 1795. In 1817, their son, Simon Jr, is believed to have committed suicide by jumping overboard from a ship returning from the East Indies.

Simon Forrester died on July 4, 1817, one of the wealthiest citizens of Salem. His last will and testament was written to ensure that his wife, children, and grandchildren, as well as the Hathorne family he loved, were well taken care of. He also made sure to include in his will, a fund to ensure that there would be a Christmas dinner and Independence Day dinner for the poor, every year in Salem. Interred with Simon and Rachel Forrester are their daughter, **Rachel Forrester** (bapt. Dec 28, 1778, d. Nov 25, 1814), and daughter-in-law, **Charlotte (Story) Forrester** (bapt. Oct 19, 1788, d. Dec 16, 1867), wife to their son John. Several of Charlotte and John Forrester's children are interred here as well; **Rachel Forrester** (b. Feb 6, 1817, d. Apr 8, 1891) and **Elizabeth Forrester** (b. Aug 14, 1820, d. May 12, 1890). **Charles Forrester** (b. Jan 14, 1819, d. Feb 7, 1864) was a grandson of Simon and Rachel, the son of Charles and Margaret (Southward) Forrester.

Fisk Tomb

The Controversial Minister & Opening The Tomb

Reverend Samuel Fisk (b. Apr 6, 1689, d. Apr 3, 1770) was the son of Reverend Moses Fisk of Braintree, Massachusetts. He graduated from Harvard College in 1708, when Harvard was mainly a school for men who pursued careers in the ministry. He was ordained in Salem in 1718 as the minister of the First Church of Salem. His time as the minister was controversial, as he brought with him his own strong opinions on the authority of the church. This led to complaints against him by the parishioners, who refused to go to the church services and brought their grievances to the ministers of Boston. It was eventually uncovered that he had been tampering with church attendance records, which lead to his dismissal in 1735.

In response, Reverend Fisk founded a new church, proclaiming it as the "First" Church of Salem. The church meetinghouse was built on what is currently the site of the Tabernacle Congregational Church (50 Washington Street). Reverend Fisk resigned as pastor on July 30, 1745, though he spent the rest of his life in Salem, and passed away in 1770. His church would keep the First Church name until 1762 when the leadership was compelled to rename it as the Third Church of Christ. The original First Church was located where the Daniel Lowe & Co. building is today (231 Essex Street), and has since moved to 316 Essex Street. The Second Church was located on Brown Street, where now stands the Salem Witch Museum (19 ½ North Washington Square).

Reverend Fisk famously gave a speech in Boston prior to the elections of May 26, 1731, in which he discussed the qualities that were most important in an elected official; "They should be faithful and true men, for they stand oppos'd to the Vicious and Ill-qualified... Persons of inflexible Justice & Impartiality, otherwise their Skill will degenerate into Craft & Cunning. For there is something due to every Man in the Community which should be rendered to him in particular."

Fisk's speech emphasized the importance of a public official's honesty, and his devotion to helping his fellow man, and never giving in to contempt or flattery. Reverend Fisk married Anna (Gerrish) Fisk of Salem on November 17, 1739. She died of smallpox at the hospital (sometimes called the Pest House) on February 20, 1761. It is likely that Anna was interred at the Pest Cemetery, a place on Roach's Point (located by modern-day Settlers Way on Collins Cove, former site of the Alms-house) where the victims of contagious disease were buried. Samuel and Anna had five children, but only one of them lived to adulthood.

Major General John Fisk Sr (b. May 6, 1744, d. Sep 29, 1797) was the only surviving son of Rev. Samuel and Anna Fisk. John Fisk was involved in many commercial and real estate pursuits. An experienced ship's commander, he was appointed command of the ship *Tyrannicide*, the first war-vessel commissioned by the state of Massachusetts, on July 8, 1776. On December 10, 1777, he took command of the *Massachusetts*. He ascended quickly through the ranks of the state militia, was promoted to Colonel, then Brigadier, and finally Major General. Outside of military life, he was engaged in charity and religious movements, and was said to have contributed very freely. In 1797, he was recorded as having died of apoplexy. Maj. Gen. Fisk was a good friend of Rev. Bentley, who said that he had dinner with Fisk every Saturday night, or several times a month. Bentley was with him when he passed, and called him, "the best and most constant of friends." Fisk was buried with military honors; artillery fired off, and all vessels in Salem Harbor flying their flags at half-mast.

Major General John Fisk was married to **Lydia (Phippen) Fisk** (b. Jun 7, 1747, d. Oct 13, 1782). The couple had about seven children, but nearly all of them died in infancy or young adulthood. Their daughter, Anna Fisk, was born June 12, 1770, and married Capt Edward Allen Jr on October 2, 1798. Betsey Fisk was born July 19, 1778, but there are no other records of her, so she may have died in childhood. **Lydia Fisk** (b. Apr 17, 1768, d. Sep 13, 1785) died young of consumption, as did her sister, **Margaret "Peggy" Fisk** (b. Apr 4, 1775, d. Oct 20, 1792). A pair of twins, Prissa and Samuel Fisk, were recorded as born February 9, 1782, but there is no further record of them either. A burial that is not recorded in this tomb but seems likely is **John Fisk Jr** (b. Feb 20, 1780, d. Feb. 7,

1801), their only son who lived to adulthood. In the late 1790s, John Fisk Jr's ship was captured by French privateers, and he was taken prisoner. Following the French Revolutionary War, American merchant vessels would be harassed and sometimes captured by French privateers, though America had remained neutral in the war. After his eventual release and return home, he suffered from intemperance. His intemperance seems to have been encouraged by the company he kept, and would lead to his death at the age of 21. After Lydia (Phippen) Fisk's death, John Fisk Sr remarried to **Patty Fisk** (b. abt. 1753, d. Nov 30, 1785), whose maiden name is unknown, and she died of consumption shortly after they were married. Fisk would marry for the third time to **Sarah (Wendall) Fisk** (b. abt. 1745, d. Feb 4, 1804)

* * *

Please note that some readers may find this section to be unsettling due to graphic depictions of corpses, and anyone with an aversion to such details may wish to skip the rest of this section.

At some point before 1795, Major General John Fisk decided to purchase a tomb for his family, which is the Fisk tomb we see today. Fisk wanted the bodies of his family that were already interred in the Burying Point to be exhumed and placed into the new tomb. Reverend William Bentley, as a close friend of the Fisks, attended this event and recorded much of what he saw in his personal diary. The following is a passage from Reverend Bentley's diary.

From the Diary of Reverend William Bentley:

June 16, 1795: The New Tombs were closed this day. As Gen. Fiske's Family had been known to me, I visited the Grave Yard, while the family was removed. English told me that he buried Rev S. Fiske in the corner of the Ground, at the projecting angle of Peele's fence, near the place in which Mr Norris lay. But as the fence had been moved & the bones we found were westward of the spot, we returned them. In removing the other Bodies the sextons were directed by the Grave Stones. The first Mrs. Fiske was found in the earth as the Coffin had broken, & the bones were gathered from the earth. Buried in 1782. The second Mrs. Fiske was found, the Coffin was broken but not so as to admit the earth. The Grave Cloathes were yet to be seen & the folds in the Shroud plainly, but as tho ' they had been applied wet to the body. The Substance of the flesh was like a liquid in which the Bones were laid & from which they could not free themselves when the Coffin was turned over, without striking with a spade on the bottom and then the small bones did not disengage themselves. Upon examing it, it was found in the Sun to be alive with a motion from the worms which covered the whole surface but which were clearly distinguished near the part on which the body rested. This Substance spread over the whole surface whether occupied by the body or not, Buried in Nov. 1785, æt .32. Lydia, eldest daughter of Gen. Fiske. Buried in Sept. 1785, æt.17. She was found with the greater part of the grave cloathes easily seperable from the bones, but no flesh remained. Her hair was as entire & in as apparently good order as when she was buried. The Bows of Silk ribbon were entire & the parts not in immediate contact with the body were as sound as ever. They looked fresh when first exposed to the air but afterwards changed to a snuff colour. I brought away one of the silk ribbons & have preserved a part of it. Margaret, 20 Oct. 1792, æt.17. The Coffin was sound & the Plate as legible as when first put into the ground. The body remained entire, & the grave cloathes, only the dark appearance in the last stage of putrefaction. Mrs Putnam, Sarah, about 22 æt., buried last year had begun to mould. The little child buried in 1783 was found in the earth & only a few bones remained. Mrs Putnam's child buried not long since, coffin was not opened.

* * *

ORNE TOMB

The Forgotten Merchant & The Fair Widow

Capt. **William Orne** (b. abt. 1751, d. Oct 14, 1815) was a prosperous mariner and merchant. Little record exists of the family's business, and few members of this branch of the Orne family line remained in Salem. William was the captain of many vessels, and the owner of many more by the time of his death. He was a shipmaster by the age of twenty-one, commanding ships such as the *Tyger*, and *Jupiter*. He took part in the American Revolutionary War as a privateer. He owned part interest in a great ship called the *Black Prince*, which was used in the Penobscot Expedition in 1779, a forty-four ship assault on the British forces in Maine. The assault was a terrible failure, and the *Black Prince* was burned to prevent capture.

After the war, William found his fortune as an owner of multiple vessels, engaging in trade beyond the Cape of Good Hope with many Asian ports. He and William Gray (mentioned in the *Gray Tomb*) co-owned the *William and Henry*; a ship that brought one of the first cargoes of imported Eastern tea to New England. He was part owner of the ships *Polly*, *New Adventure*, *Speed*, *Eliza*, *Hind*, *Pompey*, and *Junius Brutus*. Maritime trade was a treacherous business, and several of his ships met with disaster; the *Hopewell* and *Harmony* were lost at sea, and the *Essex* was taken by pirates in the Red Sea, with all crew aboard killed except for a single boy. Among the dead was the captain, his nephew, Joseph Orne.

William Orne's home was nearby to the present site of the Salem City Hall (93 Washington Street). He owned a wharf on Front Street, which was then the waterfront. In 1801, Orne sold a portion of his land to the Town of Salem, which was used to create the Howard Street

Cemetery. In 1805, he attempted to thwart Ezekiel Hersey Derby's (*Derby Tomb*) proposed construction of a bridge across the South River, which would have rendered his wharf essentially useless. Orne employed Joseph Story as his attorney, a future Supreme Court Justice. Story, from Marblehead, may be best known for delivering the ruling in the case of *United States* v. *Amistad* in 1841, which declared the capture and enslavement of a several dozen Africans kidnapped by Spanish slavers to be illegal. Despite the work of his capable attorney, Orne attempted to stop the project by quickly constructing a building precisely on the spot where the bridge was proposed to be built. The hasty move backfired, and turned the public sentiment against Orne.

Orne became a member of the Salem Marine Society in 1792 and remained so until the end of his life. The Society was formed in 1766 by a number of Salem sea captains for the purpose of providing relief to the elderly and disabled members of their profession. He had previously been a member of the society in 1774, but resigned for unknown reasons. Other prominent members of this society were Jonathan Gardner Jr (*Gardner Section*), Capt. Daniel Hathorne (*Hathorne Section*), and Col. Benjamin Pickman (*Pickman/Toppan Tomb*). Orne was one of the Directors of the Essex Bank when it first organized in 1792. He was President of the bank up until his death. William Orne was highly esteemed in business, as well as known for his hospitality and charity. When he died in 1815, Reverend Bentley noted "his habits did not admit a splendid bounty, but a close attention to business was attended with punctuality and honour."

On March 24, 1780, Orne married **Abigail (Ropes) Orne** (b. abt. 1761, d. May 24, 1813). They had six children together, however, all but one of their children died young. Their first two sons, William and George, seem to have died in childhood. **Charles Henry Orne** (b. Apr 1, 1786, d. Dec 15, 1816) married to Lucy Blanchard of Wenham, and died one year later with no children. **Joseph Orne** (b. Jan 31, 1795, d. Sep 3, 1818) married to Sally Fiske Ropes on May 19, 1817, and died of consumption the following year, leaving no children. Samuel Orne was born August 27, 1786, and removed to Cambridge, where he married Lucinda D. Howard in February, 1818. Samuel and his family would move to Springfield, Massachusetts.

Eliza (Orne) White (b. May 10, 1784, d. Mar 26, 1821) was the only daughter of William and Abigail Orne. Eliza married an attorney named William Whetmore, on May 7, 1804. They had one son, William, who died at age five. Whetmore died of consumption in New York on February 27, 1807, after a trip to the Mediterranean. Eliza, who was known to the town as Mrs. Whetmore, would remarry to the Honorable Daniel Appleton White on August 1, 1819. The White family was pleased with the match, both for the additional wealth and influence of the Orne family, and for the respect and admiration the town held for Mrs. Whetmore. Eliza was an avid reader, and by the time of her death, had in her possession a wide range of volumes, including religious sermons, the works of Shakespeare, and Hannah Glass' popular recipe book, *The Art of Cookery Made Plain and Easy - Which Far Exceeds Anything of the Kind Ever Yet Published*. Eliza died March 27, 1821, shortly after the birth of their only child, William Orne White, who became a respected minister and lived into his nineties. It is said that her universal kindness was displayed in no better way than the sight of the highest of society and the poorest of beggars grieving at her funeral.

Her granddaughter, Eliza Orne White, wrote of her family's memories of Eliza, saying "she must have had a warm and loving nature, for her two stepdaughters were passionately devoted to her." White makes note of a silhouette taken of Eliza just before her wedding to Judge White, which was then hanging in the relic room of the Ropes Mansion. She mentions that she had an earlier silhouette in her possession, and describes Eliza's appearance, saying, "It is a charming profile, spirited, if not regularly pretty... a piquant face, and with the hair worn with a high comb behind, and a dress cut down in a point in front with a little frill about the neck, the picture might stand as a portrait of gracious girlhood for all time."

Ezekiel Howard (b. abt. 1798, d. Feb 13, 1818) was the son of Rev. Bezaleel Howard of Springfield, Massachusetts. Ezekiel was a member of the senior class at Harvard University, and had been instructing at a school in Newton. He contracted typhus fever and came to Salem for care, staying in the home of Samuel Orne. He would die within a few days and was interred in the Orne Tomb.

GRAY TOMB

The Constant Deacon & The Great White Plague

Deacon **Abraham Gray Sr** (b. Jan 13, 1714, d. Feb 11, 1791) was a cordwainer, originally from Lynn, Massachusetts. He married **Lydia (Calley) Gray** (b. abt. 1722, d. Nov 27, 1788) on April 1, 1742. The family moved to Salem sometime between 1760 and 1763. Abraham Gray became the deacon of the First Church of Salem, a position he appears to have held until his death from consumption. The Gray family suffered a great deal of loss to consumption, now known as tuberculosis, or T.B., which at one time was the leading cause of death in the United States. Consumption was caused by bacteria which attacked the lungs and caused the sufferer to waste away, growing pale and thin. Hippocrates claimed that consumption was the most widespread disease of his era in ancient Greece. In medieval times, the external effects of consumption would be known as scrofula, or the King's Evil, and it was claimed that the Kings of England and France could cure it with a touch. Consumption was known by many fearsome names across the ages, such as the Great White Plague, and the Captain of All These Men of Death. Within a span of three years, six members of the Gray family died from consumption.

It is believed that most of the children of Abraham Sr and Lydia Gray are interred in this tomb. The children who died of consumption were **Abraham Gray Jr** (b. Sep 1, 1755, d. Aug 6, 1788), **Hannah Gray** (b. abt. 1763, d. Sep 14, 1790), **Francis Calley Gray** (b. Dec 19, 1762, d. Apr 27, 1790), and **Abigail Gray** (b. Sep 1, 1755, d. Nov 6, 1790). While Abraham Jr and Lydia died before the tomb was reportedly erected in 1790, they are not recorded as interred anywhere else, and it was common (as seen in the *Fisk Tomb* section) to exhume bodies which were previously buried once a family tomb was purchased. Rev. Bentley, in a diary entry on February 16, 1792, wrote that he, "saw carried into the Burying Yard as a monumental Stone to support the monument upon the Tomb belonging to the Gray family, a Stone measuring, 5 feet long, 3 high & 1 broad. It is to be placed upon the arch, & a marble to be placed upon it." The marble table-top Bentley referred to is still on top of the granite base of the tomb today.

Of the surviving children of Abraham Sr and Lydia Gray, the most influential would be William Gray. William was apprenticed to merchant Samuel Gardner, and worked as a clerk for Capt. Richard Derby Sr. During the Revolutionary War, he served under Col. Timothy Pickering at the Battle of Lexington on April 19, 1775, and served as a privateer during the rest of the Revolution. In his career as a merchant after the war, he owned forty-four vessels, many of which travelled to Asia for commerce. He served as Lieutenant Governor of Massachusetts from 1810 to 1811. William Gray was interred at Saint Paul's Church in Boston, and later, his remains were moved to Mount Auburn Cemetery in Cambridge.

MASON TOMB

The Mason Family & The Freemason Doctor

The family name of Mason on this tomb may be said to have two meanings. Members the Mason family are interred here, as was a man who was a prominent member of the Freemasons.

Doctor George Logan (b. abt. 1751, d. Jul 16, 1793) was originally from Edinburgh, Scotland. He emigrated to South Carolina, where he was a member of the secretive fraternal order of Free and Accepted Masons. He was the Senior Warden of the Union Kilwining Lodge at Charleston, South Carolina. His wife's sister was Margaret (Lockhart) Allen (*Allen Tomb*), and Dr. Logan was staying with the Allen family in their home (125 Essex Street) while journeying to the Northeast in an attempt to recover his failing health. After his funeral, the Kilwining Freemason Lodge sent a letter to the Essex Lodge thanking them for the care they took in the passing of their member. Rev. Bentley writes that when Dr. Logan was buried, it was with the Masonic rites (which he did not describe) and that Dr. Logan was, "laid out in his underclothes, as he usually dressed, without shoes."

Captain Thomas Mason (b. Jul 9, 1723, d. abt. Jul, 1801) was a profitable shipmaster, known for his contributions to charity. He was paralyzed at some point (in what way we do not know) and had retired from life at sea quite wealthy. He built a home near the Burying Point in 1755. He was the son of Thomas and Preserved (Lambert) Mason.

John Scobie (b. abt. 1764, d. Jul 23, 1823) was a native of Scotland and resided there until 1789, when he emigrated to Marblehead. In 1792, he would move to Norfolk, Virginia, and remained there for three years until he returned to Essex County, settling in Salem by June, 1795. In 1799, he pursued American citizenship, writing a letter to the Court of Common Pleas to state that he held no hereditary titles in Great Britain and swearing to uphold the Unites States Constitution. Scobie provided letters signed by Daniel Wright of Salem, and five of his associates from Marblehead which attested to his good moral character. He would marry Lydia (Mason) Maley, the widow of Capt. Benjamin Maley of Newburyport, on September 4, 1802. Scobie was a merchant, but may have fallen on difficult times in his final years. Scobie died after suffering from *delirium tremens*, a severe reaction to alcohol withdrawal. Interred with him is his daughter **Mary Scobie** (b. Aug 27, 1804, d. Oct 15, 1890).

Also interred in this tomb are **Ann Mason** (b. Feb 10, 1805, d. Aug 14, 1869) and **Abigail Mason** (b. abt. May, 1795, d. May 1, 1869) who were daughters of Jonathan and Mary (King) Mason. The sisters were never married, and lived together for most of their lives, passing away within a few months of each other.

ALLEN TOMB

The Uncertain Tomb & Tragedy at Sea

There is limited information regarding the occupants of this tomb inscribed with the name "ALLEN 1795." It was not uncommon for tombs to have occupants from multiple families, even those who may have been strangers to each other in life. There have been many cases in cemeteries of this age where an older tomb would be purchased, the occupants removed, and new people interred. In Boston, where finding space in cemeteries grew even more difficult than Salem, an enterprising gravedigger frequently bought old tombs and emptied them for sale to new owners. In the early 1800s, an attempt was made by the Town of Salem to sell off some neglected tombs, which was met with outrage from the families affected, and the proposal was withdrawn. Some tombs were eventually sold and emptied, however, and exactly who is interred in some of them today is uncertain. The same may be said for the location of the remains of those who were removed. It may be that one of these forgotten tombs became a vault for the ancient remains of those who were exhumed when their own tombs were sold.

Capt. Edward Allen Sr (b. abt. 1737, d. Jul 27, 1803) is likely the person who owned this tomb at some point. Capt. Allen's family are recorded as interred in the Old Burying Point, though records do not specifically confirm they are in a tomb. There are no other grave markers for these members of the family, and their wealth and status make them likely to have afforded the tomb. Captain Allen was originally from Berwick-Upon-Tweed, Northumberland, England. Allen immigrated to Salem in 1757 as a mariner, and soon after became a shipmaster. He captained the ships *Antelope*, *Baltick*, *Industry*, and *Neptune*. Allen would become a merchant, engaging in trade to Asian countries. Through his second wife, **Margaret (Lockhart) Allen** (b. abt. 1754, d. Aug 13, 1808), he owned land in South Carolina, which was highly coveted by merchants. Allen owned a farm on Salem Neck, by Cat Cove, which he intended to use as the summer residence for his family. However, Capt. Allen passed away unexpectedly before completion.

On January 18, 1759, Allen married to **Ruth (Hodges) Allen** (b. Oct 24 1728, bur. Oct 10, 1774), who was the widow of Israel Gardner, and the sister of Mary (Hodges) Derby (*Derby Tomb*). After her death, he married Margaret (Lockhart) Allen in 1778. Margaret was the sister-in-law of Dr. George Logan (*Mason Tomb*), and Logan was staying with the Allens when he passed away. Capt. Allen had nine living children when he passed, however, the family would face tragedy in the young deaths of their sons.

Jordan Lockhart Allen died on October 19, 1797, aged sixteen, when he drowned at the Cape of Good Hope on his first voyage to sea. Edward's son Alexander, who seems to have had a troubled relationship with his father, and suffered from intemperance, drowned at sea shortly after the death of his father. **Capt. Henry Allen** (b. abt. 1790, d. Oct 15, 1818) died of consumption at age twenty-eight. There is some conflicting information in the records of Henry's death, as the name John Henry, son of Edward Allen and aged 28, is listed as dying the same day. This may be due to confusion in Rev. William Bentley's diary, who writes that he was with John Henry when he passed on the 15th, then later writes of being with Henry Allen when he passed on the 15th. Only Henry Allen appears in Salem's Death records for that month. Capt John Allen, son of Edward Allen, died in Halifax on January 16, 1814, at the age of twenty-eight. **Betsey Allen** (b. abt. 1788, d. Sep 27, 1825), was the daughter of Edward and died of dropsy. **Edward Allen Porter** (b. abt. 1787, d. Dec 30, 1819), the grandson of Capt Edward by his daughter, Ruth (Allen) Porter, died of consumption, and is interred here as well. Ruth (Allen) Porter was the daughter of the Captain and his first wife, Ruth (Hodges) Allen. After her husband's death, she moved to New York, and died in Brooklyn at the age of eighty-nine on June 17, 1849.

Edward Allen Jr, another child of Edward and Ruth (Hodges) Allen, died in São Miguel in the Azores, Portugal on December 5, 1845, and was buried there. Edward Jr was married to Anna Fisk on October 2, 1797, and served in the Revolutionary War on the privateer *Jack* under

Capt. Nathan Brown. His enlistment card from July 1, 1780, gives his age of 24 years and height 5'4". Edward Jr had first proposed marriage to Lydia Mason, but his parents forbade the marriage to take place, and she would instead marry Capt. Benjamin Maley. Edward Jr's sister, Alice (Allen) Orne, widow of Josiah Orne III (*Hollingworth Section*), would eventually move to Pontotoc, Mississippi. She would pass away August 28, 1851 and was buried in the Pontotoc City Cemetery.

Capt. William Allen (b. abt. 1766, d. Jan 20, 1853), a cousin to this family, was born in Manchester-by-the-Sea, Massachusetts. He was the son of Malachi and Ruth (Edwards) Allen, both of whom are interred at the Old Burial Ground in Manchester-by-the-Sea. While living in Manchester, William married Hannah Edwards, with whom he had three children. Two of their daughters, Hannah and Priscilla, died young. Their third daughter, Evelina Allen, lived to the age of eighty-three. After his wife Hannah died in 1802, William journeyed to Salem, where he met his second wife, **Mary (Hunt) Allen** (b. abt. 1775, d. Aug 26, 1842). Mary was the daughter of Irish immigrant Capt. Thomas Hunt and Susanna (Palfrey) Hunt. Captain Hunt was originally from Waterford, Kilkenny, Ireland, and served as Master's Mate on the ship *Tyrannicide* under John Fisk (*Fisk Tomb*). At some point, the remains of Capt. William and Mary Allen were removed from this tomb and interred at the Harmony Grove Cemetery, where there are tombstones for both of them.

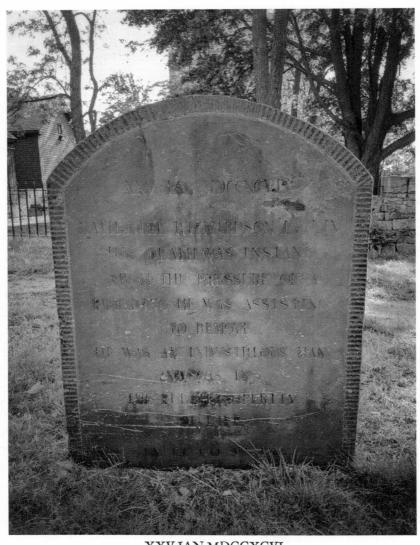

XXV IAN MDCCXCVI

NATHANIEL RICHARDSON, Æ LIV
HIS DEATH WAS INSTANT
FROM THE PRESSURE OF A
BUILDING HE WAS ASSISTING
TO REMOVE
HE WAS AN INDUSTRIOUS MAN
AND WAS IN
THE FULL PROSPERITY OF LIFE
UX ET FIL VI POS
(placed by his wife and daughter)

Charter Street Section

The Distinguished Captain & The Unfortunate Merchants

The Charter Street entrance is the newest addition to the Old Burying Point, the land purchased on June 13, 1767, from William Lander and Joseph Mottey. The iron fence at the entrance was erected by 1904. It was temporarily removed in 2020 and replaced in 2021.

Captain George Dodge (b. Apr 10, 1726, d. Jan 18, 1808) was a distinguished sea captain and prosperous merchant who placed business above all other matters. He married **Lydia (Herrick) Dodge** (b. Mar 18, 1726, d. Jul 10, 1798). Their daughters married into the affluent Cabot and Thorndike families, and their surviving sons found it difficult to live up to their father's high expectations. After the death of his wife, Captain Dodge was not one for company, even that of his own children, who were allowed only brief visits at his home. Little otherwise is known of Captain Dodge, who kept to himself but continued to amass a great fortune in his later years and worked nearly until the day he died. The tombstones for Mr. and Mrs. Dodge are immediately to the left upon entering the cemetery via Charter Street. The tombstone for George Dodge was damaged and removed at some point before 1901. Only the footstone remains, which may have been recut to show his full name and age when the tombstone was damaged.

Capt.

George Do-

-dge Obt. 1808

Æt 82

Samuel Page (b. Dec 3, 1749, d. Jun 24, 1785) was a successful shipowner who financed several privateer vessels during the Revolutionary War, including the sloop *Trenton*, and schooner *Blackbird*, which he co-owned with Walter Price Bartlett (*Gedney Tomb*). By far, his most successful ship was the schooner *Sweat*, with a total of eight carriage guns (cannons) and fifty men on the crew, captained by an experienced shipmaster, John Leach. The *Sweat* set sail in September 1778, and by spring, had captured a two-hundred-ton ship, four brigantines, two sloops, and a schooner. These ships would have sold for a great profit at auction, which was where privateers made their best money. Unfortunately for Samuel, the *Sweat*'s next venture would prove disastrous. Under the command of Jesse Fearson, the ship ran aground in Nova Scotia, where it was taken by the Loyalist infantry known as the Royal Fensible American Regiment. Despite this tremendous loss, Samuel continued financing privateers, though he died of an unknown cause shortly after the end of the war at the age of thirty-six.

Lois (Lee) Page (b. Apr 22, 1753, d. Jun 6, 1779) married Samuel Page on August 12, 1773. Their first son, Samuel Page Jr, appears to have become a merchant and mariner. Their daughter, **Elizabeth Page** (b. abt. 1776, d. Jan 5, 1799) is buried nearby, having died of a hectic fever at age twenty-three. Lois Page died just a week after giving birth to their third child, Jeremiah Lee Page, who would live to become a brick-maker, and died at age eighty-two in Danvers.

Nathaniel Richardson (b. Mar 20, 1742, d. Jan 25, 1796) was born in Woburn, and was descended from one of the founders of that town, Thomas Richardson. He was the wealthy owner of a tannery, a warehouse, several slaughterhouses, a currier's shop, and over 1,250 acres of land in Beverly, Peabody, and along the Kennebec River in Maine. The date of his death is provided in Roman numerals: XXV IAN MDCCXCVI and at the base of the stone is the Latin inscription, *UX ET FIL VI POS*, which translates to, "placed by his wife and daughter."
   Nathaniel's tombstone inscription (pictured) describes the gruesome manner of his accidental death while moving a house. Reverend Bentley further details the unfortunate event in his diary: "Just before 6 o'clock a melancholy accident happened at the corner of Daniels Street, occasioned by a building removing towards Derby Street from Essex Street. Mr N Richardson upon turning the corner took the charge of his own Oxen, and as the building slid towards the fence, the

shoe caught his great coat and before it could be known, he was thrown down and his head passed between an open joice of the building and some timber piled against the fence and it was instant death." After Nathaniel's death, his family suffered yet more tragedy. His son, Jesse Richardson, fell into terrible debt, and was forced to declare bankruptcy, losing almost all that his father had accumulated in life, and his mother was made to take on the debt. In the grips of intense depression, Jesse Richardson hanged himself February 11, 1814, at age thirty-seven. He is interred in the Howard Street Cemetery.

Joshua Richardson (b. Feb 14, 1745, d. Feb 26, 1774) was the younger brother of Nathaniel Richardson and was a provision dealer, trading in beef and lamb. He married **Anstiss (Chipman) Manning** (b. abt. 1752, d. April 27, 1821), who was a teacher. Joshua formalized his will January 18, 1774, just over a month before his death, and left one-third of his estate to his wife, and the rest to his son, Joshua Jr, directing that should his son die before age twenty-one, the inheritance would go to his brother Nathaniel's eldest son instead. The child Joshua would die in infancy shortly after his father's passing.

Anstiss Richardson would marry to Thomas Manning, a mariner who also died young. She is recorded as interred in the Burying Point, though no tombstone for her remains. Her son, **Thomas Manning Jr** (b. abt. 1778, d. Apr 1, 1798) is interred nearby to Joshua Richardson's grave, so it is likely she is buried in this section as well. Thomas Manning Jr's stone has suffered from damage over the years, and is in need of more sophisticated repair. The inscription reads:

This humble stone
is erected
To fhew where the mortal part of
THOMAS MANNING
(the only Child of
Thomas & Anstis Manning)
is deposited

Who died April 1ˢᵗ 1798

In the 21ˢᵗ Year
of his Age

Of all thofe Sorrow that attend mankind,
With patience bear the lot to thee assigned

Lucy Ann (Brooks) Brooks (b. abt. 1806, d. Jan 23, 1840) was married to Luke Brooks on September 26, 1835. She was the daughter of Capt. Anthony Brooks, and originally from Eastport, Maine. It is likely there was a distant relation between them; marrying a second or third cousin was not uncommon in these times. Lucy Ann's cause of death was listed as "palpitation of the heart," which was likely brought on by complications of childbirth. Interred with Lucy is her unnamed **Infant Daughter Brooks** (abt. Jan, 1840, d. Feb 17, 1840) who died at five weeks old. Luke Brooks, who was listed as a grocer, remarried on December 16, 1848, to Hannah Kilby. Neither of them is interred in the Old Burying Point.

Rachel Phelps (b. Jan 12, 1741, d. Sep 5, 1776) was originally from Philadelphia, Pennsylvania. Her maiden name is unknown, and the only similar name found in the Philadelphia vital records is Rachel Corson, born April 1741, daughter of Peter Corson. Rachel of Salem was married to Jonathan Phelps, and may have died soon after. The front of her gravestone is beginning to crumble, and the inscription reads:

Here lies Buried the Body
of RACHEL PHELPS
Wife of JON^A PHELPS Jun
was born at Philadelphia
Jan^r 12th **1741** Departed
this Life died Sep^t 5th **1776**

Death thou hast Conquer'd me
I by thy darts am Slain,
But Christ has conquer'd the (*thee*)
And I shall Rise again

Polly Lawrence (b. abt. 1782, d. Oct 14, 1785), **Mary Lawrence** (bapt. May 5, 1788, d. Oct 29, 1796), and **Henry Lawrence** (bapt. Dec 20, 1789, d. Aug 13, 1798) were among the 14 children of Captain Abel Lawrence and Abigail (Page) Lawrence. Captain Abel was a successful merchant, distiller, and Captain of the Salem Cadets. He was part owner of the ship *Putnam*, whose Master and Logkeeper was Nathaniel Bowditch. Young Henry was killed instantly when he was thrown from his horse in the vicinity of the Old North Meeting House, which was on the corner of

North and Lynde streets. Most children in the cemetery are listed with their parents on those stones, so a separate three like these is unusual. Most of the Lawrence family is not interred in Old Burying Point, but in a tomb in Harmony Grove that was built after both Captain Abel and Abigail's deaths. They were originally interred in the Broad Street Cemetery, then were re-interred in the tomb along with several of their adult children on July 27, 1841. There is no record at this time of these children being moved. Guests have traditionally left mementos at many of these graves. If you wish to do so, please consult the Center staff first.

Photo courtesy of Hayley Eldridge

In   Memory   of
HENRY   LAWRENCE
Son of Capt. Abel & Mrs. Abigail
Lawrence   his   death   was
instantaneous by falling from
a Horſe. Aug 13ᵗʰ 1 7 9 8
Aged 8 Years
& 8 Months

PICTURED IN THE BACKGROUND
IS THE GRIMSHAWE HOUSE
(OR PEABODY HOUSE) IN 2020
THE GEDNEY TOMB IS IN THE FOREGROUND

GRIMSHAWE HOUSE SECTION

The Eminent School Mistress & The Son Who Died at Sea

The 1770 home of Dr. Nathaniel Peabody stands to the right of the Charter Street entrance. Dr. Peabody and his wife, Elizabeth (Palmer) Peabody, lived in this home with their four daughters and three sons. The Peabody sisters, Elizabeth Palmer Peabody, Mary Tyler (Peabody) Mann, and Sofia Amelia (Peabody) Hawthorne, were well-known in their time for their active involvement in education, and in the slavery abolitionist movement. Elizabeth, the eldest sister, is credited with having founded the first American kindergarten, opening a foreign-language bookstore, as well as being one of America's first female publishers, publishing books and anti-slavery pamphlets under the name E.P. Peabody. Mary Tyler Peabody was a teacher, botanist, and civil rights reformer, who lobbied for the education of African-American children. She would marry Horace Mann, the first United States Secretary of Education. Sophia Peabody, an artist whose paintings may be found in the Peabody Essex Museum and the House of the Seven Gables, married Nathaniel Hawthorne. Hawthorne wrote a novel which takes place in the home, using the cemetery as a setting, entitled *Doctor Grimshawe's Secret*.

In more recent years, the home was owned by the late Dr. Harlan Berkley Peabody Jr, who had a great interest in historic preservation. The historic home fell into disrepair over the last few decades, and while the home is still privately owned, it has not had a regular resident in quite some time. As of 2021, the home is undergoing extensive remodeling, and is expected to be turned into a multi-family home. The following graves are located on the side closest to the Grimshawe House, behind the tombs of Orne and Forrester.

Colonel Ezra Newhall (b. May 1, 1733, d. Apr 7, 1798) was a participant in the American Revolutionary War. He was first a Captain, commanding a company of minutemen marching from Lynn on April 19, 1775. Newhall was stationed at Winter Hill during the Siege of Boston, and eventually served with Gen. George Washington at Valley Forge, present for the surrender of General John Burgoyne. He would have taken part in crossing the Delaware River with Washington, and engaged in the Battles of Trenton and Princeton. At the end of the war, he was appointed by Washington as Collector of Internal Revenue, and held that position for the remainder of his life. He married Sarah (Fuller) Newhall on April 10, 1755, and after her death, he married Alice (Basset) Newhall on May 8, 1781, who survived him. Neither of his wives are interred in the Old Burying Point. The *Salem Gazette* published a notice of his death on April 10, 1798: "He served his country in the late war with fidelity and honour; and in civil and domestic life the character of an honest man, faithful friend, tender husband and kind parent was conspicuous in him. Society suffers a real loss by his death."

Captain Joseph Lambert (b. abt. 1731, d. Aug 17, 1790) was the captain of many vessels, most of which were owned by the Derby family. Captain Lambert sailed at least fifteen lengthy voyages, travelling to the West Indies, Gibraltar, Madeira, Jamaica, Barbados, Fayal, and Lisbon. He captained brigantines such as the *Mary and Sarah* and *Ranger*, schooners the *Mercury* and *Liberty*, the snauw *Earl of Derby*, and hundred-and-forty ton, *Lydia*. On the occasion of Lambert's passing, William Bentley wrote: "He was a man of great virtues and great vices. He was the best of sons, the most kind of fathers, the most tender relation and charitable to all who applied in their distress."

John Emerson (b. abt. 1653, d. Feb 24, 1712) was a schoolteacher and served as a chaplain during the French and Indian Wars. He is an ancestor of celebrated writer, Ralph Waldo Emerson.

Susannah (Beckett) Babbidge (b. Apr 14, 1714, d. Jun 2, 1804) was a schoolteacher, keeping a two-floor school in which she would teach young children on the first floor, while one of her daughters, **Lydia Babbidge** (b. Sep 7, 1733, d. Jul 9, 1800) taught young ladies on the second floor. It is said that Susannah was quite heavyset, and preferred not to have to stand up to discipline disruptive children with a smack of her ruler, so she kept a long pole at her desk, with which she could easily strike a misbehaving student from across the room. The inscription on her gravestone reads:

In Memory of
Madam SUSANNAH BABBIDGE
Ob. June 2. 1804.
Æt. 90.
An eminent School Mistrefs for
nearly 50 years.

After being open for over thirty years, the school ceased operating around the time of Lydia Babbidge's death in 1800. Susannah herself passed away four years later at age ninety. Her advanced age did not seem to slow Susannah down, however, as Rev. Bentley notes during her 1803 visit to the Crowninshield house, in her ninetieth year, "She possesses great vivacity, was able to go with us to all parts of the house... She had a distinct recollection of all the first members of the second church." The school in which she and her daughter taught has since been torn down, and was likely set on modern-day Washington Street (then called School Street) near the Lyceum Hall.

Abigail (Bartholemew) Willoughby (b. Aug 6, 1650, d. Sep 3, 1702) has a tombstone which is a replacement for a double-tombstone which formerly stood in this place or nearby, and lists only Abigail's epithet. The original tombstone was shared with her husband, **Nehemiah Willoughby** (b. abt. 1647, d. Nov 6, 1702). Nehemiah was originally from Charlestown, and married Abigail, who was from Salem, on January 2, 1672. Nehemiah was a merchant, co-owner of the ketch *Frances and Mary*, served as a selectman, and was a town constable in 1679. The original stone had a death's-head design over each panel, and bore this inscription:

HERE LYES INTERRE[D]
y[e] BODY OF
MR. NEHEMIAH
WILLOUGHBY AGED

55 YEARS DEC[D]
NOVEMBER y[e] 6TH

1702

HERE LYES INTERRE[D]
y[e] BODY OF MR[S]
ABIGAIL WILLOUGHBY
WIFE TO M[R]. NEHEMIAH

WILLOUGHBY AGED 52
YEARS DEC[D] SEP[T] YE 3[d]

1702

Mary (Preston) Rantoul (b. Sep 17, 1755, d. Jul 17, 1816) was the widow of Capt. Robert Rantoul. They married on October 15, 1774. She was re-married to Samuel Very on September 26, 1793. There seems to have been an unusual end to this second marriage, which Rev. Bentley details in his diary. Samuel apparently agreed to a divorce, one urged by Mary's family, and consented to be found, with witnesses, being in bed with another woman. No date is given for this event, however, if it occurred after 1805, a divorce on grounds of infidelity would mean Mary Rantoul would lose none of her estate (see *Elizabeth (Derby) West; Derby Tomb*). An arrangement such as this would benefit the Rantoul family, who may have seen Very as the proverbial "gold-digger," and would explain why she is buried under her first husband's name. Mary Rantoul died only ten days after her son, **William Rantoul** (b. abt. 1794, d. Jul 7, 1816). William was the clerk of the barque *Camel*, and died at sea of scurvy. He is recorded as "a young man of excellent character."

In Memory of
MR. WILLIAM RANTOUL.
son of
Mrs. Mary Rantoul.
who died at sea
July 7, 1816
Aged 22 years

1922 Map

Graves of Greatest Historical Interest

This bronze map, placed here in 1922, shows the locations of "Graves of Greatest Historical Interest." If using the book as a guide, from this point we will move forward along the inner belt of the cemetery walkway before returning to this spot and proceeding along the outer belt. The 1922 map does not include the paths of the cemetery, and references some tombstones which no longer exist, such as those of Capt. John and Anstiss Crowninshield (*Turner Section*, photo in *Missing Gravestones*). There are also several errors on the map, indicating Capt. John Turner (*Turner Tomb*) in the incorrect location, and providing the wrong name for Nathaniel Ward (*Ward Section*) referring to him as "Jonathan Ward." As of the printing of this book, it is unknown if any corrections will be made to the bronze map. The map itself is nearly a hundred years old, making it an historic landmark.

THE GEDNEY TOMB

GEDNEY AND BARTLETT TOMBS

The Witch Trials Judge & The Secret Spice

This tomb features a sandstone table-top which remains in mostly legible condition. An inscription on the top of the tablet indicates it was repaired in 1894.

John Gedney Esq. (b. abt. 1599, d. Aug 8, 1686) arrived in Salem in 1637 on the *Mary Ann* out of Yarmouth. A vintner, he was licensed to sell wine and other alcohol at his tavern, which was known as the Ship's Tavern. Gedney's tavern also served as an inn, and would have been located roughly where the House of the Seven Gables is today. He was married to Mary Gedney, whose maiden name and vital information are unknown. He remarried to Catherine Clark, whose daughters, Hannah and Susanna, would marry John's sons (their step-brothers) Bartholemew and John Jr, respectively.

Colonel Bartholemew Gedney (b. Jun 14, 1640, d. Feb 28, 1697) was one of nine judges on the Court of Oyer and Terminer; the official name of the court of the Salem Witch Trials. Gedney is one of only two judges of the Court found in this cemetery. He was a son of John and Mary Gedney, and on October 22, 1662, married his step-sister **Hannah (Clark) Gedney** (b. Nov 11, 1643, d. Jan 6, 1696). Gedney was a physician, judge, military officer, and successful merchant in Salem, taking over the Ship's Tavern from his father. In 1678, Gedney was appointed Deputy of the General Court, and would eventually become a councilor to Governor Joseph Dudley. Gedney continued this position under the next governor, Sir Edmund Andros. Andros' reign came as the head of the Dominion of New England, established after the revocation of the Massachusetts Bay Colony's charter. Andros was incredibly unpopular, and brought high taxes, disallowed town meetings, voided landowner's rights, and forced Puritan towns to accept Anglican Churches to be established. Following the Glorious Revolution in England, where William of Orange overthrew King James II, an angry mob stormed Boston and forced Andros to step down. Gedney was tasked with making a list of all the illegal activities committed under Andros' administration.

In 1692, Gedney was appointed as the first Chief Justice of the Court of Common Pleas, and would be appointed to the Court of Oyer and Terminer that same year. Gedney had served as a magistrate along with John Hathorne and Jonathan Corwin, with whom he was reportedly good friends. Gedney would frequently provide the members of the Court with food and entertainment at the Ship's Tavern immediately after hearing cases during the Witchcraft Hysteria.

Gedney's voice is rarely heard in records of the Court until the examination of Captain John Alden, who was the son of a Mayflower Pilgrim, and was a respected military officer. In Thomas Brattle's report of the examination, (see chapter on *Criticism of The Witch Hysteria*) he reported that Alden appealed to Gedney as an associate of his in the past, saying that Gedney must know his character. Gedney replied that he had always thought of Alden as an honest man, but could not be sure given the evidence against him. The evidence largely consisted of the spectral accusations of the afflicted, who also claimed that Alden gave guns and ammunition to the Native Americans, and fathered Native American children. Alden refuted these claims, and asked Gedney how it could be that he could afflict the children simply by looking at them, but he could not do so to the judges. His question went unanswered, and Captain Alden would escape from the Boston jail and flee to either New York, or more likely, to his family home in Duxbury, Massachusetts in September of 1692, reportedly claiming to relatives that the "Devil" was after him, and surviving the Hysteria.

Also interred in this tomb are Hannah and Bartholemew Gedney's daughters, **Bethiah (Gedney) Willoughby** (b. May 27, 1672, d. Nov 24, 1713), who married Francis Willoughby, and **Lydia (Gedney) Corwin** (b. Apr 17, 1670, d. Dec 23, 1700) who married Capt. George Corwin. Captain Corwin was the High Sheriff of Essex County during the Witch Hysteria, and was responsible for the pressing of Giles Corey. Lydia Corwin's husband is buried in the Broad Street Cemetery. It was Lydia Corwin who was forced to pay restitution on her husband's behalf to Philip English, as further discussed in the Hollingworth Section. Bartolemew Gedney's son, **Dr. Samuel Gedney** (b. Nov 2, 1675, d. Sep 18, 1705), a physician like his father, is interred here, as is his infant son, **Samuel Gedney Jr** (bapt. Jul 5, 1702, d. Sep 8, 1702).

Capt. Jonathan Carnes (bapt. May 29, 1757, d. Dec 8, 1827) was an adventuring shipmaster and shrewd merchant who made the single greatest contribution to Salem's age of legendary maritime prosperity. Jonathan and his brother, John Carnes Jr, were both privateers during the Revolutionary War, though John Jr's exploits would earn him greater distinction, he would also gain a reputation as a villain and untrustworthy scoundrel. After the war, both brothers served as shipmasters for the Derbys. John Jr married Lydia Derby, to the dismay of her family and friends. He was lost at sea off the Cape of Good Hope in 1797. Jonathan married **Rebecca (Vans) Carnes** (bapt. Feb 5, 1764, d. Nov 9, 1846) on April 26, 1784. Rebecca came from a wealthy family who were partners in the Boston banking firm Freeman & Vans.

In 1790, Jonathan Carnes was captain of the *Cadet*, the first Salem vessel to traverse the uncharted waters on the western coast of Sumatra. In 1791, Jonathan commanded the snauw *Grand Sachem* for Elias Hasket Derby (*Derby Tomb*). The *Grand Sachem*'s voyage to India lasted several years, and the ship was bound for Salem in 1794. However, on October 7, 1794, Jonathan Carnes returned to Salem empty-handed. The ship had been wrecked off the coast of Bermuda. The entire crew survived, but the ship and cargo were lost. Captain Carnes would have apologized profusely to Derby, however, his apology may have hidden his excitement, for he kept to himself information that was far more precious than Derby's cargo.

During a stop in Sumatra, Carnes had discovered an area where pepper grew in abundance. Pepper was one of the world's most sought-after spices, and Americans had been forbidden from trading in pepper under English rule. Pepper could be not only be used to season meat, but to preserve it, which was exceptionally valuable for economies that relied on maritime trade. In secret, Carnes met with his mother's relatives, Jonathan and Willard Peele, as well as Ebenezer Beckford of Salisbury, and told them of his discovery. If they went in together on a venture, they could turn an extraordinary profit, so long as no one else got there first. The Peeles and Beckford outfitted the schooner *Rajah* for a voyage to Sumatra. The ship would have a crew of ten men, with Jonathan as the captain, and his brother Samuel as first mate. Only the brothers knew the ship's intended destination before it left port on November 3, 1795. The vessel carried a load of lumber, brandy, gin, and tobacco for trade. Stowed away in a barrel was eight thousand dollars in Spanish silver to help the sale should it be needed.

Arriving in Cape Town on March 18, 1796, Carnes sent a letter to his investors to update them on his progress. As was customary, these letters would have been picked up by vessels travelling to America and sent for delivery. When the *Rajah* finally arrived in Padang, Sumatra, the pepper season was coming to an end. Carnes knew he could turn a profit with what was available, but it would fall far short of his promises to the investors. He made the decision to remain in Sumatra until the following year, when the next pepper crop was ready to be harvested and sold. The crew of the *Rajah* stayed in Sumatra for eighteen months while the pepper grew. Whether Captain Carnes was able to relay this decision to wait over a year to his investors (or to his family) is unconfirmed.

At last, the crop was harvested and purchased. Carnes loaded the *Rajah* with as much pepper as the ship could hold and set sail homeward. On January 27, 1797, the *Rajah* was attacked by a French privateering vessel. The attackers had mistaken the American ship for a British ship and were determined to take the prize. In the fighting, a French officer was killed, and a member of Carnes' crew lost his hand. In the case of attack by pirates or privateers, eight thousand dollars in bills was kept on board with direction that it was only to be used to bribe an attacker not to plunder the ship. Carnes did not need to offer the money as the French crew realized their error and apologized.

The *Rajah* arrived at New York in the early summer of 1797 with the first bulk load of pepper to enter the United States. The Peeles hid their records well, and even the family's papers obscure the details of the voyage and cargo, keeping their Sumatran secret safe from prying eyes. However, it became known that the investors in the *Rajah* had made a seven-hundred-percent return on their investment. Every New England merchant wanted to know where Carnes had picked up this extraordinary load of pepper, but he refused to tell. Eager merchants may have tried to pry the information from the *Rajah*'s crew. Carnes had prepared for this possibility, and most of the sailors did not know where the ship had gone, some of the crew believing that they had spent over a year in Burma.

For the next voyage to Sumatra, the *Rajah* was either converted to a brigantine (which had a larger hold) or a new brigantine with the name *Rajah* was built. The Salem Gazette announced on July 20, 1798, that the ship was bound for Sumatra. However, while the destination was known, the route Carnes took was not, and so the location remained a secret. The *Rajah* returned to Salem on October 15, 1799, with a load of 158,544 lbs. of pepper. The ship headed out again and returned in July of 1801 with 147,776 lbs. By this time, the location of his secret port became known, and other merchants sent their vessels to trade. Carnes made several more voyages before he settled in as a successful merchant in a home at what is now 315-317 Essex Street. From his travels, Carnes gave many "curiosities" to the East India Marine Society; an elephant's tooth, a large oyster shell, a two-stemmed pipe, and boxes with worked thin plates of gold from Malaysia. Ship records show him as 5'5" with a dark complexion. He was initiated into the Essex Lodge of Freemasons on November 2, 1780. His exploits would make such an indelible mark on Salem's history that a Sumatran Acehnese pepper merchant with a Salem ship in full sail is pictured on the official City Seal and flag to this day.

Bartlett Tomb

Walter Price Bartlett (bapt. Dec 11, 1743, d. May 15, 1824) is interred in a tomb nearby to the Gedney tomb. He was a shipowner, and a mariner who served as first mate on the *Mary*, captained by David Ropes (see *Ruth Ropes Jr; Ropes Section*). The vessel travelled to St. Croix, and Castle Harbor, Bermuda. He was the son of Joseph Bartlett, and married Elizabeth (Norris) Bartlett around 1769. This tomb is believed to be the oldest in the cemetery, first constructed in 1650 and repaired by Mr. Bartlett in 1809. It is presently unconfirmed who else may be interred with Mr. Bartlett; the sandstone table-top bears Bartlett's name only. Whose tomb it was prior to Bartlett's is presently unknown, nor is it known if any of the remains from 1650 are still within.

Sarah (Whitfield) Higginson (b. abt. 1620, d. Jul 8, 1675) is interred nearby to, but not in, the Bartlett Tomb. She was the first wife of Rev. John Higginson (*Bradstreet Tomb*). She was the daughter of Rev. Henry and Dorothy (Sheafe) Whitfield. She was born in England and migrated with her family to America in 1639. The family settled in Guilford, Connecticut, where her father became the leader of the colony there. She married Rev. John Higginson and came with him to Salem in 1659. Her mother and father had returned to England, and that had been the Higginsons' intent as well, however, a storm forced them to go to Salem, where they stayed. Her great-grandchildren are interred nearby to her (see *Gardner Section*).

SAMUEL SHATTOCK y^e
SON OF SAMUEL & SARAH
SHATTOCK AGED 17 YEARS
& 14^W DECD DECEMBER y^e 14
1 6 9 5

Shattock Section

The Persecuted Quaker & The Bewitched Boy

This section begins nearby to the Bartlett Tomb, continuing until the McIntire Section. Here are interred a number of the members of the Shattock family, who were Quakers. The Old Burying Point is not a churchyard, however, all of those interred here belonged to denominations of Protestantism. This would also mean that there was no restriction on interring unbaptized children in the Old Burying Point.

Samuel Shattock Sr (b. abt. 1630, d. Jun 6, 1689) was a feltmaker and hatter, as well as one of Salem's earliest Quakers. A number of Quakers had begun migrating to New England, despite harsh punishments for openly practicing their religion. Quakers, also known as Friends, were persecuted in colonial New England for beliefs which the Puritans considered heretical. These beliefs included the ability for any member to speak during worship, including women and children, when they felt inspired by God. Shattock and his wife had been respected members of the Salem church, however, they would soon begin attending Quaker meetings.

Shattock was frequently imprisoned and punished along with the other members of the small Quaker congregation. However, despite the danger they faced, Shattock and his wife, **Hannah Shattock** (b. abt. 1624, d. Sep 14, 1701), continued to attend Quaker meetings. Punishments for Quakers were cruel and barbaric, and could include severe floggings, and mistreatment while imprisoned. Several were partially stripped of their clothing and harshly whipped while being forced to march across several towns. Their homes or property could be confiscated, Shattock himself lost half his house and land while imprisoned. A Quaker man could have his ears cut off, and a woman could have a hole burned in her tongue with a hot iron. The sentence of death by hanging was frequently handed out to Quakers, their bodies removed of all personal affects, and disrespectfully thrown in ditches. The persecution of Quakers in Massachusetts grew so rampant, that by 1659 the law allowed for any person to arrest, strip, and flog any nonresident Quaker they found to be in their town without permission.

In September of 1658, Salem magistrate William Hathorne ordered a constable to forcibly enter a Quaker meeting. The constable did so by breaking down the door with an axe and arresting Shattock and the other worshippers. After a short, perfunctory trial before Simon Bradstreet, the men each were given ten stripes (lashes). They also received a sentence of banishment from the colony, not to return on penalty of death. They refused to leave, and in May 1659 were called before Governor Endecott, who gave them a final deadline of two weeks to leave the colony or face execution.

Samuel Shattock and Nicholas Phelps took the opportunity to leave the colony on a ship bound for England, in an attempt to make a complaint to Parliament regarding the cruel treatment of their fellow Quakers. They arrived to find the government in chaos following the fallout of the death of Oliver Cromwell in 1658. The Quakers were forced to wait until the restoration of the monarchy under Charles II was complete. The wounds of the Puritan revolution that had ended in his father's execution were still fresh to young King Charles II; the body of Cromwell was exhumed and beheaded, and nine men convicted of regicide were hanged, drawn and quartered, including the former minister of Salem Town's church, Reverend Hugh Peter, who had served as Cromwell's chaplain.

In September 1661, Shattock and Phelps were finally able to present their argument before the King. Charles II had a missive written for all governors of the New England colonies which ordered that any Quaker who had been imprisoned or placed under the sentence of death be released and sent to England for trial. Effectively, the missive served as a rebuke to the American governors, and took the law out of their hands regarding the corporal and capital punishment of Quakers. The following November, at a meeting of the Massachusetts general court, the missive from the king was reluctantly accepted, and all corporal and capital punishment of Quakers was ordered to cease.

Samuel Shattock Sr's return to Salem with the missive is dramatized in John Greenleaf Whittier's poem, "The King's Missive." Below is an excerpt of the poem, published in 1892:

The door swung open, and Rawson the clerk
Entered, and whispered under breath,
"There waits below for the hangman's work
A fellow banished on pain of death—
Shattuck, of Salem, unhealed of the whip,
Brought over in Master Goldsmith's ship
At anchor here in a Christian port,
With freight of the devil and all his sort!"

Twice and thrice on the chamber floor
Striding fiercely from wall to wall,
"The Lord do so to me and more,"
The Governor cried, "if I hang not all!
Bring hither the Quaker." Calm, sedate,
With the look of a man at ease with fate,
Into that presence grim and dread
Came Samuel Shattuck, with hat on head.

"Off with the knave's hat!" An angry hand
Smote down the offence; but the wearer said,
With a quiet smile, "By the king's command
I bear his message and stand in his stead."
In the Governor's hand a missive he laid
With the royal arms on its seal displayed,
And the proud man spake as he gazed thereat,
Uncovering, "Give Mr. Shattuck his hat."

He turned to the Quaker, bowing low,—
"The king commandeth your friends' release;
Doubt not he shall be obeyed, although
To his subjects' sorrow and sin's increase.
What he here enjoineth, John Endicott,
His loyal servant, questioneth not.
You are free! God grant the spirit you own
May take you from us to parts unknown."

Several Quaker families were involved in the 1692 Salem Witch Hysteria, including Samuel Wardwell Sr, who was hanged as a witch on September 22, 1692 (see *Victims of the Salem Witch Trials*). Another was Thomas Maule, who accused Bridget Bishop of witchcraft, though he would come to be an outspoken critic of the Court of Oyer and Terminer. Bridget Bishop would also be accused of witchcraft by the son of Samuel Shattock Sr.

Samuel Shattock III (b. Sep 7, 1668, d. Dec 14, 1695) was the son of Samuel Shattock Jr and Sarah (Bruckman) Shattock. Samuel III was the firstborn of the couple, and, in a deposition against Bridget Bishop in 1692, Samuel Shattock Jr claimed she was responsible for their son's ill health. Samuel Jr said that in 1680, when she was known as Bridget Oliver, the widow of Thomas Oliver, she began to practice her magical arts on their son Samuel, who was then about two years of age. He claimed young Samuel "was taken in a very drooping Condition and as she came oftener to the house he grew worse and worse." The boy would suddenly fall over "as if he had been thrust out by an invisible hand." Samuel III's condition grew worse; suffering from fits, gasping for air, crying until he exhausted himself from crying and fell asleep, only to awaken again crying and moaning. This continued for many months, until, as his father claimed, "understanding decayed so that we feared (as it has since proved) that he would be quite bereft of his wits; for ever since he has been stupified and void of reason."

The Shattocks suspected witchcraft was the cause of their son's illness, though they did not immediately suspect Bridget. The boy's behavior suggested to them that he was being controlled somehow. Samuel Jr explained how his son would sometimes stand on a wooden board outside and would not come to them, no matter how they called, until he could be physically helped from the board. He would walk to the edge of the board and hold out his hands as if trying to go to his mother, but could not step from the board himself, even when offered money or cake.

An unusual event occurred when an unnamed stranger visited the Shattocks. According to Samuel Jr, he had a conversation with the stranger who said that "we are all born, some to one thing and some to other." Samuel Jr asked the stranger what it was that young Samuel had been born to, and the man replied, "he is born to be bewitched and is bewitched." Samuel Jr pressed him, telling him he could not know that, but the stranger replied that the boy was bewitched by a neighbor whom the boy's mother had argued with, and that the witch had claimed that Goody Shattock had too much pride and would have her pride in her child taken away. Samuel Jr then recalled previous arguments his wife Sarah had with Goody Bishop, including a recent one in which Bishop demanded that Sarah beat Henry Williams, a servant who lived with the family, and went away muttering in a threatening manner, not long before the boy fell ill. Samuel recalled that Bishop had begun visiting their home for seemingly trivial reasons at this time. Bishop had brought "a pair sleeves" to be dyed, and the money she had paid them mysteriously disappeared from a locked box, as Henry Williams reported to him.

Nothing is known of the stranger who professed to know so much about the ways of witches and of the particular witch who was afflicting the Shattocks. However, he seems to have been someone whom Samuel Jr was willing to risk believing. The stranger offered to help the family undo the curse by taking young Samuel with him to Bridget's home, where, under the pretense of getting a pot of cider from her, the stranger would obtain some of her blood. When the stranger returned, it was young Samuel who had been bloodied instead. Bridget had been angered by the appearance of the stranger demanding cider from her, and chased him off with a spade. Spying the boy outside, the stranger claimed Bridget had scratched the child's face and said, "thou rogue what dost thou bring this fellow here to plague me." Young Samuel's fits worsened after this encounter; requiring constant looking after lest he fall into fire or water, and lying still and seeming dead when he did fall. Without the benefit of modern medicine and awareness of mental health, the Shattocks had to conclude their son was bewitched by Bridget Bishop. However, there was little they could do to fight it. It is likely they may have tried folk remedies against witchcraft, as Roger Toothaker and his family were known to do. However, if they did, it certainly was not mentioned before the court. Using magic to combat witchcraft was considered as bad an offense as witchcraft. The Toothakers had been forced to confess to witchcraft, and Roger had died in jail.

When Bridget Bishop was accused of witchcraft in 1692, the Shattocks saw their chance to end the affliction they had struggled with for so long. Samuel Jr and Sarah Shattock submitted testimony on June 2, 1692, against Bridget Bishop before the court clerk, Stephen Sewall. The Shattocks also served as sworn witnesses to Bishop's acts of witchcraft against Abigail Williams, likely seeing their own son's torments mirrored in the fits of the afflicted girls. Bridget Bishop was convicted of witchcraft and hanged June 10, 1692; the first victim of the Salem Witch Hysteria. Samuel Shattock III died three years later at the age of seventeen. It is not recorded whether there was any sign of improvement in his health upon the death of his supposed tormentor, nor is his actual cause of death.

Priscilla (Hodges) Jayne (b. Dec 29, 1788 d. Jul 18, 1810) was married to John Jayne, an auctioneer, on November 2, 1809. There is little record of her besides this ornate tombstone, which has suffered damage, the top portion broken off and re-attached. It appears she may have died of consumption while her husband was at sea. Several days after her death, Rev. Bentley prayed with Mary Andrew, her mother, for Priscilla, and for her daughter's husband, who was at sea. "As we have no Methodist society," Bentley wrote, "he worships with the Baptists. His unoffending little wife in a Consumption, at the last hour resigned herself calmly to the disposal of her new friends. Thus sympathy is made to trifle with salvation." Priscilla Jayne's inscription, written by her husband, reads:

Erected to perpetuate
the remembrance of
PRISCILLA JAYNE,
the affectionate consort of
JOHN JAYNE,
Born Dec 29, 1788;
Died July 18, 1810.

How oft I gazed prophetically sad!
How oft I saw her dead, while yet in smiles!
In smiles she sunk her grief, to lessen mine,
She spoke me comfort, and increased my pain.
When such friends part,
Tis the survivor dies.

In Memory of
Mr SAMUEL MᶜINTIRE
Who died Feb. 6 1811

Æt 54

He was distinguished for genius in Architecture,
Sculpture, and Musick; Modest and sweet manners
rendered him pleasing; Industry, and Integrity
respectable.; He professed the Religion of Jesus
in his entrance on manly life; and proved its
excellence by virtuous Principle and unblemished conducᵗ

McIntire Section

The Genius Architect & Hawthorne's Inspiration

Samuel McIntire (bapt. Jan 16, 1757, d. Feb 6, 1811) was a woodcarver and architect of great distinction. He is considered by many to be the most skilled American woodcarver of his time, though his career was cut short by his sudden and unexpected death. He was the son of Joseph and Sarah (Ruck) McIntire. On August 31, 1778, he married **Elizabeth (Field) McIntire** (bapt. Oct 13, 1754, d. Oct 16, 1815). She was the daughter of Samuel and Priscilla (Ingles) Fields. Samuel's father was a housewright, and woodworking could be said to run in the McIntire blood. Reverend William Bentley said that he encouraged young Samuel to turn his eye towards literature on a variety of subjects, and that this began McIntire's lifetime of appreciation and practice of the arts.

He began his career in woodworking by crafting the figureheads of many Salem vessels. He soon turned to furniture, cabinet-making, and interior design. The plans for many of the grand mansions he designed are held by the Peabody Essex Museum. He was known for carving elaborate and exquisite pieces that were often adorned with his signature sheaves of wheat. One of his most famous pieces was a hand-carved wooden profile medallion of President George Washington, completed in 1802, which was created from a sketch McIntire made of the President during his only visit to Salem, which occurred in 1789. He also created busts of philosopher Voltaire, and Governor John Winthrop. A true renaissance man, McIntire was skilled as a musician, and had a talent for repairing and improving instruments. McIntire died quite suddenly at the age of 54 after complaining of "some obstruction in the chest."

Reportedly, this was the result of a pneumonia that McIntire developed after diving into the icy waters of the North River to rescue a drowning child.

McIntire's home and workshop were located at 31 Summer Street; however, both were torn down. Regrettably, a number of his lauded creations have been lost to the progression of time and industry in Salem. McIntire designed several public buildings which no longer exist, such as the former Court House (which was demolished to make way for the railroad) and the North and South Meeting houses. However, some of his work may still be seen today around the historic McIntire District of Salem, which encompasses areas including Broad Street, Federal Street, Chestnut Street, and Essex Street. McIntire redesigned the interior of the Cotting-Smith Assembly House (136 Federal Street), transforming it into a private home, which is now owned and maintained by the Peabody Essex Museum. The Pierce-Nichols House (80 Federal Street), which he designed in 1782, is another PEM property, as is the Gardner-Pingree House (128 Essex Street). The Derby Summer House in Danvers was designed by McIntire and still stands on Glen Magna Farms. The companion one-room Derby-Beebe Summer House, sometimes called the McIntire Tea-House, is currently in the Federal Garden of the PEM, and viewable from Brown Street.

A number of private homes in Salem today have a mantle or staircase with McIntire's elegant touch. Long after this master craftsman's death, his work is still highly desired. One piece of McIntire's set a new world record for Federal furniture at a 2011 Christie's auction; a McIntire mahogany chair, which had belonged to the Derbys, was sold for $662,500.

Hannah (Hammonds) McIntire (b. Jun 2, 1780, d. Jan 14, 1862) is interred beside her father-and-mother-in-law. She was the daughter of Benjamin and Mary Hammonds and married **Samuel Field McIntire** (b. Jan 26, 1784, d. Sep 27, 1819), the only son of Samuel and Elizabeth McIntire, on January 15, 1804. Her husband carried on his father's business of woodcarving, though he did not achieve the success of his father. Samuel Field McIntire died September 27, 1819, which was blamed on intemperance. He is interred in the Old Burying Point, though no tombstone exists for him. Together, the couple had seven children, none of whom remained in Salem.

Deliverance Parkman (b. Jun 3, 1651, d. Nov 15, 1715) was a shipwright, mariner, shipowner, and merchant. Parkman's home, which stood on the corner of Essex Street and North Street, was built in 1673 and torn down in 1833. The house was believed to have inspired the home in Nathaniel Hawthorne's short story, "Peter Goldwaithe's Treasure," as well as elements of the home in *The House of the Seven Gables*. Hawthorne wrote of Parkman's home in his personal notes, stating that, "one of the ancestors of the present occupants used to practice alchemy."

Deliverance Parkman was married four times, and there are tombstones for three of his wives nearby to him here. His first wife was Sarah (Veren) Parkman, daughter of Hilliard and Mary (Conant) Veren. They were married October 9, 1673, when he was about twenty-two and she was eighteen. They were married nine years before she died, and her cause of death is unrecorded, as is her place of burial. His second wife was **Mehitabel (Waite) Parkman** (b. Sep 15, 1658, d. Dec 7, 1684), originally of Malden, Massachusetts. The date of the marriage is unrecorded; however, she was only twenty-six when she died. Deliverance's third wife was **Margaret (Gardner) Parkman** (b. Jul 14. 1664, d. Mar 25, 1689), they were married in Marblehead on June 3, 1685, when she was twenty-one and he thirty-four. Margaret would pass away four years later, and Deliverance would marry for the final time to **Susannah (Clarke) Parkman** (bapt. Mar, 1643, d. Feb 19, 1728) on September 18, 1704, when he was aged fifty-three and she sixty-one. She outlived him and did not remarry, being interred beside her husband when she passed.

The Lynde Tomb circa 1900, courtesy of The Phillips Library Collection.

SAORED

to y^e Memory
of the Honble BENJ LYNDE Esqr
Who fuſtained with nſefulneſs and dign
=ity in his native Province
The high Offices of
A Repreſentative, a Counſillor &
One of y^e Juſtices of y^e ſuperior Court.
In which Laſt Capacity
His Honored Father & He Com-
pleated beyond Example no leſs
a Period than Sixty Years.

He was born in the year 1700. & on
y^e 3d of october 1781 with an hope
full of Imortallity He reſigned his
ſpirit Into ye hands of his Redeemer.
Reader would,ſt thow Know his worth
Thow muſt inſpect ye register of Heaven

LYNDE AND BROWNE TOMBS

The Boston Massacre Judge & The Unmarked Tomb

The tablet of the Lynde Tomb is an example of how poorly marble has lasted over the years in historic cemeteries. The names which were listed on the marble table-top slowly eroded over time, so that no trace of them remains. The table-top also cracked in three places and needed to be restored in 2016, as did the granite block and bricks that make up the tomb entrance. Now, the tomb is in much better condition, though there are still no names. The tablet-top once read:

Hic Depositae Sunt
Reliquœ BENJAMINIS LYNDE, Armigeri
Prov. Maſs Juſtic Capitatis. Ob. 28. Jan. 1744 Ætat 79.
MARIÆ LYNDE Conjugis Suœ,
Honº GULIELMI BROWNE, Armigeri Filiœ
guœ, Obiit. 12. Julii. A.D. 1753. Ætat. 74.
Mr WILLIAM LYNDE Merch't.
Died the 10th May. A.D. 1752. Ætat. 57.

The Latin inscription translates as follows:

Here lies the
Remains of Benjamin Lynde, Esquire.
Chief Justice of the Province, died Jan 28, 1744 age 79
Mary Lynde, his Wife
Daughter of the Honorable William Browne Esq,
died July 12, 1752 at aged 74

The Honorable Benjamin Lynde Sr Esq (b. Sep 22, 1666, d. Jan 28, 1745) was a highly educated and universally respected judge. Lynde graduated from Harvard College and studied law in London. Upon graduation, he chose to return to the American colonies, one of few learned men of English university to do so. His grammar school years were under schoolmaster Ezekiel Cheever Sr, whose son Ezekiel Cheever Jr was deputized as a court stenographer for the examinations of the Salem Witch Trials, and is responsible for a large portion of the records of the Trials we have today. Lynde passed the bar in 1692. On April 27, 1699, he married **Mary (Browne) Lynde** (b. abt. 1679, d. Jul 12, 1753) the daughter of the Hon. William Browne of Salem, Judge of the Common Pleas for Essex County.

In 1712, Lynde was appointed a judge of the Superior Court. He replaced Samuel Sewall as Chief Justice of the Province in 1728, an office which he held until his death. Lynde had mastered the Greek and Latin languages, and loved the work of Roman poet, Horace. He had a favorite horse, named Rosy, whom he frequently rode to Boston. The Boston Evening Post eulogized him on his passing as follows: "Inflexible justice, unspotted integrity, affability and humanity were ever conspicuous in him. He was a sincere friend, most affectionate to his relations, and the delight of all that were honored with his friendship and acquaintance."

The Honorable Benjamin Lynde Jr Esq (bapt. Oct 5, 1700, d. Oct 5, 1781) is best known for his role as one of the presiding judges in the prosecution of British soldiers involved in the Boston Massacre. He was a graduate of Harvard College and received his master's degree at Cambridge. He married **Mary Bowles (Goodridge) Lynde** (b. abt. 1709, d. May 31, 1790) on November 11, 1731. Mary was noted as a lady of 'strong character.' Lynde was appointed a special Judge of the Court of Pleas for Suffolk in 1734, and became the Standing Judge of the same court in 1739. In 1745, he was appointed to the Superior Bench of the Province.

In 1770, during a sudden protest against the treatment of colonials in Boston by British soldiers, a jeering throng surrounded a group of British soldiers, who discharged their weapons into the crowd. This resulted in the deaths of several civilians, and would become known as "the Boston Massacre." The ensuing riot was quelled only when the mayor assured the people of Boston that a fair trial would be held, and justice served. It was reported that Justice Lynde acted with impartiality. He presided over the separate trials of both the officer, Captain Prescott, and the soldiers. The attorney for the defendants was John Adams, the future second President of the United States. Captain Prescott was cleared of charges in the case, and attention then moved on to the soldiers themselves.

In his remarks to the jury in the soldiers' trial, March 5, 1770, Justice Lynde carefully instructed them to be aware of whether the soldiers were guilty of murder or of the lesser charge of manslaughter. This was a particularly tricky case for one soldier, Matthew Kilroy, as he had a history with one of the victims, and reportedly had claimed that he wanted revenge. Lynde said to the jurors that "this taken alone would suggest a malicious intent to this man... had he gone down and joined the soldiers of his own accord, but that was not the case; he was ordered there by his superior officer whom he was obliged to obey."

Kilroy and Private Hugh Montgomery were found guilty of manslaughter. The soldiers were spared the hangman's noose by "benefit of clergy," an obscure plea that could save one from a death sentence, merely by reading the Bible passage Psalm 51, verse 1; "Have mercy on me, Oh God, according to your unfailing love, according to your great compassion, blot out my transgressions." In medieval times, usually only the clergy were literate, so reciting the Psalm would result in a more lenient punishment. The soldiers' thumbs were branded with an M (for Murder), which meant they could never again seek "benefit of clergy."

Lynde was appointed a Chief Justice in 1771, but resigned due to controversy over judges being paid their salaries by the crown, as one of many difficult political issues leading up to the American Revolutionary War. In the spring of 1781, when he was eighty years old, Justice Lynde was kicked by a horse and never recovered, dying the following October. Also entombed here is his daughter **Hannah Lynde** (b. Aug 17, 1735, d. Dec 21, 1792).

Primus Lynde (b. after 1722, bur. Jun 14, 1787) was an enslaved African American man who was a longtime servant of the Lynde family. He is first mentioned in the will of **William Lynde** (b. Oct 27, 1714, d. May 10, 1752), the brother of Benjamin Sr, and uncle to Benjamin Jr. In William Lynde's will, dated April 7, 1752, he leaves, "To my Negro man Primus the interest of £100" (equal to $30,000 today), an extraordinary amount to bequeath to a servant at the time, especially an enslaved person. Primus' age is not given, but William Lynde indicates that he is not yet thirty years old as of 1752. Primus married Jane, listed as "servant of George Small," in Danvers, on December 30, 1757. At some point, Primus' service transferred to Benjamin Lynde Jr, who seems to have had great affection for Primus, as he is mentioned many times in Lynde's diary as accompanying him to Boston.

In Lynde's 1776 last will and testament, he writes, "I give my negro man Primus his Freedom, provided he get security that he shall be no more charge to my estate, if he grows old and unable to support himself." Primus may have been granted his freedom soon after, as Lynde's diary records on June 13, 1777, "My man Primus left us." Primus is recorded in the Danvers records as marrying a second time, to "Rose, servant of wid. Miriam Putnam, Sept. 14, 1777." The Vital Records of Salem list Primus with the last name "Lynde," as does Judge William Pyncheon in his personal diary. Pyncheon records attending the funeral of Primus Lynde on June 14, 1787. Given Primus' relationship to the Lynde family, especially Benjamin Jr, the likelihood that he was interred in this tomb is high. If indeed Primus is in the Lynde tomb, he is one of the few African Americans interred at the Old Burying Point (see *Missing Stones*).

THE LYNDE TOMB IN 2020
THE SLATE PANEL WHICH HELD THE INSCRIPTION
IS GONE, AND THE WRITING ON THE TABLE-TOP
HAS WORN AWAY

Browne Tomb

Close by to the Lynde Tomb is the Browne Tomb. The table-top of this tomb has been lost, and whatever once supported the table-top, whether it was table legs or a stone base, has also been lost. However, the table-top still existed in 1891, when the inscription below was recorded. Even at that time, much of the inscription was illegible.

WM. BROWNE
FAMILY
TOMB
Erected
1801

\<Coat of Arms\>

HERE LYETH	HERE LYETH
INTERRED Y^e BODY OF	INTERRED Y^e BODY OF
WILLIAM BROWN ESQ.	M^rs. SARAH BROWN
AGED 79 YEARS.	WIFE OF WILLIAM BROWN
WHO DEPARTED THIS LIFE	ESQ. AGED ABOUT ...
Y^e 20 OF JANUARY	YEARS DEPARTED THIS LIFE
1687/8	Y^e 19th OF FEBRUARY ....
	Here lyth ...

Any other names listed below Mr. and Mrs. Brown on the tomb are lost. There is some confusion as to whether William Brown died in 1679 or 1688, which may be due in part to the legibility issues on the tomb. As there is a donation by William Brown Sr. listed as being given to the Grammar school on December 18, 1682, then again in 1687 and 1688, we will assume the correct date of his death was 1688.

William Brown Esq (b. Mar 1, 1608, d. Jan 20, 1688) emigrated from the village of Raydon, in Suffolk, England. He arrived in Salem in 1635, and married **Sarah (Smith) Brown** (b. abt. 1614, d. Feb, 1668) of Wenham. In 1659, he joined with William Hathorne, George Curwin, and Walter

Price to create the Company of the Western Plantation, whose goal was to further the fur trade, and establish a plantation fifty miles west of Springfield, Massachusetts. It is unclear if the plantation was ever established, as the venture seems to have been eventually abandoned. From 1680 to 1683, Brown served as an Assistant to Governor Simon Bradstreet. After the Massachusetts Bay Colony's charter was revoked and the Dominion of New England declared in 1686, the name William Brown then appears as an Assistant to Sir Edmund Andros, however, it is supposed that this is his son, Major William Brown Jr. His other sons made names for themselves in the colony as well; Reverend Joseph Brown became the minister of Charlestown, and Samuel Brown became an enterprising Salem merchant.

Capt. Benjamin Brown (b. abt. 1648, d. Dec 7, 1708) was a son of William and Sarah Brown. His interment in the Browne Tomb on December 13, 1708, is recorded by Rev. Samuel Sewall, who was invited to be a Bearer by Benjamin's brother, Maj. William Browne Jr. Benjamin Brown was a merchant who left money in his will for the Salem Church to buy a baptismal font. He left £200 to create a scholarship for poor Salem scholars to attend Harvard College, as well as money towards making attendance free for the Grammar School, and £20 towards building an Alms-house for the poor. He had in his service a Native American enslaved person by the name of Peter, whom he willed to his brother, Maj. Browne. Rev. Nicholas Noyes (see *Bradstreet Tomb*) was at Benjamin Brown's bedside when he died.

Hilliard Veren (bapt. May 3, 1621, d. Dec 20, 1683) is buried nearby to the Browne Tomb. Veren was born in Salisbury in Wittshire, England. His father was Philip Veren, and the family arrived in Salem in 1635. Hilliard Veren had the important duty of serving as a clerk of the new colony. He performed nearly all clerical duties, serving as a clerk of the writs, clerk of the courts, register of deeds, register of probate, and collector of customs. His signature is found on nearly every important document from the colony, and he is named as an executor in numerous wills. This was in addition to his own business as a merchant, as well as his duties to the militia. Veren was married to Mary (Conant) Veren, the daughter of Salem's founder, Roger Conant. His son, Hilliard Veren Jr, died at Barbados in 1680.

John Sanders (b. Nov 1, 1640, d. Jun 9, 1694) was an influential merchant who owned a wharf at the bottom of the hill on which the cemetery sits, near Central Street. He was one of the prominent citizens of Salem who signed a petition for a new meetinghouse in June, 1680. The old meetinghouse proved too small and could then only hold two thirds of the population. Beside him is his wife, **Hannah (Pickman) Saunders** (b. abt. 1640, d. Mar 18, 1707), who was the daughter of Nathaniel and Tabitha (Dike) Pickman, the first of the Pickman family in Salem, who are mentioned in more detail in the chapter on the Cromwell Section. Her epithet reads:

HERE LYES BURIED
Y^e BODY OF M^{RS}
HANNAH SAUNDERS
FORMER^{LY} WIFE TO
M^R. JOHN SAUNDERS
AGED 65 YEARS
DIED MARCH Y^e. 18th.
1706/7

The use of "formerly wife" as opposed to "widow" or "relict" is an interesting choice. Nearby is interred their daughter, **Elizabeth Sanders** (b. Aug 28, 1678, d. Jun 23, 1708), who is provided with the prefix "Mrs," though there is no record of her marriage, and her maiden name is the same. It is possible this was a mistake on the stone by the original carver, or when the letters were re-cut.

HERE LYES Y^e BODY
OF Mrs ELIZABETH
SANDERS DAUGHT^R
OF Mr JOHN & HANNAH
SANDERS AGED 30
YEARS DEPARTED
THIS LIFE JUNE Y^e
23rd 1708.

Capt William
Bowditch Marn^r
Deceas^d y^e 28th of May
1728 aged 64
years and 9 Months

BOWDITCH SECTION

The Tragic Bride & "Detestable Superstition"

H ere may be found members of some of Salem's oldest families. The history of Salem is filled with the names of Bowditch, Felt, and Hunt. Most notably, this would be the family of famed American navigator, Nathaniel Bowditch.

Elizabeth (Boardman) Bowditch (b. abt. 1780, d. Oct 18, 1798) was the wife of Nathaniel Bowditch, a mathematician who revolutionized nautical navigation with the release of his book, *The New American Practical Navigator* in 1802. Elizabeth was known for her intelligence and amiable nature, and many of their friends applauded them as a wonderful match. Elizabeth was the daughter of Francis and Mary (Hodges) Boardman. Her father died at sea in Haiti when she was twelve, and Elizabeth lived with her mother and siblings, of which she was the second-eldest. Elizabeth and Nathaniel Bowditch were married on March 25, 1798, in a ceremony performed at the Boardman's home by Rev. William Bentley. Bowditch's family was not a wealthy one, and the young couple could not afford their own home, so they lived with her mother in the Francis Boardman House at 82 Washington Square East. It was not long after their wedding that Nathaniel had to set back out to sea on the ship *Astrea*, bound for Europe.

In December 1798, while in Alicante, Spain, Nathaniel received the terrible news that his wife had died. Elizabeth had contracted consumption and died at the age of eighteen, having been married for only seven months. Nathaniel could not return home to grieve at his wife's grave until the following April. Bowditch returned the dowry he had received and all the bridal gifts, giving them to his mother-in-law, saying that he felt he had no right to them. Nathaniel did not write about his feelings regarding the death of his wife, however, one of his close friends, Judge Daniel Appleton White, gave a eulogy after Bowditch's death and mentioned Nathaniel and Elizabeth's short marriage, saying "A momentary vision of bliss had thus flitted before him and vanished forever, leaving no trace of itself in his path of life." This statement may have been particularly poignant coming from Judge White; his own wife Eliza (Orne) White (*Orne Tomb*) died less than two years after their wedding.

After Elizabeth's death, Nathaniel Bowditch grew closer to his cousin, Mary Hodges Ingersoll. The two were childhood friends, and it is thought that Mary was Nathaniel's first love, however, she had previously rejected his affection. Mary Ingersoll and Elizabeth Boardman had been close friends, and it is possible that Elizabeth's fondness for Nathaniel may have been the reason for Mary's prior rejection of him. However, after Elizabeth's death, Mary and Nathaniel fell in love. On a voyage to Manila in 1799, he began to write to Mary at every chance he could, sending letters home via fellow sailors bound for Salem. They were married on October 28, 1800.

Nathaniel and Mary had eight children together, and moved into a home that is now located at 9 North Street, where they lived until 1823, when the family moved to Boston. Their fourth son, **Charles Ingersoll Bowditch** (b. Dec 1, 1809, d. Feb 21, 1820) died of a throat distemper at the age of ten, and is interred nearby to Elizabeth. Their eighth child was a daughter whom they named Elizabeth Boardman Ingersoll Bowditch. Nathaniel and Mary Bowditch are buried in the Mount Auburn Cemetery in Cambridge, Massachusetts.

Captain William Bowditch (b. Sep 1663, d. May 28, 1728) was a mariner who joined Captain Richard More and others in the taking of Port Royal in Nova Scotia. He famously wrecked a ship in Salem Harbor on an unknown ledge which was subsequently called Bowditch's Ledge. A tall granite marker was placed at the location, which collapsed in 2018. He was the great-grandfather of Nathaniel Bowditch. His tombstone, seen at the start of this section, is nearby to the outer path and almost opposite the Hollingworth tombstone.

Here lies the remains of
Mrs. ELIZABETH BOWDITCH
wife of
Mr. Nathaniel Bowditch
Who died Oct 18th
1 7 9 8
Aged 18 years

Habbukak Bowditch (b. Jan 5, 1737, d. Jul 28, 1798) was the husband of Mary (Ingersoll) Bowditch and the father of Nathaniel Bowditch. Habbukak was a cooper, who is someone skilled in the craft of making barrels, casks, buckets, and similar items. Habbukak learned the trade of a cooper when he was young, and then set out to sea, becoming a shipmaster, taking ships laden with cargo to the Caribbean. Habbukak was remembered for his intelligence despite his lack of a formal education, and unfortunately, for his problems with alcoholism. Nathaniel was the fourth of their seven children, and shortly after his birth, the family removed to small, two-room home in Danvers. They were a family of little means, and poverty played a large role in their lives, especially as the American Revolutionary War raged around them. Perhaps preferring not to risk his life by returning to the dangers of the sea, Habbukak once again took up his old trade of coopering, and the family of seven children returned to Salem. Habbukak worked to ensure that his children could receive an education, as several of his sons proved to be talented mathematicians. Nathaniel recounted being teased by his classmates for going to school in winter wearing his summer clothes, for the family could not afford warm winter clothing. Once a year, the family would receive a small donation from the Salem Marine Society to help their struggling situation, and they would often rely on the kindness and generosity of their friends and neighbors.

Habbukak's wife, Mary Bowditch, died December 16, 1783, though her cause of death and burial site are unconfirmed. Shortly after Mary's death, Habbukak took his son Nathaniel out of the cooperage and sent him to be apprenticed as an accountant. Tragically, Habbukak's daughter, Elizabeth, died after suffering a fall in 1791, and was buried at the churchyard of Saint Peter's Church at 24 St. Peter Street. His sons, Habbukak Jr and Samuel, went out to sea, as their father and brother had, and Samuel died at sea in 1794. Four months after Nathaniel married Elizabeth Boardman, Habbukak suffered from a stroke which left him paralyzed. He died shortly after, and was interred here, having seen only just the beginning of the history-making rise to prominence of his son.

Ebenezer Bowditch Jr (b. May 10, 1800, d. Aug 22, 1825) was the son of **Ebenezer Bowditch Sr** (bapt. Nov 23, 1766, d. Jul 23, 1830) and **Mary (Appleton) Bowditch** (b. abt. 1772, d. May 17, 1819). He was a desperate young man who took his own life at the Salem almshouse, a shelter built for the poor and homeless. It was not impossible at the time for a Protestant who committed suicide to receive a cemetery burial, as it was for some other faiths existing in New England at the time. By the late 1700s, it was thought and accepted by many that suicide was the result of temporary insanity, the victims declared as *non compos mentis*. Another Salem man, William Obear, hanged himself in 1816 and was refused burial in Saint Peter's Cemetery, which was Episcopal. Reverend Bentley had Obear buried in the Howard Street Cemetery, and called the practice of refusing burials for suicides a "detestable superstition."

William Gedney Esq. (b. May 28, 1668, d. Jan 24, 1730) was the son of John and Susannah (Clark) Gedney, and brother to Bartolemew Gedney (*Gedney Tomb*). He succeeded George Corwin as High Sheriff of Essex County, serving from 1696 to 1708 and again from 1710 to 1715. Sheriff Gedney took part in the capture of the pirates of the *Charles*, which is detailed in the entry of the Honorable John Turner II (see *Turner Tomb*). He married **Hannah (Gardner) Gedney** (b. Apr 16, 1671, d. Jan 4, 1704), who is buried beside him.

Deacon Lewis Hunt (b. Mar 23, 1746, d. Oct 23, 1797) was a baker and a deacon of the First Church. He ran a baker's shop out of his ancestral home, known as the Lewis Hunt House, named so for his seafaring ancestor. The gabled mansion stood at the corner of Washington Street and Lynde Street, until it was torn down in 1863. He was the son of **William Hunt** (b. Aug 5, 1701, d. Sept 19, 1780) and **Eunice (Bowditch) Hunt** (b. Mar 22, 1707, d. Aug 30, 1764). Lewis would marry **Sarah (Orne) Hunt** (b. Jun 7, 1750, d. Nov 17, 1781) on November 22, 1770, and they were married until Sarah's sudden death at age thiry one. On April 7, 1782, Lewis married **Mary (Bowditch) Hunt** (bapt. Jun 15, 1760, d. Mar 18, 1829). Deacon Hunt joined a group of prominent Salem patriots who signed a letter to Governor Thomas Gage on June 21, 1774, protesting the closure of Boston Harbor, which had been done as a punishment for the Boston Tea Party. Gage was residing in Danvers at the time and had been sent a letter from the Tories in Salem commending the closure and welcoming the influx of shipping to Salem. Deacon Hunt signed the opposing letter, which questioned if closing the port was fair to the people of Boston, who had "subdued the dreary wilderness" and stating that Salem harbor was not suited to take on the heavy trade that flowed through Boston.

George Felt III (b. abt. 1657, d. Feb 24, 1730) was a block-maker by trade; he carved woodcuts used for printing. His grandfather, George Felt Sr, was one of the first settlers of North Yarmouth. His father, George Felt Jr, was killed in battle against Native Americans in Casco Bay in 1677, serving under the command of John Hathorne (*Hathorne Section*).

Katherine (Shafflin) King (b. abt. 1626, d. Dec 15, 1718) was a member of an early Quaker congregation in Salem. Her husband, William King, a cooper by trade, was charged with blasphemy, and stood trial for this crime in 1681. William was well-liked in his community, but was believed to be "distracted," and suffered from delusions. He believed that he had been gifted by God with supernatural abilities, and could walk on water, and force speech or impose silence on others This offended Thomas Maule, who argued with King over his supposed blessings, and provoked him to make an official statement about it before the magistrates. King agreed to do so, and exclaimed before Bartholemew Gedney that he was "the son of God." Gedney was forced to act on this, and King was tried for blasphemy before the Court of Assistants at Boston.

Katherine provided a petition to the Court regarding the wrongs Maule had done to her husband, and how her husband had been provoked by Maule to appear before the magistrate. Maule's intention seems to have been to turn the community against King, but quite the opposite occurred, and his neighbors supported King, whom they felt was mad, but harmless. They tolerated King's ranting, likely due to the loyalty and affection the community felt for Katherine. William King was imprisoned for two months, whipped, jailed again, and eventually freed. This was a fairly lenient sentence, considering the heretical nature of his crime, however, the Court likely took into consideration his supposed madness.

HERE LYES BURIED
THE BODY OF M^R
GEORGE   FELT
DEC^D FEB^{RY} y^e 2
17 2 9 30 IN y^e 74th
YEAR OF HIS AGE

HERE LYES INTER^D
y^e BODY OF CO ^ ^{LO} JOH^N
HATHORNE ESQ^R
AGED 76 YEARS
WHO DIED MAY y^e 10th
I 7 I 7

Hathorne Section

The Hanging Judge & Bold Daniel

Here are buried several members of the Hathorne family, from whom Salem's most famous author, Nathaniel Hawthorne, is descended. Nathaniel Hawthorne himself is interred at the Sleepy Hollow Cemetery in Concord, Massachusetts.

Colonel John Hathorne (b. Sep 4, 1641, d. May 10, 1717) was the son of William Hathorne, a notoriously harsh Puritan magistrate and soldier. He married Ruth (Gardner) Hathorne on January 22, 1675. Nathaniel Hawthorne, who was the great, great grandson of John Hathorne, recalls William Hathorne's "bitter persecution" of the Quakers, most notably an incident when he had a Quaker woman stripped to the waist and whipped in the street. "His son," Nathaniel says, "inherited the persecuting spirit."

John Hathorne was a magistrate of Salem in 1692, and would be appointed as one of nine judges of the Court of Oyer and Terminer, which presided over the Salem Witch Trials. He is one of only two judges of the court interred in the Old Burying Point, Bartolemew Gedney (*Gedney Tomb*) being the other. Hathorne is sometimes referred to as the "Hanging Judge," which is a misinterpretation of his actual role in the trials. Hathorne served as a spokesman for the other judges of the Court, interrogating the accused, while it was the duty of the jury to determine innocence or guilt.

Hathorne's role in the 1692 hysteria began when he presided over the questioning of three women accused of witchcraft, Sarah Good, Sarah Osbourne, and Tituba Indian. The "afflicted" children were present at Ingersoll's Ordinary, a tavern in Salem Village, where they repeated their accusations, writhing and convulsing in alleged spectral torment. Tituba, an enslaved Native American woman who was purchased by Reverend Parris in Barbados, confessed to witchcraft, though she would later claim it was false, and that she had been forced to confess. The magistrates prodded her further to try and confirm the names of other witches in the community. This act was technically a breach of common witch interrogation procedure; a confessed witch's accusations would usually be thrown out as lies. After all, what better way could the Devil use to wrongly condemn an innocent person than to have a confessed witch accuse them? This practice would continue throughout the accusations of 1692, despite a warning from Reverend Cotton Mather against it (though later he would seem far more accepting of its use). Hathorne would continue to serve as a principal interrogator during the months leading up to the start of the trials, with the same scenario playing out in nearly all of the depositions. On May 27, 1692, Hathorne was appointed by Governor William Phips as one of the judges of the Court of Oyer and Terminer.

The court documents of the Oyer and Terminer sessions from June through October of 1692 are lost, however, many of the arraignments and depositions have survived, and give remarkable insight into how the grand jury trials operated. A judge, Hathorne typically, would pose questions to the accused that assumed their guilt, and demanded explanation for the torments from which the afflicted were suffering. Statements made by the accused in their defense were often met by outcries from the afflicted, both at the stand and in the audience. It is unlikely that the final courtroom appearances differed greatly from these grand jury trials, which were held at the Salem Village Meeting House, and open to the public. The afflicted, originally a group of young women between the ages of ten and twenty, but later expanding to over forty men and women of all ages, served as the bulk of the evidence against the accused. Common wisdom of the time indicated that children, being untainted by sin, could see the works of witches and the devil, which was invisible to adults. Those afflicted by witches were also thought to have a part of the witch's spirit within them, allowing the witch to torment them, but also allowing the afflicted to see the witch's hand in afflicting others. These forms of evidence would be referred to as "spectral."

Governor Phips would halt the Court of Oyer and Terminer in October 1692 amid controversy over the spectral evidence accepted during the trials, among many other complaints. A new court would be created to handle the remaining cases, which still numbered over a hundred. Hathorne was not appointed to this court, though many of the previous Oyer and Terminer judges were. This new court found only five individuals guilty, all of whom were pardoned by Phips. The remaining cases were dismissed, including that of Tituba Indian. Of all the judges that took part in the original court, only two publicly expressed discontent; Lieutenant Nathaniel Saltonstall, who stepped down due to the sentence of death on Bridget Bishop, and Reverend Samuel Sewall of Boston, who publicly apologized for his role in the trials afterward.

John Hathorne remained a respected and important figure in Salem following the end of the Court. In 1696, he received his military commission, and joined Colonel Benjamin Church in laying siege to Fort Nashwaak in Acadia. The attack was a failure, and Church blamed the defeat on Hathorne's incompetence. Hathorne remained active in the military and attained the rank of Colonel in 1711. He owned a home located on modern-day Lapin Square Park on Washington Street, which visitors will notice is the site of the "Bewitched" statue, erected in 2005. He also owned property on 'Hathorne Hill' in Danvers, the eventual site of the notorious Danvers State Lunatic Asylum, also known as Danvers State Hospital.

In 1965, Hathorne's gravestone was repaired and set into a granite case. In 1986, Salem resident Everett Philbrook found that the gravestone had fallen out of the casing. To prevent theft of the historic stone, Mr. Philbrook carried it to the Salem Police station. "As I walked," Mr. Philbrook says, "I imagined that Judge Hathorne was watching me, and taking me for a thief, was making a terrible judgment about my motives." The stone was soon replaced into the granite casing. Mr. Philbrook is today the museum store manager of The House of the Seven Gables, where Judge Hathorne's legacy is retold as part of the history of his descendant.

It was Nathaniel Hawthorne who added the 'W' to the family name. Local folklore holds that he did so in order to distance himself from his infamous ancestor, though this is not affirmed in any of the author's works or personal letters. What is known for certain is that during Hawthorne's lifetime, the standardization and reform of spelling was a highly relevant topic, and surnames were important to the argument. When the family was still in England, prior to William Hathorne's migration to the colonies, one of the spellings they had used was 'Hawthorne.' Nathaniel Hawthorne did, however, give his readers a glimpse into his personal feelings for his great, great grandfather in the introduction to *The Scarlet Letter*, stating that he "made himself so conspicuous in the martyrdom of the witches, that their blood may fairly be said to have left a stain upon him. So deep a stain, indeed, that his dry old bones, in the Charter Street burial ground, must still retain it."

Captain Daniel Hathorne (bapt. Aug 22, 1731, d. Apr 18, 1796) was a hero of the American Revolutionary War. While Col. Jon Hathorne's name is remembered with infamy, his grandson's has been celebrated throughout the years. A successful Salem shipmaster, he captained privateer vessels for the Derbys and many others during the war. One of his vessels was attacked by a British vessel carrying two hundred and fifty soldiers under the command of General Howe. The captain and crew fought off the boarding party, and Hathorne's bravery would be commemorated by the ship's surgeon, who wrote a ballad, "Bold Hawthorne" about the battle and Hathorne's heroics. The following is an excerpt of the ballad published in 1892, in which the British snauw, filled with troops under Howe's command, bears down on their ship and launches an attack with a boarding party.

She was prepared with nettings,
And her men were well secured,
And bore directly for us,
And put close on board;
When the cannon roared like thunder,
And the muskets fired amain,
But soon we were alog-side
And grappled to her chain.

And now the scene is altered,
The cannon ceased to roar,
We fought with swords and boarding-pikes
One glass or something more,
Till British pride and glory
No longer dared to stay,
But cut the Yankee grapplings,
And quickly bore away.

Our case was not so desperate
As plainly might appear;

Yet sudden death did enter
On board our privateer.
Mahoney, Crew, and Clemmons,
The valiant and the brave,
Fell glorious in the contest
And met a watery grave.

Ten other men were wounded
Among our warlike crew,
With them our noble captain,
To whom all praise is due;
To him and all our officers
Let's give a hearty cheer;
Success to fair America
And our good privateer.

The name of the surgeon is not recorded, and while the battle is attributed to Hathorne's time on the ship *Fair American*, a ship bearing that name is not listed among the catalogues of Salem privateer vessels. It is possible that the name of the ship and the events of the battle have been confused as the ballad has been retold throughout the years. Hathorne was once the captain of the schooner *True American*, but he did not engage in a battle such as the one described during that time. On October 28, 1776, while Hathorne served as captain of the brigantine *Sturdy Beggar*, he was engaged in battle for two hours with an unnamed British ship. Three of his men were killed and ten wounded, exactly as described in the song. It may be that the battle described in the song actually took place on the *Sturdy Beggar*.

Following the war, Captain Hathorne continued his career at sea, travelling to the West Indies. He had the misfortune of losing the ship *Mary Ann* off the coast of Martinico. At one time, he owned the home now known as the Nathaniel Hawthorne Birthplace, once located on Union Street, and now moved to the property of the House of the Seven Gables. Buried beside him are his wife **Rachel (Phelps) Hathorne** (b. Jun 1, 1734, d. Apr 16, 1813), as well as their daughters, **Eunice Hathorne** (b. Oct 4, 1766, d. May 10, 1827) and **Sarah (Hathorne) Crowninshield** (bapt. May 22, 1763, d. Jan 14, 1829).

Nancy (Bickford) Mudge (bapt. Nov 22, 1778, d. Jan 9, 1801) was the wife of Capt Joseph Mudge. She married Capt. Mudge on August 10, 1799. She would pass less than two years later. Her tombstone was originally located in the Ropes section, where the footstone remains. When the headstone was moved here, and why, is uncertain. It is likely that her body is still interred there, and was not moved here with the tombstone. Her tombstone carries a loving inscription from her husband:

This Monumental
Inscription is dedicated
Sacred to the Memory of
Mrs. NANCY MUDGE
Confort of Capt JOSEPH MUDGE
Of LYNN
who died Jan^{ry} 9 1801
Ætat 22.

Thou fair example of our rising youth
Of Modesty, of Wifdom, Prudence, Truth
In Joys sedate, in suffering much compof'd
Serene through life, & peaceful when it closed
Of softest maners and a virtuous, mind
Courteous to all, benevolent and kind
Go live with GOD, who calls the hence away,
Go reign with him in everlasting day
Yet take our tears, Mortalitys relief
Until we share your joys, forgive our grief
These rites this Monument this verse receive
Tis all a Hufband, all a Friend can give.

Stone in 2020

HERE
LYETH BURIED
YE BODY OF CAP^T
RICHARD MORE
AGED 84 YEARS
DIED 1692
MAYFLOWER

PILGRIM

Stone prior to 1901
The Only Mayflower Gravestone
George Ernest Bowman

More Section

The Mayflower Passenger & The German Immigrant

This section is placed where the inner belt and outer belt of the cemetery paths meet. This plot was once fenced in, like the Robert Peele Lot, but the wooden fence was removed long ago.

Captain Richard More (bapt. Nov 13, 1614, d. 1696) has a gravestone encased in a bracket for protection. This is the only known gravestone of a Mayflower passenger still in existence that was erected at the time of their death. More's gravestone has the words "Mayflower Pilgrim" etched into it; however, those words and the date "1692" were not included on his stone when the old mariner passed away. In fact, during his lifetime, no one referred to the passengers on board the Mayflower as "Pilgrims," instead calling them the "First Comers" or the "Old Planters." In Plymouth, those Mayflower passengers who sought a new, religious colony were called "Saints" while those on board who sought wealth and opportunity were called "Strangers." Richard More was on the Mayflower through no choice of his own, and he was not a "Saint" by any means. More would become known as a smuggler, borderline pirate, and may have worn the literal Scarlet Letter.

Much like the rest of this intriguing rogue's life, his journey to Salem began with skullduggery and deceit. In 1620, Richard's father, Samuel More of Shropshire, England, divorced his wife Katherine on the grounds that she had been unfaithful. Samuel declared that Richard and his siblings, Ellen, Jasper, and Mary, were not his children, but rather those of a local rascal named Jacob Blakeney. Katherine did not deny this, and claimed to have been first married to Jacob before being forced into an arranged marriage to Samuel, who was her fifth cousin. The court sided with Samuel, who sold the children into seven years of indentured servitude to the financiers of the Virginia Colony, which included his employer, Lord Edward Zouche.

Richard was the only one of the children to survive the passage to Plymouth and the harsh first winter. He likely would have been serving food to the colonists and Wampanoag tribe at the first Thanksgiving. At the age of twenty, he was back in England with Plymouth colony's accountant, Isaac Allerton, who was starting his own merchant colony in Kennebec, Maine. It appears Allerton took the young Richard as an apprentice, paying sixty pounds to Samuel More. Whether Richard ever saw his estranged father or mother during this or any other voyage to England is unknown. Richard and Allerton returned to Massachusetts on the *Blessing*, where Richard would have met **Christian (Hunt) More** (b. abt. 1616, d. Mar 18, 1676), the twenty-year-old stepdaughter of Richard Hollingworth, who was immigrating to Salem with his large family.

Richard More and Christian Hunt were married in Plymouth in 1636, and had their first child, Samuel, in 1640, which was unusual for Puritans in New England as they often had children in their first year of marriage. This may have been a sign of trouble with the young couple, who would eventually have seven children together. In 1638, Richard seems to have become involved with another woman, during one of his trips to London in 1638. "Richard Moore mariner of Salem" married Elizabeth Woolnough on October 23, 1645, at Saint Dunstan's of Stepney parish. The couple had a child, Elizabeth, who seems to have been about the age of eight, conceived around 1638, and baptized March 1646. Bigamy was punishable by death in Oliver Cromwell's Protectorate, so it is likely More entered into this second marriage without disclosing his first marriage, or perhaps he was forced into this marriage by the Woolnoughs, since the child was born out of wedlock. One month after the baptism, Richard was charged with "being taken in the company of a lewd suspicious woman and a common feildwalker (slang for 'prostitute'), and for assaulting a child about eight years of age (most likely his own)." Rather than answer for the charges, he returned to Salem and left his London wife to answer in his place.

By 1649, Richard's family in Salem had grown considerably. Christian had given birth to Thomas More, **Caleb More** (bapt. Jan. 31, 1645, d. Jan 4, 1679), Joshua More, Richard More Jr, Susannah (More) Dutch, and **Christian (More) Conant** (b. abt. 1652, d. May 30, 1680). That

October, the family moved to their home on the South River, near the Burying Point. If you exit the cemetery through the Witch Trials Memorial, turn right to walk down Liberty Street to Derby Street, then turn left and walk one block to Hawthorne Blvd. To your left is the Lydia Pinkham Memorial Clinic at 250 Derby Street, which sits on the land the More family's home, tavern, and wharf was built. A plaque still stands to the left of the clinic, declaring this as the site of the former home of Richard More.

It was also on this site that the plunder of war was stolen from Richard. In 1654, during a raid on Port Royal in Nova Scotia, Captain More took possession of a large, ornate church bell worth three hundred pounds. The bell was meant to be delivered to Beverly, but More decided to keep it for himself. He kept it in his yard and refused to hand it over to the claimants from Beverly. Whether he meant to keep it as a spoil of war, or more likely, sell it, the bell was stolen from his yard while he was on a voyage to the Caribbean. Soon after, a new, large bell appeared at the Beverly Church. This incident was but one of many times Richard More flouted the law. When the restored monarchy declared there was to be no shipping between the colonies without first going to England, More took an active part in smuggling as an inspector who could declare cargo travelling from one colony to another "unfit for sale" and then unload it to be sold in the colonies, likely earning himself a generous fee or cut of the profits.

More retired from the life of a seafarer in 1668 and turned his home into a tavern. There were fourteen taverns and ordinaries in Salem at that time, and More's became a haven for sailors, where fighting and cursing were commonplace. After his wife Christian died in 1678, Richard would marry **Jane (wd. Crumpton) More** (b. abt. 1631, d. Oct 8, 1686), who worked as a bartender in his tavern. The only other employee of the tavern was an African woman named Judeth, whose status as either an indentured servant or enslaved person is unknown. Richard and Jane More operated the tavern for another ten years, however, the couple began to slowly decline in their fortunes and Richard sold off his land holdings piecemeal. The tavern license expired in 1682, and on October 5, 1686, Jane More died at the age of fifty-five.

As was common with many taverns of the time, More's tavern was a place to settle legal matters without the formality of a court. The most notable of these events to be handled at More's tavern was the case brought against Giles Corey by John Proctor, who claimed that Corey had burned part of his roof. The issue was amicably resolved with the conclusion that the fire had been accidentally started by Proctor's servant, which was attested to by Jane More. Richard More later stated that Proctor and Corey "showed great love for each other," and split their drink bill. In 1692, Proctor and Corey become integral parts to the story of the tragic witch hysteria that was brewing within the town, Proctor hanged as a witch and Corey pressed to death.

There was one final act of the drama to play out in the life of Richard More: in July of 1688, when he was past the age of seventy, he faced the charge of adultery with a married woman. The woman's name was not provided, indicating she was probably not a member of the church. According to English law of the time, the proper punishment for him would have been to stand on a gallows with a noose around his neck to symbolize the seriousness of his offense (punishable by death previously), thence to be whipped with no more than forty lashes. He would then have been forced to wear a two-inch-long "A" upon his upper garments; the infamous 'Scarlet Letter.' The whipping post was located on the grounds of modern-day Salem Common, where all public punishments, excepting hanging, were carried out. As there was no gallows in Salem at the time, it is unclear whether he was made to suffer some, or all of these torments. What is certain is that Richard More was excommunicated from the church under the eyes of the junior minister, Reverend Nicholas Noyes, and the elder minister, Reverend John Higginson. More would suffer from this humiliation for two years before his public apology was accepted on April 26, 1691, and he regained admittance to the church. Captain Richard More died at sometime before 1696, though the actual date and cause of death are unknown, and the stone is engraved with 1692. The tombstone of the man who began as an unwanted child and became a First Comer, an extraordinary shipmaster, an incorrigible rogue and an adulterous lout, is every bit as deceptive and controversial as the man himself; mislabeling him as a Pilgrim, and perhaps even engraved with the wrong date of death.

Buried beside Captain More is his first wife, Christian (Hunt) More, whose stone is engraved with the Latin phrase *Hodie Mihi Cras Tibi*, which translates to "Today me, tomorrow you," a common and morbid expression for 17th century headstones. To the right of Capt. More is his second legal wife, Jane (wd. Crumpton) More, whose original maiden name is unknown.

Jane Crumpton had arrived in Salem on the *Friendship*, captained by Captain More's son, Richard Jr. With her was her husband, Samuel Crumpton, who was killed shortly afterward by the Nipmuc tribe in the Battle of Bloody Brook, a one-sided massacre in South Deerfield, Massachusetts. Jane Crumpton married Richard More sometime before 1678. The side panels of her tombstone are decorated with foliage, which may be seen in many gravestones of the time. It is interesting to note the death's head figure on her stone is not a skull, as seen on Christian More's, but a winged soul effigy, which was just starting to become popular in Puritan Massachusetts.

Caleb More (bapt. Jan. 31, 1645, d. Jan 10, 1679) was the third son of Richard and Christian More. Caleb More was a mariner who died at the age of thirty-four, and did not have any children, nor was he married. His cause of death is unknown, however, there was a report published in 1677 by Richard Hutchinson that was noted as "Being a True and Perfect account brought in by Caleb More, Master of a Vessel Newly Arrived from Rhode Island," and provided the details of the death of King Philip (Metacomet) of the Wampanoag. Is it highly likely this account comes from the same Caleb More of Salem, and aside from this tidbit, his baptismal record and his tombstone in the Old Burying Point, there is no other historical note of him.

Christian (More) Conant (b. abt. 1652, d. May 30, 1680) was the youngest daughter of Richard and Christian More. On August 1, 1676, she married Joshua Conant Jr, the grandson of Salem's founder, Roger Conant. They had one child, named Joshua Conant III, who was baptized May 12, 1678. Christian Conant died at the age of 28, her cause of death unknown. After she died, Joshua Jr moved to modern-day Truro in Barnstable County. No further record of her husband or son could be found.

The empty frame in this section was for the double-headstone of two of the More family who died as children. The stone on the right was for **Barbara Dutch** (bapt. Dec 2, 1677, d. Apr 10, 1678), eight-month-old child of Richard More's daughter, Susannah (More) Dutch, and her husband, Samuel. The stone on the left was for **Samuel More** (b. Nov 16, 1673, d. Nov 24, 1673) the nine-day-old son of Richard More Jr and his wife, Sarah. It is unclear if he is named for his great-grandfather back in Shropshire, or for Richard Jr's older brother, Samuel, who took part in King Philip's War, fighting against the Narragansett tribe.

War seems to have had an ill effect on the elder Samuel, and he became known as a ne'er-do-well. With a group of his shiftless friends with him, he took to the roads at night to harass and bully travelers. He was sentenced to have a "B" branded into his forehead with a hot iron, to be known as a "brigand" to one and all. After this, he seems to have slipped out of Salem, and his place of burial is unknown.

While the tombstones have been lost, a recording of the Charter Street Cemetery inscriptions from 1901, by William Dennis Devereaux, has saved the inscriptions.

SAMUEL SON
TO RICHARD &
SARAH MORE.

AGED 9 DAYES
DEC^D NOVE^R ye 24.
1673

BARBARAH
DAUGHTER TO
SAMUEL & SUSANNA
DUTCH. AGED 8
MONTHS. DEC^D.
APRIL ye 10.
1678.

Mehitable Higginson (b. Mar 26, 1764, d. Jul 19, 1846) is memorialized with a large, stone plaque embedded in the earth here. Her mother was a Loyalist during the Revolution, and was highly respected in the community. She was a schoolteacher in Salem alongside her mother for many years, and they were both considered uncommonly well educated. Her nickname was "Hitty."

George Heussler (b. abt. 1751, d. Apr 3, 1817) was a native of Alsace, Germany and was the first resident of Salem to be a gardener by profession. He designed the gardens of the Derby Estate in Danvers, which is now on the property known as Glen Magna Farms. Most of his work had been for the Derbys, and after the passing of Elias Hasket Derby, he would do similar work by request for other families, as well as owning a gardening shop. The inscription on his tombstone reads:

SACRED
To the Memory of
MR. GEORGE HEUSSLER
Obt. Apr 3, 1817.
Æt. 66.

Precious in the sight of the Lord
is the death of his saints.

George married **Abigail (Russell) Heussler** (b. abt. 1753, d. Apr 21, 1799) with whom he had a daughter, **Elizabeth Heussler** (bapt. Jan

10, 1790, d. Nov 1, 1823) who died at age 33. After the death of Abigail, George married **Elizabeth "Jenny" (Lunt) Heussler** (b. abt. 1761, d. Mar 10, 1821) of Danvers, whose inscription reads:

SACRED
To the Memory of
MRS. ELIZABETH,
Relict of the late
Mr. George Heussler,
Obt. March 10, 1821
Æt. 60.

So waits my soul to see thy grace
And find a brighter day.

Rebekah Whitford (b. abt. 1737, d. Apr 14, 1744) was the daughter of Samuel and Rebekah (Hawks) Whitford. Her mother was originally from Lynn, Massachusetts, and her parents were married on November 10, 1732. Rebekah was a descendant of the *Mayflower* passenger Isaac Allerton, to whom Capt. Richard More was apprenticed. Her father Samuel was a fisherman, and the family was deeded the home of Walter Whitford by Rebekah's uncle John Hawkes Jr, which is included in the *Mayflower Deeds and Probates*. There is a local ghost story about a child buried alive that has been attributed to this grave, however there is no historical evidence to support the anecdote. It may be that the somber epitaph on her tombstone inspired the tale.

HERE LYES Yᵉ BODY
OF REBEKAH WHITFORDᴰ
DAUGᵗʳ OF SAMˡˡ &
REBEKAH WHITFORD.
DIED APRIL Yᵉ 14ᵗʰ.

1 7 4 4 IN HER 7ᵗʰ
YEAR, *Being Willing to die.*

The Robert Peele Lot

Robert Peele Lot

The Chained Plot & The Prisoner of War

The sight which will most likely dominate your attention in this area would be the chained Robert Peele Lot, and the great tree growing within it. In many older cemeteries, families may have paid for a fence or barrier to be placed around a particular grave or plot. In the Charter Street cemetery, the Robert Peele Lot is the only one with such an existing barrier; a heavy chain supported by granite blocks surrounds the plot. There are records of a fence once existing around the More family plot, but there are no remnants of that fence existing. Family members are often grouped together, but this was by no means a requirement. Building a fence could serve as a way of preserving the area to ensure only your immediate family members (or other relations) would be buried in this area.

Interred within this plot are members of the Peele family, whose history in Salem goes back to the early days before the Witch Hysteria. The Peele lineage is often difficult to verify, as there were numerous Robert Peeles throughout the generations.

Roger Peele (b. Jan 25, 1676, d. 1728) the son of Samuel and Ann (Wallis) Peele and was born in London, England. Roger arrived in Salem sometime before 1709, as on November 15th of that year, he married **Margaret (Bartoll) Peele** (b. Feb 11, 1682, d. Aug 1728), which was her second marriage, being formerly married to a Kempton. They had three children: Roger Jr, Samuel, and **Robert Peele Sr** (b. Aug 12, 1712, d. April 29, 1773). Robert Peele Sr was a tailor, who married **Mary (Bartlett) Peele** (b. May 10, 1730, d. May 4, 1771) in Marblehead in June of 1753.

Their son, **Robert Peele Jr** (b. Jan 4, 1737, d. Jun 12, 1792), followed his father's profession, and was a highly prosperous tailor. On December 1, 1768, he married **Elizabeth (Ropes) Peele** (b. abt. 1743, d. Aug 6, 1770). One of their sons, **Josiah Peele** (b. Feb, 1765, d. Jun 20, 1784), died at the age of twenty, and seems to have a portrait carved into his stone, more specific than a usual soul effigy. It is one of only two examples of a portrait tombstone in the cemetery. After Elizabeth died in 1770, Robert Jr remarried to **Eunice (Sterns) Peele** (b. abt. 1733, d. Jun 20, 1780) on June 11, 1771.

Another son of Robert Sr and Mary Peele, **William Bartoll Peele** (b. Dec 17, 1738, d. Mar 4, 1817), was a merchant, and married Elizabeth (Beckett) Peele. Their son, another **Robert Peele** (b. Apr 19, 1767, d. Mar 21, 1842), continued the family tradition by becoming a tailor as well as a merchant and shopkeeper. His first wife, **Elizabeth "Betsey" (Smith) Peele** (b. Aug 21, 1768, d. Dec 18, 1828) was a member of the Singing Company at the East Church. Their daughter, **Elizabeth Ropes Peele** (bapt. Mar 10, 1816, d. Oct 27, 1882) is interred with them in the Peele Lot, as are their two of their sons, **Robert Peele Jr** (b. abt. Mar, 1794 d. Apr 4, 1874) and **Josiah Peele** (b. abt. Nov, 1796, d. Jul 3, 1822). The brothers share a double-headstone. Josiah was a mariner, and died of a fever in Havana on the brig *Chase*. After the death of Elizabeth Peele, Robert Jr remarried to **Sarah (Brown) Peele** (b. Oct 4, 1770, d. Jan 20, 1854)

Timothy Lindall (b. Jun 3, 1642, d. Jan 6, 1699) has one of the most memorable tombstones in the cemetery. A skeleton is depicted on the left, a memento mori that may be symbolic of Death itself. To the right is Father Time, a scythe in his hand and an hourglass depicted on his head. The tombstone is shown in the *Tombstones and Symbols* section.

A prosperous merchant and shipowner, Timothy Lindall represented Salem in the Massachusetts General Court along with John Hathorne. He married **Mary (Veren) Lindall** (b. abt. 1648, d. Jan 7, 1732) whose mother, Mary (Putnam) Veren, was the widow of Lt. Thomas Putnam Sr of Salem Village. Mrs. Lindall ran a store for more than twenty years after her husband's death, with the assistance of her daughters, Sarah and Rachel. The Latin inscription on Timothy Lindall's gravestone reads, *Sanctorum Memoria Sit Beata*, meaning "Blessed Be the Memory of the Saints."

James Lindall (b. Feb 1, 1676, d. May 10, 1753) the son of Timothy and Mary (Verin) Lindall, was aboard his father's ketch *Exchange* when the ship was taken by the French off of Block Island on August 6, 1697. James was taken hostage by the French, and carried to Placentia in Newfoundland until a ransom was paid for him. He married Elizabeth (Corwin) Lindall on December 15, 1702. Elizabeth was the daughter of Jonathan Corwin; judge of the Salem Witch Trials and former occupant of the house museum today known as the Old Witch House or Corwin House, the only building left standing in Salem with a direct connection to the Witch Hysteria. She would die a few years later on May 19, 1706. It is unconfirmed if Elizabeth is interred in the Old Burying Point. Many of the Corwins are buried in the Broad Street Cemetery, including her father and mother, however, there is no grave recorded for her there.

James married next to Mary (Higginson) Weld Lindall in May of 1708. Mary Lindall's death may have occurred in 1718, however, if she is interred here, there is no grave marker for her. The couple had seven children, yet only four lived to adulthood. Not far from James Lindall's tombstone, is a triple-tombstone for their young children, **Veren Lindall** (b. May 14, 1711, d. Apr 29, 1712), **Rachel Lindall** (b. Aug 9, 1714, d. Sep 6, 1714) and an **Unnamed Son** (b. Apr 25, 1709, d. same).

Stephen Cleveland (b. Oct 8, 1741, d. Oct 8, 1801) is believed to be the first commissioned captain of the Continental Navy. On August 2, 1792, he was a grand juryman and engaged in the pursuit of a slave-trader named Sinclair. The man was accused of having beaten his crewmembers to death, and barricaded himself in a second-floor room he was renting. Cleveland, the Sheriff, and others rushed the door, and Sinclair leapt out of the window, where an officer apprehended him. Stephen Cleveland was an ancestor of the future President of the United States, Grover Cleveland.

Pickman/Toppan Tomb

The Wandering Colonel & The Witch Hunter's Brother

Directly behind the Grimshawe House is the tomb which holds members of the Pickman, Toppan, and Barton families. The table-top is more legible than any other in the cemetery, and bears the most names. The Pickman/Toppan family would be caught up in the upheaval and passions of the American Revolution.

Colonel Benjamin Pickman Jr (b. Nov 7, 1740, d. May 12, 1819) was the son of Col. Benjamin Pickman Sr and Love (Rawlins) Pickman. Like his father before him, Benjamin was a successful merchant, and the owner of a number of vessels. He would marry **Mary (Toppan) Pickman** (b. Aug 29, 1744, d. Apr 28, 1817), the daughter of **Dr. Bezaleel Toppan** (b. Mar 7, 1705, d. Aug 8, 1762) and **Mary (Barton) Toppan** (b. Oct 5, 1715, d. abt. Jun, 1776). Benjamin Jr. graduated from Harvard in 1759, and was a Colonel in the 1st Essex Regiment. When it became clear that war between England and the colonies was inevitable, Pickman, a Tory, said that he did not believe that the colonies had grounds for rebellion and could not, in good conscience, take up arms against English soldiers. Not long after the events of Leslie's Retreat on February 27, 1775 (see *Capt. Richard Derby, Derby Tomb*), Pickman would decide to flee, and boarded a ship bound for Bristol on March 11, leaving his wife and children behind. According to Pickman, he had consulted with his wife on this decision, and she fully supported the flight. Pickman knew it would be quite some time before he returned, although he may not have suspected it would be ten years before he saw his family again.

Mary Pickman remained in Salem with their four children, Benjamin III, Thomas, William, and Mary. As a Loyalist family in a fiercely pro-Revolution community, the Pickmans faced harassment and persecution from their neighbors. At one point, Mary began the process of moving the family to Halifax, Nova Scotia, however, in the end she chose to stay in Salem. After the death of Mary's mother in June of 1776, her sister, **Anna Toppan** (bapt. Nov 20, 1757, d. abt. Dec, 1777), came to stay with the family and give comfort, company, and assistance with the raising of the children. The following year, however, Anna died of consumption.

Mary may have felt her family was cursed by this dreadful disease. In her younger years, she had been the caregiver for her brother, **Thomas Toppan** (bapt. Jun 18, 1738, d. Apr 23, 1758), when he contracted consumption and died soon after in 1758. The next year, her nineteen-year-old sister **Sarah Toppan** (bapt. Jul 20, 1740, d. Oct 17, 1759) died of the same disease, as did her other brother, **Willoughby Toppan** (bapt. Nov 5, 1735, bur. May 10, 1760), the following year in 1760. All four of Mary's siblings, as well as her mother and father, are buried in the Pickman/Toppan tomb. Having watched most of her family die of consumption, Mary was understandably concerned for her own health. In 1770, she spent several months at Stafford Springs, a mineral spring in Stafford, Connecticut, that is thought to be America's first health spa.

Benjamin began sending letters to Mary once he arrived in Bristol, England. Many of the letters he sent home were kept by the family, however, he kept very few of the letters sent in reply to him. This may have been due to the constantly transient nature of his time in England, staying sometimes no more than a few months in one place. He does not seem to have engaged in much business during this time, aside from inspecting manufacturing centers; his diary records almost daily entries of visiting friends and relatives for dinner or tea, taking long walks to neighboring villages, attending lectures or reading books to pass the time. It is unknown how much money he brought with him; however, he does note a distinct decline in his accommodations and diet, and several times requests that his wife send him money.

It would often take several months for letters to be passed between them, with letters handed to friends and confidants who might be travelling to the same areas. Communication between the couple was frequent at first, but soon the flow of letters slowed. After sending a letter telling her husband of her mother's death, Mary seems to have ceased sending him any letters at all. Each of Benjamin's following letters urges his 'dearest Polly' to write him back, but for more than three years she sent him no response. After the declaration of peace between England and the colonies, Benjamin sent her a letter in 1783 declaring his intent to return home. Mary replied to this letter with elation to the news, writing "I have no doubt every obstacle will in a short time be removed." However, the Banishment Act of Massachusetts remained in place, which forbid the return of Massachusetts residents who had fled to England, under penalty of death. Benjamin sent another letter stating he could not return, and asking her to bring the family to England. Shortly after he sent the letter off, he received a letter from Mary expressing great joy and relief that he would be returning home soon. When Mary received his letter stating that he was not coming back, she did not send a reply, instead, Benjamin seems to have begun primarily communicating with his son, Benjamin III.

In 1784, Benjamin Pickman would find his way to return home cleared, and had some of his belongings shipped ahead of him. That August, he had a trunk full of books shipped home with instructions to Mary to burn one of them, a copy of Ovid's *Epistles*. Benjamin Pickman III met his father in London, and was taken by his father around the countryside to meet his associates and friends before continuing his journey to France. When his son came back to England, Pickman returned home with him in April of 1785. Benjamin Pickman was received warmly by his friends, neighbors, and associates. He was elected treasurer of the town, a position he held for nineteen years in total. Pickman would also carry the duty of Overseer of the Poor, and would have been in charge of collecting a "poor tax" to help administer relief in the way of food, clothing, and shelter to those in need. He would also have worked with other Overseers regarding health, transiency, crime, and the welfare of children. At times, the Pickman family struggled financially, but retained their dignity and the respect of their neighbors, even if they had not seen eye-to-eye during the Revolutionary War. In their beautiful Essex Street home, which has since been torn down, the Pickmans entertained guests such as Alexander Hamilton, Count Luigi Castiglioni of Italy, and President James Monroe.

Mary Pickman would suffer from a "raising of the blood" in 1809, which she survived while under the careful hand of **Dr. Thomas Pickman** (b. abt. 1774, bur. Jan 5, 1817), her son, who had graduated from Harvard in 1791 and became a doctor. However, her health suffered greatly during the event, and she was confined to her home for the remainder of her life. The old curse of consumption would claim another victim from Mary Pickman's family in January, 1817, as Dr. Thomas Pickman himself would pass away from the illness. Dr. Pickman was interred in this tomb, but at some point was removed to the Harmony Grove Cemetery in Salem. Mary Pickman was said to have remained dignified and cheerful, despite her failing health, and would pass away a year later in 1817. Reverend Bentley wrote of her, "I had the highest respect for her... She had a fine person, a dignity of deportment, a correct behavior with her servants, a reverence from her children & took the first place among the ladies by their full consent."

Benjamin Pickman, who had meticulously recorded his time in England in his diary, seems to have forsaken it upon his return. His diary picks up again seven years later, as he looks to retirement from his duties as treasurer. Pickman began to spend most of his time travelling with his youngest daughter, Love Rawlins Pickman, named for his mother, who was born April 10, 1786. His final diary entry is December 3, 1818; "All my family dined with me being Thanksgiving day." Pickman died May 12, 1819, and his cause of death was listed as "old age, or consumption." Reverend Bentley memorializes Col. Pickman in his diary, noting that he was known around town simply as "The Colonel," and was respected and esteemed by many sorts of people. "Till the close of life he retained his suavity of manners, his inquisitive but unoffending temper, his power to recommend himself and to retain in his friendship every man with whom he had ever conversed."

The others interred in this tomb are recorded as:

Dr. Thomas Barton (b. Jul 11, 1680, d. Apr 28, 1751), his wife **Mary (Willoughby) Barton** (b. Sep 1, 1676, d. Jan 23, 1758), and their son, **John Barton** (bapt Dec 5, 1711, d. Dec 21, 1774). It was recorded that when Dr. Barton passed, he had received enough funerary rings as to fill a quart mug, showing that he was highly respected in the community.

Dr. Bezaleel Toppan (b. Mar 7, 1705, d. Aug 8, 1762) and his wife, **Mary (Barton) Toppan** (b. Oct 5, 1715, d. abt. Jun, 1776). Dr. Toppan graduated from Harvard in 1722. He was pastor of the first church at Newbury, and may have preached the first sermon delivered in Concord, New Hampshire. They were the parents of Mary (Toppan) Pickman and her four siblings.

Thomas Toppan (bapt. Jun 18, 1738, d. Apr 23, 1758) the brother of Mary (Toppan) Pickman, died of consumption at age 20, a disease which he seems to have suffered from for a full year. A student of Harvard, he was noted as "an uncommonly handsome, interesting and promising young man" by Benjamin Pickman III in his writings. Also interred here are **Mary Anne Pickman** (b. Dec 9, 1800, d. Jan 2, 1809) the daughter of Benjamin Pickman III and Antiss (Derby) Pickman, as well as her brother, **Hasket Derby Pickman** (b. Mar 12, 1796, d. Oct 22, 1815).

There is another Pickman family tomb in Salem, which is located at the Broad Street Cemetery. Colonel Benjamin Pickman Jr's notable father, The Honorable Colonel Benjamin Pickman Sr, is listed as interred in that tomb, as are many of his siblings. Benjamin Jr. and Mary Pickman's youngest daughter, Love Rawlins Pickman, is interred at the Harmony Grove Cemetery in Salem.

Dr. John Swinnerton (b. abt. 1633, d. Jul 6, 1690) and his wife, **Hannah (Bartholemew) Swinnerton** (b. Feb 13, 1642, d. Dec 23, 1713), are interred nearby to the Pickman/Toppan Tomb. Dr. Swinnerton was a prominent physician in Salem Town, and had attended on young Nathaniel Mather, the brother of Cotton Mather, as well as Thomas Oliver, the second husband of Bridget Bishop. Nathaniel Hawthorne took particular note of this stone, which he noted was, "moss-grown, deeply sunken. One to 'Dr. John Swinnerton, Physician' in 1688; another to his wife." Hawthorne used the doctor's name in his novel *The House of the Seven Gables*. Julian Hawthorne, Nathaniel's son, referred to the real Dr. Swinnerton as, "the old quack doctor," in his writings, passing blame on him for the Witch Hysteria. However, it is likely Julian confused Swinnerton with Doctor William Griegs (who diagnosed Betty Parris as bewitched), as Dr. Swinnerton died before the Witch Hysteria, so his reputation, in that respect, should remain safe.

Nathaniel Mather (b. Jul 6, 1669, d Oct 17, 1688) is buried nearby to the Pickman/Toppan Tomb and the Robert Peele Lot. Nathaniel is the only member of the famous Mather family of Boston to be interred in Salem. His father, Reverend Increase Mather, was a minister of the Old North Church in Boston and the president of Harvard College. Nathaniel's elder brother, Reverend Cotton Mather, was also a minister of the Old North Church, but may be best known for his controversial role in the Salem Witch Trials as a counselor to the judges, and to Governor William Phips. Nathaniel Mather was accounted as a brilliant young man whose passion was the pursuit of knowledge. By the age of sixteen, he could speak conversationally in Latin and Greek, and when he graduated from Harvard College, he delivered an oration entirely in Hebrew. Nathaniel tutored his younger brother, Samuel Mather, in the classical languages.

Cotton Mather wrote a brief biography of his late brother, and wondered if his dedication to his books may have contributed to his death. "While he thus devoured books, it came to pass that his books devoured him. His weak body could not bear the toils to which he used himself." Nathaniel had always suffered from ill health, and did not expect that he would live a long life. Therefore, he used the time he had to the fullest extent, to expand his mind as well as his devotion to God. He wrote, "The Lord does not require me to neglect the body, but to have my body for a few days or years - I say few, for they cannot be many - to be wholly at the service of my soul; and to be willing that the union between them should be dissolved.; the soul taking its flight to the everlasting bliss; the body being laid in the dust, until the resurrection in the last day. With my body I must expect to lose all the pleasant enjoyments of this world - liberty, library, study and relations; and yet, in a higher sense I shall not lose them." Nathaniel Mather was recuperating in Salem from a surgery on a tumor in his leg, when he passed away on October 17, 1688. His tombstone appears on the cover of this book.

Nathaniel Hawthorne certainly was familiar with Mather's story, and wrote in his notebook of discovering Nathaniel Mather's grave by accident. Hawthorne's future wife, Sophia Peabody, lived in the Grimshawe House, and one day, he was looking over the tombstones behind the house. "M_ Peabody has trained flowers over (the Pickman) tomb, on account of her friendly relations with Colonel Pickman." As he got down on his knees to look at the stones by his feet, he recalls, "It affected me deeply, when I had cleared away the grass from the half-buried stone, and read the name. An apple-tree or two hang over these old graves, and throw down the blighted fruit on Nathaniel Mather's grave - he blighted too."

MEMENTO MORI

M^R
NATHANAEL MATHER
DEC^D OSCOBER Y^e 17
1688
An Aged perſon
that had ſeen but
Nineteen Winters
in the World.

157

SIMON BRADSTREET

ARMIGER EX ORDINE SENATORIO IN COLONIA MAS-
SACHUSETTENSI AB ANNO 1630 USQ: AD ANNUM
1673 DEINDE AD ANNUM 1679 VICE GUBERNATOR
DENIQ: AD ANNUM 1686 EJUSDEM COLONIAE COMMU-
NI & CONSTANTI POPULI SUFFRAGIO GUBERNATOR
VIR JUDICIS LYNCEATO PREDAEDITUS. QUEM NEC
MINAE NEC HONOS ALLEXIT REGIS AUTHORITATEM
& POPULI LIBERTATEM AEQUA LANCE LIBRAVIT
RELIGIONE CORDATUS VIA INNOCUUS MUNDUM ET
VICIT ET DESERUIT DIE XXVII. MARCIJ ANNO DOM:
MDCXCVII ANNOQ: R.R'S GUILLIELMI TERTII IX ET
AETATIS SUAE XCIV

BRADSTREET AND WAINWRIGHT TOMBS

New England's Nestor & The Old Ministers

The Bradstreet Tomb and the Wainwright Tomb are at the summit of the small burial hill, overlooking modern-day Central Street. The metal plaque on the side of the tomb is a recreation of a plaque which was once engraved in the table-top. The inscription is provided first in Latin, as it was originally, and translated into English.

SIMON BRADSTREET

ESQUIRE IN THE SENATE OF THE MASSACHUSETTS COLONY FROM THE YEAR 1630 TO THE YEAR 1673, THEN LIEUTENANT GOVERNOR TO THE YEAR 1679, AND AT LAST, UNTIL THE YEAR 1686, GOVERNOR OF THE SAME COLONY BY THE GENERAL AND DETERMINED VOTE OF THE PEOPLE. HE WAS A MAN ENDOWED WITH KEEN JUDGMENT WHOM NEITHER THREATS NOR HONORS COULD SWAY. HE WEIGHED THE AUTHORITY OF THE KING AND THE LIBERTY OF THE PEOPLE IN EVEN SCALES. IN RELIGION DEVOUT AND UPRIGHT IN HIS WAYS HE VANQUISHED THE WORLD AND RELINQUISHED IT ON THE XXVIITH DAY OF MARCH IN THE YEAR OF OUR LORD MDCXCVII, AND IN THE IXTH YEAR OF KING WILLIAM THIRD, AND OF HIS LIFE THE XCIVTH

THIS TABLET, PRESERVING THE INSCRIPTION FORMERLY ON THIS TOMB WAS PLACED HERE IN 1917

This particular tomb has a well-documented history. Reverend Samuel Sewall records being present at the burial of Governor Simon Bradstreet in the tomb, which he states is new at that time. It is unknown if anyone may have been interred in this tomb prior to Bradstreet. Sewall was also present for the burial of Reverend John Higginson in this same tomb.

The next recorded action taken involving the tomb is actually recorded inside the tomb itself. It appears it fell into a state of disrepair in the mid-1700s, and required maintenance. This writing was discovered when the tomb was opened again in the 1890s, likely to prepare for the final interment within. The inscription was discovered within the entry arch of the tomb, indicating that work may have been done in 1751. The inscription reads:

(W)

1751
Ri[c]haRD
W + CloW

(S) 1751 : R.P. :: D.E. 1751 (N)
1751
(E)

It is presumed, based on other examples of similar inscriptions, that this is stating whom the work was done by, and when the work began and ended.

A record of the tomb appears in a Bill of Sale in 1789, sold by the estate of Colonel Benjamin Pickman Sr., to Col. John Hathorne and Capt. Samuel Ingersoll. In 1835, as space within the cemetery grew sparse and the tombs of old showed signs of disintegration, there was a proposal to clean out any unclaimed and neglected tombs so that they might be re-sold. While this effort was mostly thwarted by the descendants of the old families of Salem, it is reported that a member of either the Hathorne or Ingersoll family removed the remains of the former occupants of the Bradstreet tomb and placed them into a nearby and unmarked hole. Both Colonel Hathorne and Captain Ingersoll are believed to still be entombed here, as is Captain Ingersoll's daughter, Susanna Ingersoll, whose unique engraved iron casket with a glass window has been con-firmed to remain within the tomb.

Governor Simon Bradstreet (bapt. Mar 18, 1604, d. Mar 27, 1697) has often been referred to as the "Old Nestor" of colonial Massachusetts. The nickname, which we first see bestowed on him by Rev. Cotton Mather, refers to the legendary wise old king of the Greeks in Homer's, *The Odyssey*. In his advanced age, Bradstreet was very much involved in colonial politics, and was relied upon by the Massachusetts Bay Colony when wisdom and temperance were required to handle a difficult situation.

Simon Bradstreet was born in March of 1602, in Hobling, a village of Lincolnshire, England. His father died when he was only fifteen years old, and the boy was taken in by a friend of his father's, Thomas Dudley, steward to the Earl of Lincoln. Bradstreet grew up in the Earl's household and took on many duties. He was given admission to Emanuel College to assist as a governor to the Earl of Warwick's son, but the young noble never attended. Instead, Bradstreet became governor to one of the Earl of Lincoln's brothers studying there, in the hopes that his studiousness and conscientious habits would rub off on the idle and indifferent young noble. Bradstreet graduated with a Bachelor of Arts degree, though whether the Earl's brother ever did is unknown. Bradstreet learned the running of the great house so well, that when Dudley relocated to Boston, Massachusetts for a time, Bradstreet took over as steward. In 1628, Bradstreet fell in love with Anne, Dudley's young daughter, she being sixteen at the time, and he twenty-five. Anne contracted smallpox shortly after they were engaged to be married, and her chances of survival were slim. She overcame the deadly illness after a difficult battle, and the two were married once she was well, however, her health would suffer for the rest of her life due to this illness.

In 1630, Simon and Anne (Dudley) Bradstreet would accompany Thomas Dudley, Governor John Winthrop, William Hathorne, and other officials of the new Massachusetts Bay Colony, on the voyage to the American colonies. The journey was a long and difficult one, with cramped and uncomfortable quarters, fraught with danger from the harsh weather and the threat of Spanish privateers, as well as mischief and fighting among the passengers due to the intolerable conditions. Their arrival in Salem was much anticipated by all on board, however, their spirits fell when they came ashore at last and found the village in dire conditions due to disease and famine.

Anne Bradstreet and the other wives of the officials stayed behind in Salem, while Bradstreet, Winthrop, and Higginson went to Charlestown. They found this town in the same desperate situation as Salem. Anne would join Simon at Boston, and eventually move to Cambridge. Simon Bradstreet served as Assistant Governor from 1630 to 1644, during which time he moved from Cambridge, to Ipswich, and then Andover. After his tenure, he remained active in colonial politics, including being one of the commissioners who helped to establish the border between New Amsterdam (eventually New York, held by the Dutch) and New Haven (in Connecticut, held by the English).

Bradstreet would then be tasked with handling one of the most difficult challenges facing the colony. The English Civil War had seen Charles I executed by the militant Puritan faction lead by Lord Protector Oliver Cromwell, but with Cromwell's death, the monarchy had been restored, and the future of the Massachusetts Bay Colony was in question. Only the most prudent and learned statesmen could be sent to address the new king, and in June 1661, Simon Bradstreet and John Norton set sail for England to meet with the newly crowned Charles II to renew the colony's charter. He returned with the new charter, and a promise from the King for a good degree of tolerance to the colony's rights. However, many in the colony felt that Bradstreet and Norton had allowed the King to take too much while giving very little in the arrangement of the new charter.

Anne (Dudley) Bradstreet died on September 16, 1672, and is buried in North Andover. She is best known for her works of poetry, and is considered to be the first American poet of the colonies, and many of her writings survive to this day. A wonderful example of her tender lyrical style may be found in this poem, dedicated to her husband. The date of the poem is unconfirmed, as it was published undated in the posthumous poetry collection published by her family in 1678.

"To my dear and loving husband"
by Anne Dudley Bradstreet
If ever two were one then surely we,
If ever man were loved by wife, then thee;
If ever wife was happy in a man,
Compare with me ye women if you can.
I prize thy love more than whole Mines of Gold,
Or all the riches that the East doth hold.
My love is such that Rivers cannot quench,
Nor ought but love from thee give recompense.
Thy love is such I can no way repay,
The heavens reward thee, manifold I pray.
Then while we live in love let's so persevere,
That when we live no more, we may live ever.

In 1673, Simon Bradstreet was again appointed an assistant governor, until the death of Governor Leverett in 1679. At that point, Simon Bradstreet became the new Governor, which lasted until 1686 when the old charter was revoked by King James II. The Governorship would then be replaced by the Presidency of the Dominion of New England. The new role was extremely unpopular, as was the disastrous Presidency of the harsh and tyrannical, Sir Edmund Andros. King James was forced to abdicate his throne in 1689, and King William and Queen Mary ascended to the throne. This sparked revolution in Massachusetts, and Bradstreet is thought to have been one of the organizers of a mob that formed in Boston and ousted Andros in 1690. Simon Bradstreet then remained as an interim governor for the Massachusetts Bay Colony, until the appointment and arrival of the new Governor, Sir William Phips, in May 1692. This placed Bradstreet as the governor of the colony when the Witch Hysteria erupted in Salem.

Bradstreet was expected to attend the examinations of Elizabeth (Bassett) Proctor and Sarah (Towne) Cloyce at the Salem Meeting House on April 11, 1692, to see the proceedings with his own eyes, however he was prevented from going due to ill health. It would not have been Bradstreet's first brush with witchcraft accusations. In Andover, during April of 1659, he was called to bear witness to an accusation of witchcraft against John Godfrey. Job Tylar, his wife, and three teenaged children, claimed Godfrey had command of a familiar; a large black bird that did his bidding and sought to harm Tylar's wife. Bradstreet did not handle this accusation with the rushed judgment of the magistrates of Salem, and it would be five years before the case made its way to court.

Would the events that unfolded in Salem have played out any differently had the cautious and tolerant Governor Bradstreet been present, rather than his deputy governor, Thomas Danforth? Danforth later regretted allowing the witch hunt to continue, having only advised the magistrates to rely less on spectral evidence, but otherwise allowing them to proceed with their own preferred methods. Perhaps the learned governor would have reminded the magistrates, as Reverend Cotton Mather would later, that the accusations they accepted from those who had confessed to witchcraft should have been immediately dismissed, for the servants of the Prince of Lies could not be expected to tell the truth.

Reverend Samuel Sewall, a friend and confidant of Governor Bradstreet, attended Bradstreet's funeral and was a pall-bearer. Sewall describes the event in an entry from his diary dated April 2, 1697:

"*The wether clear'd and was warm. About 3 was the Funeral; Bearers, Mr. Danforth, Major Gen. Winthrop, Mr. Cook, Col. Hutchinson, Sewall, Mr. Secretary; Col. Gedney and Major Brown left the Widow; I bore the Feet of the Corps into the Tomb, which is new, in the Old Burying place. Mr. Willard, Capt Checkly, Capt Hill, Capt Williams, Capt Belchar &c. There. Mr Bromfield, Mr. Eyre. Probably very many would have assisted, had not the weather been discouraging. Three Volleys, but no Great Guns, by reason of the Scarcity of Powder.*"

Anne (Downing) Bradstreet (bapt. Apr 13, 1633, d. Apr 19, 1713) was the second wife of Governor Bradstreet, who outlived him by sixteen years. Her first husband, Captain Joseph Gardner, had been killed in the Narragansett Swamp Fight of 1675. She was the executor of Gardner's will, and inherited quite a large amount of property and money. When she married Simon Bradstreet the following year, she insisted that he agree to sign a pre-nuptial agreement. Her brother, Sir George Downing, was the namesake of Downing Street in London, England, which is known for being the official residence of the Prime Minister.

Reverend John Higginson (bapt. Aug 6, 1616, d. Dec 9, 1708) was born in Leicestershire, England, and arrived in Salem with his father, Reverend Francis Higginson, aboard the *Arbella*. In those days, a Puritan would not simply be admitted into a congregation because they wanted to, but had to be put forward by senior members of the congregation and agreed upon. At the age of thirteen, John was accepted into his father's church. His father would be considered the first Teacher of the new colony in Massachusetts, but died shortly after his arrival in Salem. John Higginson became well-respected in the new colony despite his young age.

Higginson moved to Hartford, Connecticut to teach at a grammar school, and became an assistant to Reverend Henry Whitfield. Higginson married the reverend's daughter, Sarah (Whitfield) Higginson (*Gedney Tomb*), in Whitfield's granite home; a building that still stands in Guilford, Connecticut today. After the death of his mother in 1659, he was returning to London when a terrible storm forced his ship to return to the nearest port, which happened to be Salem. The town was then in need of a new minister, and asked Higginson to stay on as the Teacher of the Church, a position started by his father thirty years earlier. He remained in that post until the end of his life, in 1708.

John Higginson was the minister in Salem Town during the terrifying times of the Witch Hysteria. The Salem Meeting House in which he preached formerly stood on the ground where the Daniel Lowe & Company building is today (231 Essex Street). This meeting house did not serve as the site of the actual trials of the Court of Oyer and Terminer, though some significant events during the Hysteria did take place there, such as the examinations of Elizabeth Proctor, the arrest of John Proctor, and the excommunications of church members Giles Corey and Rebecca Nurse. The actual trials were held in the Town House, which was torn down over a century ago, and would have been in the center of modern-day Washington Street in Town House Square. There is a plaque at 72 Washington Street recognizing this site.

Rev. John Higginson, despite being the elder minister of the Salem Church, rarely appears in the records of the Court of Oyer and Terminer. His son, Col. John Higginson Jr., was a Justice of the Peace, who signed several testimonies and confessions in 1692. Rev. Higginson's daughter, Anna (Higginson) Dolliver, was accused of witchcraft for afflicting Mary Warren and Susannah Sheldon. She was examined by the magistrates, and during her examination, she confessed to having created poppets to try and ward off witches that she believed were afflicting her brother. She was not convicted of witchcraft, and was believed to have been mentally unwell.

Rev. Higginson himself testified in favor of one of the accused, Sarah Buckley, on January 2, 1693. He stated:

"I cannot refuse to bear witness to the truth, viz that during the time of her living in Salem for many years in Communion with this Church having occasionally frequent converse & discourse with her I have never observed my selfe nor heard from any thing other that was unsuitable to a Conversation becoming the Gospel; and have always looked upon her as a serious Godly woman."

In his later years, Reverend Higginson would endure a great deal of tragedy, as he lost several of his adult children to smallpox, and another to a mysterious disappearance while on an expedition to Africa. The Reverend's second wife, **Mary (Blackman) Higginson** (b. abt. 1637, d. Mar 9, 1709) is buried beside the Bradstreet tomb, with a tombstone that features three deaths-head designs.

On December 5, 1708, Samuel Sewall was present when Reverend John Higginson, Salem Town's longtime minister, was interred in this same tomb. "In the afternoon, the aged and Excellent Divine Mr. John Higginson is laid in Gov Bradstreet's Tomb... Was laid in the Tomb a little before Sunset, had a very Serene, and a very Cold Aer."

Rev. Nicholas Noyes Jr (b. Dec 22, 1647, d. Dec 13, 1717) has not officially been confirmed as having been interred in this tomb, however, there is good indication that this was the site of his burial. Noyes was buried in Salem, as Rev. Samuel Sewall confirms. Rev. Bentley refers to the Bradstreet tomb as being the resting place of the Governor, "and with him are lodged the Old Ministers." The tomb did not exist when the ministers prior to Higginson died, and those who came after would be buried elsewhere; Rev. George Curwen in the Corwin Tomb of the Broad Street Cemetery, and Rev. Samuel Fiske in the Fisk Tomb. Therefore, "the Old Ministers" would likely be a reference to Higginson and Noyes, both of whom served Salem for decades, and were the faith leaders during the Salem Witch Hysteria.

Nicholas Noyes was born in Newbury, Massachusetts, the son of Rev. Nicholas Sr and Mary (Cutting) Noyes. He preached for thirteen years as the minister of Haddam, Connecticut. He served as chaplain to the Connecticut Regiment during the Great Swamp Fight in December of 1675, which saw European colonial forces attack Narragansett settlements. In the end, the colonists killed or captured over a hundred Narragansett tribe warriors, and killed anywhere from several hundred to a thousand non-combatants, including women and children.

Noyes was called to Salem in October of 1683, and ordained as a minister of the First Church in Salem on November 14, 1683. Serving under Rev. John Higginson, who was the Elder Minister, Noyes was an energetic and powerful speaker. Remembered for being "unusually corpulent," Noyes was a large man who seems to have had a commanding presence, but an eloquent way with words. Samuel Sewall records that Noyes was officiant for the marriage of Aaron Porter and Susan Sewall in Salem on October 22, 1713, and during the ceremony, Noyes stated, "love is the sugar to sweeten every condition." Aaron and Susannah Porter were the parents of Jane (Porter) Sparhawk, who would marry **Rev. John Sparhawk** (b. Sep 1, 1713, d. Apr 30, 1755), another First Church of Salem minister interred in the Bradstreet Tomb.

In 1692, as the Salem Witch Hysteria swept through the community, Noyes was a close friend and colleague of the magistrates who would become the judges of the Court of Oyer and Terminer. Noyes was present during many of the examinations, and took an active part in the assault upon the accused. As Martha Corey nervously chewed her lip, and the afflicted fell in agony before her, Noyes insisted, "I believe it is apparent she practiseth Witchcraft in the congregation." Noyes pulled out metal pins from the bodies of the afflicted during the examination of

Mary Clark, including a pin stuck in Mary Warren's neck. As Capt. John Alden referred to the Providence of God in his defense, Noyes interrupted and asked what right Alden had to speak of God. On September 21, 1692, Noyes signed a petition to give a reprieve of one month to confessed witch Dorcas Hoar, so that she could properly prepare her soul for execution.

Noyes may be best known for demanding confessions from the condemned witches at their executions. As he left Gallows Hill on September 22, where eight victims were hanged in a single day, Noyes was recorded as saying, "What a sad thing it is to see, eight firebrands of Hell hanging there." It is an oral tradition from the time that Sarah Good, who was hanged July 19, 1692, said to Noyes, "God will give you blood to drink." (see *Sarah Good; Witch Trials Memorial*) This would be a reference to Revelations 16:6 "for they poured out the blood of saints and prophets, and You have given them blood to drink."

During this time, there were many who believed that they were seeing the prophecies of the Biblical Book of Revelations coming true in the world around them. Noyes, indeed, was one of those who held this belief that the end of the world was at hand. This dreadful belief may help us to understand why Noyes was so prejudiced against those accused of witchcraft; he may have believed that they were the harbingers of the End of Times. Samuel Sewall, a longtime friend of Noyes, noted that he and Noyes frequently clashed on the interpretation of Biblical prophecy, specifically the Book of Revelations. Noyes told Sewall that he believed that the 1697 Treaty of Ryswick, which ended the Nine Years War between France and a coalition of European nations, including England, had been the beginning of a 1,260-day period which would lead to the awakening of "the Beast of the bottomless pit." Noyes believed that the 1700 death of King Charles II of Spain, and the War of Spanish Succession that followed, was this event, signaling the impending fall of Sodom and Gomorrah. Noyes also quarreled with Sewall about the Fifth Seal; Revelations 6:9-11, a Bible verse about the souls of martyrs crying out for God's vengeance on behalf of "those who had been slain for the word of God and for the testimony which they held." It is an interesting conversation for these two men to have had, when they were both so deeply involved in the executions of innocent people in 1692. Noyes notably did not sign the petition set forth by several ministers from Essex County in 1703 to reverse the decisions of the Court of Oyer and Terminer.

Noyes remained the minister of the First Church of Salem following the death of John Higginson. Sewall and Noyes were at dinner together on Dec 9, 1708, when Paul Dolliver [son of Anne (Higginson) Dolliver] told them Rev. Higginson was breathing his last. Noyes said they would come once they had finished dinner, and when they arrived at Higginson's house, "he expired two or three minutes before we got into the room." Another young minister, Rev. George Curwen, soon joined the First Church in 1714, but died three years later, one month before Noyes.

In 1713, Noyes fell ill, but seemed to recover from this illness in good fashion. However, he suddenly took ill again a few years later on December 12, 1717, and died the next day. His cause of death was not officially recorded, but local folklore says he died of a brain aneurysm, which caused blood to appear in his mouth as he died, the alleged "curse" of Sarah Good coming true.

Samuel Sewall was unable to attend his friend's funeral in Salem due to the snow and cold, and wrote in his diary, "A sore Loss to Salem and New England, He was *Malleus Haereticorum* (The Hammer of Heretics)! My most excellent and obliging friend. Salem will be now much less pleasant to me, since I have not my constant Friend to meet me there."

Capt. Samuel Ingersoll Sr (b. Apr 14, 1760, d. Jul 15, 1804) and his brother-in-law, **Col. John Hathorne** (b. May 29, 1749, d. Dec 15, 1834) bought the Bradstreet Tomb from Col. Benjamin Pickman Jr. (*Pickman/Toppan Tomb*), who had inherited it from his father. Col. John Hathorne was the great-grandson of the Col. John Hathorne of the Court of Oyer and Terminer (*Hathorne Section*), and was the brother of Samuel Ingersoll Sr's wife, **Susannah (Hathorne) Ingersoll** (b. May 21, 1749, d. Dec 6, 1811). Col. Hathorne and his sister were the first-cousins-once-removed of author Nathaniel Hawthorne.

Samuel Sr purchased the Turner-Ingersoll house from John Turner III (*Turner Tomb*), a mansion which has come to be known as The House of the Seven Gables. The home was the subject of a novel by the same name written by Nathaniel Hawthorne, who was born just a few weeks before Samuel Sr's death. Samuel Sr captained his schooner, the Peacock, on a voyage to the West Indies. He was accompanied by his son, Capt. Ebenezer Ingersoll, who was his only surviving son, since family had lost **Samuel Ingersoll Jr** (b. abt. 1775, d. Jul 21, 1797) to consumption. While at sea, both Samuel Sr. and Ebenezer fell ill after performing intensive work to stop a leak in the boat. Samuel Sr died before the ship arrived home in Salem. Ebenezer was required to remain quarantined on the boat, and died of fever at one o'clock on July 22, 1804. Ebenezer Ingersoll was not interred in the Bradstreet Tomb, though it is the resting place of his family. Reverend William Bentley recorded that his funeral and burial were at the Pest Cemetery on Roach's Point. Bentley would reminisce in his diary about his evenings spent with Samuel Sr, stating that he was "friendly, quiet, and industrious... (I) enjoyed in no house with more pleasure the friendly pipe, than at Capt. Ingersoll's."

Susanna Ingersoll (b. abt. 1784, d. Jul 13, 1858) was the daughter of Samuel Sr and Susannah (Hathorne) Ingersoll. Her mother died in 1811, so at twenty-seven she was left alone with the management of the Turner-Ingersoll mansion. The family of her uncle, Col. John Hathorne, immediately attempted to take advantage of her, and seemingly laid claim to the home. They demanded access to all of the rooms and apartments as Susanna grieved her mother. Reverend Bentley, a longtime friend of her mother, wrote in his diary that he was with Susanna when she was "beset by the Col's family with the ferocity of tigers" and that Susanna was distressed, and asked for his help. The Reverend was more than willing to come to her aid, saying, "I took such charge as she desired of me and for which I expect their vengeance." He called the family "savages" and, fearful that they would steal the valuables from the home, Bentley hid the money and keys until Susanna felt well enough to manage it herself, which she would then do quite capably.

Susanna Ingersoll's mother had already begun acquiring real estate shortly before her death, and she followed this same path. As renewed war with Britain became inevitable, many coastal families were eager to sell their homes and flee. Ingersoll purchased many of these properties, and offered mortgages to those families who wanted to keep their homes, but sought an escape from wartime Salem. By the time of her death, she had purchased or sold over sixty-two properties, and had earned her own fortune in real estate, compounded with that which she had inherited.

Perhaps as a result of the bitter split with the rest of her family, Ingersoll chose to withdraw from being active in Salem society, reportedly becoming somewhat of a recluse. She did, however, have a small social circle with whom she enjoyed card games; including her second-cousin, who was seventeen years her junior, Nathaniel Hawthorne. Hawthorne is thought to be one of the few men who were allowed into the home. It is believed that during one of their many talks about the history of the grand old home, Hawthorne would find his inspiration to craft his story *The House of the Seven Gables*. Hawthorne himself denied that the home in the story had any relation to a real house in Salem, despite some evidence to the contrary.

Horace L. Connolly Ingersoll (b. abt. 1808, d. Sep 12, 1894) was the adopted son of Susanna Ingersoll. Connolly was a friend of Nathaniel Hawthorne's in those days, and said that Hawthorne had written him a letter stating that he enjoyed hearing about how the Turner-Ingersoll House had once had seven gables and that, "I think I shall make something of it." Connolly inherited the home on Susanna Ingersoll's death, and changed his last name officially to Ingersoll on November 16, 1858. Susanna Ingersoll had a great deal of affection for her adopted son, and sent him to school to become a minister, which he did, though later he chose the path of a lawyer. After her death, he spent a great deal of money repairing and restoring the old house, however, he also began to practice medicine without a license. He was sued and forced to sell the mansion, ending his days in a state of poverty. He would be interred in the Bradstreet Tomb alongside his adopted mother.

Rev. James Diman (b. Nov 29, 1707, d. Oct 8, 1788) was a longtime minister in Salem, and is likely to have been interred in this tomb, being an "Old Minister." That he was buried in a tomb is confirmed by Rev. Bentley's diary, however no specific tomb was named. It is also possible that he was buried in the Pickering Tomb of the Broad Street Cemetery, as he had married into the Pickering family.

Originally from Long Island, New York, James Diman graduated from Harvard College in 1730, and afterwards served for a time as the Harvard Librarian. For nearly fifty years, he was the minister of Salem's East Congregational Church. On December 18, 1743, he married widow Mary (Pickering) Orne, the daughter of Lois and Timothy Pickering. Together, they would have five children before she passed away on December 14, 1787. In 1783, he was paired with a junior minister, the twenty-four-year-old Rev. William Bentley. Their relationship was a contentious one, and for two years, Diman exluded Bentley from ceremonies such as baptisms and communion. The palpable tension between the ministers lead to a vote amongst the parishioners on October 19, 1785, which called for Diman to withdraw from his position as their spiritual leader in favor of Bentley. In 1786, Diman refused to share his Church records with Bentley, and later accosted Bentley in the street, demanding that money he was owed by the congregation be taken from Bentley's salary. Reverend Diman died in 1788, having never made amends with Bentley, nor redeemed his standing with the community.

Wainwright Tomb

Francis Wainwright Sr. (b.abt. 1623, d. May 19, 1699), was a merchant who migrated to Ipswich, Massachusetts from Chelmsford, England. Francis Sr served both in the Pequot War and King Phillip's War. He was not a resident of Salem, but died while in Salem and was interred here. He married Philippa (Sewall) Wainwright, who died in 1669, and is buried in Ipswich. Before Philippa died, they had a son, **Francis Wainwright Jr** (b. Aug 25, 1664, d. Aug 3, 1711). Like his father, Francis Jr served in the military, and commanded soldiers at an unsuccessful siege on Port Royal, Nova Scotia, in 1707. He fell ill on July 29, 1711, two days before he was to marry his second wife, Eliza Hurst, and died five days later.

The Wainwright tomb, where they are interred, is next to the Bradstreet Tomb, and was lost for a time. Photographs of the Bradstreet Tomb from the 1892 show nothing to mark the existence of the Wainwright Tomb, and the available Burial Records show no burials specific to this tomb. The tomb was rediscovered in 1894, and a new table-top and base were erected. Is it unlikely that the two Wainwrights were the only people interred in this tomb, and our research continues in an attempt to confirm the identities of the others.

The inscription on the table-top reads:

HERE LYETH BURIED
Y^E BODY OF
FRANCIS WAINWRIGHT SEN
AGED 76 YEARES.
DECEASED Y^E 19 OF MAY
1699.

FRANCIS WAINWRIGHT JR

TOMB LOCATED AND
TABLET RESTORED
1894

In memory of
SAMUEL BARNARD ESQ.
who departed this life
*November 21*th

Anno Domini 1 7 6 2

in the 78th Year
Of his Age

Ropes Section

The Venerable Mansion & The Doctor's Prayer

A few steps down the path from the Bradstreet tomb is where several members of the venerable Ropes family are interred. The first of the Ropes family in Salem, George Ropes, arrived in Salem some time before 1637. He and his wife Mary joined the Salem Church on March 15, 1642. Some of the early Ropes family members were cordwainers, or shoemakers. This profitable profession was carried on through several early generations of the Ropes family.

Daniel Ropes Sr (bapt. Jun 13, 1737, d. Oct 8, 1821) was a cordwainer and trader. Daniel Sr owned a tract of land described as running from "the training-field" (i.e., Salem Common) to St. Peter's Church, which would encompass the area of modern-day Brown Street. He married **Priscilla (Lambert) Ropes** (b. abt. 1739, d. Sep 22, 1808), the sister of Capt. Joseph Lambert (*Grimshawe Section*). The Lambert family lived in a mansion house near the corner of Essex Street and Becket Street. Daniel Sr and Priscilla had twelve children, including a pair of twins, though only seven would live to adulthood. One of their sons was Captain Daniel Ropes Jr, a privateer during the American Revolution. In July of 1779, he was captain of the brig *Wild Cat*, a vessel of seventy-five men and fourteen guns. The *Wild Cat* took a British schooner, but soon after their ship was captured by a frigate, and Captain Ropes was imprisoned at Halifax.

Eventually, he would secure his release and return to the sea. In 1821, his ship went down off the coast of England, and though he managed to find his way to London, he died there of fever.

George Ropes Sr (b. Oct 17, 1727, d. Oct 30, 1755) was the brother of Daniel Ropes Sr. George was a mariner who was married to Mary (Deane) Ropes on November 28, 1754. They had one son, **George Ropes Jr** (b. Sep 18, 1755, d. Mar 28, 1756), however, George Sr died soon after the child was born. In fact, the child died before the father's will could be executed, and among the accounts there was the item: "Charge of the sickness of child and funeral of it." He gave to Mary a third of his property, which was customary for a widow, as well as the remainder of George's property, "as sole heir-at-law to her son George Ropes decd, the only son and heir of George Ropes decd." George Jr is interred with his father, and his name appears at the bottom of the tombstone. Mary would remarry to Samuel Waters in 1760, and died of consumption in 1806; her burial site is unconfirmed.

Ruth Ropes Jr (bap. Dec 20, 1768, d. Jul 25, 1797) was the niece of Daniel Sr and George Sr, daughter of their brother, Capt. David Ropes. Her mother was Ruth (Hathorne) Ropes. Her father was commander of the *Jack*, and was killed in battle against a British sloop-of-war off the coast of Halifax on May 28, 1782. Ruth was not married, and died at the age of twenty-eight.

This side of the Ropes family were cousins to the Honorable Nathaniel Ropes Jr, who owned the stately Ropes Mansion at 318 Essex Street, and from whom the mansion derives its name. Judge Ropes was a Loyalist during the American Revolution and, as he was dying of smallpox, a mob assembled around his home and began to vandalize it. The crowd broke the windows of his home and threatened to drag him outside. The judge died the very next day. The Ropes Mansion is currently owned by the Peabody Essex Museum, and is available for public tours. The beautiful flower garden behind the mansion is accessible to the public for free, day and night. The mansion is often best known to Haunted Happenings visitors for appearing in the Disney film "Hocus

Pocus." Though the name of Ropes is the one most identified with this mansion, it was originally built by Samuel Barnard Esq, who is interred in this section.

Samuel Barnard Esq. (b. Dec 1, 1684., d. Nov 21, 1762) was a wealthy merchant who had the home now known as the Ropes Mansion built in 1727. In his will, Barnard left a great deal of money for the benefit of Salem's poor. Buried beside him is his second wife, **Elizabeth (Williams) Barnard** (b. Jan 1, 1707, d. Nov 9,1753), the daughter of William and Christian (Stoddard) Williams. Samuel Barnard's first wife was **Rachel (Lindall) Barnard** (b. Dec 3, 1686, d. Aug 30, 1743), who is buried beside her parents, Timothy and Mary (Veren) Lindall, near the Robert Peele Lot. Rachel was the widow of Samuel's brother, Thomas Barnard Jr. After Samuel Barnard's death, his son sold the mansion to Judge Ropes.

Capt. James Very (bapt. Apr 29, 1764, d. Dec 24, 1814) was a shipmaster who suffered an unfortunate incident in 1795. He left Salem in November 1794, bound for the Cape of Good Hope. However, when he returned to Salem six months later, he arrived empty-handed. Caught up in currents off the coast of Brazil, he could not get the ship free, and returned to Salem without having landed in any ports. This would have been embarrassing for the captain, and likely would have damaged his reputation. However, later that summer, he made a successful voyage to the West Indies. On February 3, 1805, James married **Abigail (Grant) Very** (b. abt. 1771, d. May 2, 1838), which was a second marriage for both of them. James was previously married to **Polly (Palfray) Very** (b. Oct 7, 1764, d. Mar 5, 1804), and Abigail had been married to Zachariah Brooks, who had died shortly after their marriage.

Doctor Moses Little (b. Jul 7, 1766, d. Oct 13, 1811) graduated from the University of Cambridge, England, in 1787. He studied medicine with Dr. John Barnard Swett, then emigrated to Alexandria, Virginia. He was recommended by Dr. Swett to the Reverend William Bentley, with whom he became good friends. Dr. Little began his practice in Salem, and was known as a respected surgeon. In 1798, he married **Elizabeth (Williams) Little** (b. Apr 25, 1774, d. May 29, 1808). Elizabeth, whom Bentley called "one of the best of women," died of consumption at the age of thirty-four. Dr. Little would also contract consumption and pass away after struggling with the deadly illness. Dr. Little asked Bentley to be at his side when he died. Despite ill-will between Bentley and Dr. Little's in-laws, the Pickerings, the family requested that Bentley perform the funeral service. Dr. Little's tombstone is shown in the *Tombstones and Symbols section*, and the inscription reads:

HERE LIES
THE BODY OF
MOSES LITTLE M.D.

WHO DIED 13. OCT. 1811;

AGED 45 YEARS.

PHTHISIS INSATIABILIS!
PATREM, MATREMQUE
DEVORASTI;
PARCE, O! PARCE
LIBERIS.

     The Latin of the tombstone is not entirely accurate, but the meaning translates to:

Insatiable Consumption!
Father and Mother
Thou Has Devoured;
Spare, O! Spare
The Children.

The three children of Dr. and Mrs. Little are not buried here with them, however, they all died young. Despite the heartfelt prayer on their father's tombstone, they are all believed to have died of consumption. Henry Little died at sea on March 31, 1826, at the age of twenty-three, while on the ship *Coral* of Boston. Francis Little died June 21, 1828, at the age of twenty-three, in Newbury, Massachusetts. Elizabeth Little Jr. died in Boston in 1820, at age twenty.

Hannah (Cook) Archer (b. abt. 1714, d. May 21, 1767) was the wife of **Nathaniel Archer** (b. Apr 17, 1710, d. Jun 10, 1772). The back of her tombstone is scratched out, likely with the tools of a stonecutter. It could be that a mistake was made on the tombstone, and the artisan scratched out the mistake and re-did the inscription. Another possibility is that this tombstone was reused from another grave that, for whatever reason, no longer needed a marker. The front of her tombstone is badly overgrown with lichen at this time, and reads:

In Memory of
Mrs HANNAH ARCHER
Wife of M^r.
NATHANIEL ARCHER Who died May 21, 1767
Aged 53 Years
& 9 Months

what's humane life,
Where nothing long can stand:
Time flyes, our glory fades
And death at hand.

In Memory of
MRS. LOUISA M.
Wife of
MR. DANIEL S. TRASK
Who died Sept. 12. 1837
Aged 31.

There is a world above,
Where parting is unknown
A long eternity of love,
Formed for the good alone.

Ward Section

The Harvard Librarian & The Lonely Grave

Passing by the back of the cemetery on the Central Street side brings you to the area where many of the old Ward family are buried. This is roughly where there would have been a path cut through the trees to the original site used for burials in 1637, known here as the Cromwell section. The wall that lines the west side along Central Street currently belongs to the restaurant Casa Tequila, one of several restaurants over the decades which have inhabited this spot, including Murphy's Pub, Spirits, and Roosevelt's. Many of the graves in this area belong to the Ward family.

Miles Ward Sr. (b Mar 11, 1672 d. Aug 30, 1764) was the son of Joshua and Hannah (Flint) Ward. Ward Sr was a well-known joiner and chairmaker in the town. He married **Sarah (Massey) Ward** (b. Jul 25, 1669, d. Nov 20, 1728), on Sept. 16, 1697. Miles Ward's family was a vast one; he was quoted as claiming that by the week before his death, his family had seen nineteen weddings, ninety-one children and grandchildren, and twenty-seven fourth-generation children.

Elizabeth (Webb) Ward (b. Dec 27, 1709, d. Apr 13, 1737) was the daughter of John and Elizabeth (Phippen) Webb, and married Miles Ward Jr. Elizabeth Ward died in childbirth at the age of twenty-eight. The names of her children are listed on the connected stone, all of whom died before adulthood. One daughter, Abigail (Ward) Bass, survived to adulthood, married, and had children of her own. Abigail Bass is interred at the North Cemetery in Portsmouth, NH. The children who died young are listed with their mother; **Sarah Ward** (b. Oct 19, 1728, d. Aug 10, 1729),

Elisabeth Ward (Feb 7, 1729, d. Apr 11, 1737), **Abigail Ward** (b. Apr 16, 1731, d. May 22, 1731), **Anne Ward** (b. Mar 22, 1735, d. May 2. 1737), and **Ebenezer Ward** (b. Apr 12, 1737, d. Apr 13, 1737) who was the last of Elizabeth's children and lived only a few days. The gravestone today is in poor condition and overgrown with lichen, and was in terrible condition even twenty years ago. The obscured inscription was engraved across two panels. The inscription read:

Here lyes ye body of
Elifabeth Wife of Miles
Ward Junr died 13th April 1737
In her 28th Year Elizabeth
their dau^{tr} died Apr ye 11th
1737 in her 8th Year
Ebenezer their fon died
Apr ye 13 1737 Aged 18
hours Anne their daut^r
died May ye 2^d 1737 in
her 2^d year

Sarah dau^{ter}
of Miles and Elizabeth
Ward died Augst y^e
10th 1729 Aged 9 m^o
& 20 days Abigail
Their Dau^{tr} died y^e
22nd of May 1731
Aged 5 weeks

Nathaniel Ward (b. July 29, 1746, d. Oct 12, 1768) was the Librarian of Harvard College, and died unexpectedly at the young age of twenty-three. He was the son of Miles Ward Jr and his second wife, Hannah (Derby) Ward. The inscription on his tombstone gives a detailed account of the young man's life and the grief of his family at his loss. His intelligence, affability and honesty were written of with glowing and verbose praise by his friends and colleagues at Harvard. This intensive epithet engraved on his tombstone was likely written by Reverend Joseph Willard, President of Harvard College. The photo presented here is from before 1914, by photographer Frank Cousins (courtesy of the Philips Library), and shows the stone before lichen growth obscured the inscription.

In this Grave are depoſited
The Remains of NATHANIEL WARD A.M.
Late *LIBRARIAN* of *HARVARD COLLEGE*
Whom
A penetrating Genius
Improved by extenſive Acquaintance
With the liberal Arts and Sciences
Rendered ſuperior to moſt
His native good Senſe
And literary Accompliſhments
Attracted univerſal Notice
While amiable Dispoſition And ſocial Virtues
Eſpecially,
His ſingular Franknefs and difsembled Benevolence
Gained him the Eſteem and Love of all
He was a dutiful Son and affectionate Brother
A faithful Friend and agreeable Companion
A Sincere Piety towards God
Crowned his other Virtues,
And promiſed a Life emmencly uſefull
But ah Blaſted Hope
in the Vigor of Youth
Amidſt happy Proſpects
Cut off by a raging Fever
He breathed forth his Soul
October XII in the Year MDCCLVVIII aged XXIII

Samuel Ward (b. Apr 30, 1740, d. Jul 21, 1812) was the brother of Nathaniel Ward. He was a naval officer at the Customs House, and married **Priscilla (Hodges) Ward** (b. Feb 11, 1749 d. Jun 2, 1822) on January 2, 1768. Together they had over a dozen children, twelve of whom survived Samuel. It appears that he suffered from mental health troubles, and was considered to be an eccentric personality. He found himself constantly in debt, which the State forgave on account of his "delirium." Rev. Bentley knew the family quite well, and remarked upon Samuel's passing that he was, "A man who took an active part in everything without doing much good or being well-informed." Samuel served in the Massachusetts Legislature. Bentley compliments Priscilla as being quite attractive, but says that she did not pick her friends wisely, and that her personality was perhaps as eccentric as her husband's. Samuel frequently changed his religious affiliations, as Bentley says, "I have never seen a man of greater zeal and less knowledge in the affairs of the Church." The tombstones of Samuel and Priscilla Ward may be lost or illegible.

Mary (Archer) Reed (b. Apr 1, 1776, d. Sep 29, 1796) was the wife of Daniel Reed Jr. She died at the young age of twenty of an unnamed illness, a fact which is memorialized in her epithet:

In Memory of
Mary Reed
wife of Daniel Reed Junr.
Who died Sept 29th 1796
Aged 20 years & 6 months.

Friends nor Phisicians could not save
My mortal body from the grave.
Nor can the grave confine me here,
When Christ the son of God appears.

Close by to this grave is the triple-tombstone for the daughters of Dr. Francis and Lydia (Phillips) Gathman. **Lydia Gathman** (bapt. Jul

15, 1713, d. Jul 20, 1716), **Rachel Gathman** (b. Feb 27, 1715, d. Aug 22, 1716), and **Lydia Gathman** (bapt. May 3, 1719, d. Aug 13, 1719). The children would have been born in the home known as the Pickman House (see *Goult-Pickman House*), and most likely would have died there as well. In 1704, Dr. Gathman, who was originally from Hamburg, Germany, would travel to London to serve as a witness against Capt. Thomas Larrimore in connection with the piracy of Capt. John Quelch (see *John Turner Jr; Turner Tomb*). On his journey home, he was captured by French privateers and detained for fifteen months before being released. Dr. Gathman petitioned the Massachusetts General Court for restitution, as he was captured while performing official duties, and was awarded £50.

Louisa M. (May) Trask (b. abt. 1806, d. Sep 12, 1837) has a grave set at the farthest point of the cemetery, at the edge of the Derby Street wall. This lonely gravesite is one of the most memorable and mysterious places in the Old Burying Point. Facing the retaining wall on the corner of Central Street and Derby Street, this grave holds the fascination of visitors and locals alike. Often, there will be burned-down candles, flowers or trinkets left at her grave. Perhaps those who leave items do so to recognize the melancholy solitude of this lone grave. A single tree grows beside the headstone.

Louisa M Trask was born Louisa M. May. Her parentage is uncertain, but a search of births in the Early Vital Records does not show a Louisa M. May born in Massachusetts, so she may have come from another state, or perhaps from England. She married Daniel S. Trask on November 15, 1827. They had two children, Joseph Henry Trask, who died at age sixteen of typhus on February 10, 1845, and Nancy Caroline Trask, who married William J. Lee. Louisa's cause of death is unknown. Her husband Daniel remarried on February 6, 1838, to Abigail Currier. Daniel died of palsy on May 28, 1869, and is buried in the Howard Street Cemetery.

HERE LYES INTERRD
THE BODY OF MR
CALEB PICKMAN WHO
DIED JUNE 4TH 1737 (BEING
STRUCK WITH LIGHTNING)
AGED 22 YEARS

My Times Are in thy Hand
O Remember My Life is Wind.

CROMWELL SECTION AND PIERCE TOMBS

The Oldest Gravestone & The Scottish Immigrant

There are two tomb entrances which sit close to the back wall of the cemetery, which do not have table-top makers. One tomb has no surviving writing on it, and is believed to be the resting place of **Asa Pierce** (b. Mar 21, 1754, d. May 1, 1820) and his wife, **Anna (Mansfield) Pierce** (b. Apr. 28, 1765, d. Apr 29, 1842).

The other tomb has the following inscription:

NATHAN PIERCES
TOMB
ERECTED 1801
ENDOWED 1889

Nathan Pierce Sr (b. abt. 1749, d. May 22, 1812) was born in Newburyport, and had a successful business in tobacco growing and manufacturing. Upon his death, Rev. Bentley wrote of him in his diary, saying he, "had a strong mind, and all the firm virtues, one of the favorite sons of Nature and living good." He married **Rebecca (Allen) Pierce** (b. Jun 12, 1743, d. Jul, 1815), the daughter of Robert and Rebecca Allen. Rebecca was first married to John Hill Sr on January 21, 1764. John Sr died some time before 1770, and Rebecca married Nathan Sr on July 21, 1770. They had five children living when Rebecca died: George Pierce, Sarah (Pierce) Needham, Elizabeth (Pierce) Philips, and Rebecca Allen (Pierce) Upton.

Only one of the sons of Nathan Sr and Rebecca is recorded as interred in this tomb. **Nathan Pierce Jr** (b. Nov 12, 1775, d. July 6, 1848) was married to **Betsey (Glover) Pierce** (b. abt. 1778, d. Jul 8, 1835) on Oct 26, 1801. Betsey was the daughter of Ichabod and Mary Glover, and died of palsy at age 57. Two of their children are interred in the tomb with them; **Mary A Pierce** (bapt. Dec 25, 1803, d. Dec 7, 1871) and **Ellen Pierce** (b. Dec 9, 1806, d. Mar 11, 1875). Also interred here is Betsy (Glover) Pierce's sister, **Priscilla Glover** (bapt. Aug 30, 1783, d. Apr 9, 1856).

Further down the path is where the oldest section of the cemetery may be found. While there are many gravestones from the 1700s through the 1800s in this area, there are likely to be numerous unmarked graves from the 1600s whose wooden markers, coffin rails, or gravestones have long since disappeared due to the weathering of the elements, the passage of time, the rising tides, or vandalism. Lady Arbella Johnson, Reverend Francis Higginson, and Roger Conant, are just a few of Salem's ancient residents who are believed to be interred without any markers.

Doraty (wd. Keniston) Cromwell (b. abt. 1606, d. Sep 27, 1673) was the wife of **Philip Cromwell** (b. abt. 1610, d. Mar 30, 1693), which was at least her second marriage, as she was previously the widow of Allen Keniston. She has oldest existing gravestone in the Charter Street Cemetery. The tombstone appears to have been extensively repaired at some point, and the death's head and lettering re-cut. There was damage done to the stone sometime between 1890 and 1922, and the stone was removed for repair. It is unconfirmed at this time just how the gravestone was damaged, however, there are photographs in the Farber Gravestone Collection which show most of the center panel, death's head, and left border destroyed.

The appearance of the stone in its present condition is remarkably different from the original, as may be seen in the photographs provided. The front face of the stone appears to have been ground down, which would have made the stone thinner. "*Memento Mori*" was still beneath the death's head circa 1892-1901, but the phrase is no longer visible. The crossbones symbol on the left side border was replaced with an hourglass identical to the one on the right, and the death's head itself is a pale imitation of the elaborately carved one that existed previously. A telling sign of the grinding-down is the large chip in the top of the stone in the older photograph, which is still present, though much smaller, in the modern photograph. It is possible that the stone was damaged during the Great Salem Fire of 1914, which caused damage to other tombstones in this area of the cemetery (see *Missing Stones*).

Philip Cromwell arrived in Salem sometime around 1642. He was the owner of a butcher shop that sat where the Hotel Salem is today (209 Essex Street). An enterprising merchant, he had several ketches in his small fleet of merchant vessels: the *Trial of Salem, William,* and *Betty.* He was successful enough in his ventures that he could also be a moneylender; Elianor Hollingworth (*Hollingworth Section*) mortgaged her home to Cromwell after the disappearance of her husband, William Hollingworth Sr. Philip Cromwell was appointed a constable in 1660.

Cromwell was married at least four times in his long life. His first wife, whose name is lost, chose not to leave England when her husband decided to make Salem his permanent dwelling-place. She died sometime before 1649 as this is when Philip married Doraty. After Doraty's death in 1673, he married **Mary (wd. Lemon) Cromwell** (b. abt. 1611, d. Nov 14, 1683) on November 19, 1674. Mary Cromwell's maiden name is unknown, her surname comes from her first husband, Robert Lemon. After her death, Philip married Margaret Cromwell, whose maiden name is unknown, and the marriage date is not recorded. Margaret is mentioned as his wife in his will, which was written March 3, 1688.

John Cromwell (b. abt. 1635, d. Sep 30, 1700) was the son of Philip Cromwell and his first wife. He emigrated to America with his father, married Hannah Barney, and left no children when he died. He took over his father's slaughterhouse and butcher shop. For seven years, he actually had land rights to the cemetery, in a manner of speaking. The town leased it to him in 1681 so that he could harvest the herbaceous vegetation growing there, with the consideration that burials would take place as usual. Any money that he paid the town for the lease was put towards the local grammar school. When he died in 1700, he was in possession of currency from Spain, England, and the colonies, including ten pieces of gold, a gold ring, five guns, and six swords.

DORATY CROMWELL TOMBSTONE CIRCA 1890-1915
FRANK COUSINS

HERE LYES Y^e BODY
OF DORATY WIFE TO
PHILIP CROMWELL
AGED 67 YEARS
DEC^D SEPT^R Y^e 27
1 6 7 3

Given the age of this section, it is likely that other members of the Cromwell family who died in Salem may be buried here with no existing markers. These relatives may be Philip's brother, Thomas Cromwell, a tailor from Malmesberry, Wiltshire, England, who came to live with his brother in Salem and died in 1686. Thomas had two daughters with his wife Ann; the first was Jane, who married Jonathan Pickering, and the second, Anne, who married Benjamin Ager. Upon Ager's death, Anne then married David Phippen. David died at Falmouth, Maine, during King Phillip's War, when he was killed while carrying a flag of truce. The family had been living in Boston and returned to Salem after David's death. Her burial place is unknown, though she may be here with the rest of her family.

Mary (Bright) Corry (b. abt. 1621, d. Aug 27, 1684) was the wife of Giles Corey, a victim of the Witch Hysteria in 1692. Many visitors to the Old Burying Point have mistaken Mary Corry for Martha Corey, Giles' third wife, who was hanged as a witch. Even the 1880 Salem Guidebook erroneously refers to Mary Corry as "Martha Corey, of witchcraft fame, and one of the executed," which may be due in part to legibility issues of the stone's inscription at the time. However, none of the victims of the Witch Hysteria are interred in this cemetery. Information on the victims of the Hysteria is included in the Salem Witch Trials Memorial section.

Mary Bright (or 'Brite') began her journey to Salem in 1662 when Captain Richard More bought her services as an indentured servant in Virginia. Her birthplace is uncertain, but she arrived on a ship from London. Mary worked at Captain More's tavern, where she would meet her husband, Giles Corey. They were married on April 11, 1664. The couple lived in Salem Fields, known today as part of the town of Peabody. In August 1673, in a case that was handled at Captain More's tavern, she was accused of cursing, overindulging in liquor, and beating her servant. This case seems to have been resolved without issue, and her good character was attested to by one of Captain More's daughters, most likely Christian (More) Conant. This accusation of beating may have been regarding the unfortunate servant Jacob Goodale, whom Giles was later charged with beating to death. The inscription on her tombstone reads:

MARY CORRY
Yᵉ WIFE OF
GILES CORRY
AGED 63 YEARS
DYED AUGUST
Yᵉ 27 1684

Benjamin Pickman (b. abt. 1645, d. Dec 31, 1708) was the son of the first of the Pickmans in Salem, Nathaniel and Tabitha (Dike) Pickman. The Pickmans were one of Salem's oldest families, tracing back to the 1630s, when Nathaniel Pickman emigrated to Salem from Bristol, England. It was documented that in 1639 he was granted land on the south side of Forest River Park, "next unto the widow diks (Dike's) land." It is possible that Nathaniel and Tabitha Pickman are also buried in this section of the Old Burying Point, however, no tombstone or contemporary account of their burial exists. Nathaniel Pickman owned a house near where Charter Street meets Central Street, which was sold by his heirs to Timothy Lindall in 1698. Nathaniel was a carpenter who built the town stocks and whipping post. Per his will, he would have been buried "in the buryinge place neere my wife."

Benjamin Pickman was a shipmaster who made his life on the sea, right up until his final years. On July 27, 1677, he married **Elizabeth (Hardy) Pickman** (bapt. Feb 28, 1650, d. Oct 19, 1727). The Pickman family Bible remembers Benjamin as, "maintaining during life the character of an honest, friendly man." Their tombstones are presently almost completely illegible due to lichen growth. The inscription for Benjamin reads:

HERE LYES Yᵉ BODY
OF BENJAMIN PICKMAN
AGED 63 YEARS &
3 MO DEPARTED THIS
LIFE DECEMBER Yᵉ 31ˢᵗ
1708

The inscription on the gravestone for Elizabeth reads:

Here Lyeth y^e
Body of M^{rs}
Elifabeth Pickm^{an}.
who Dec^d the
19 ^{Oct} 1727 Aged
77 years

Caleb Pickman (b. Jun 16, 1715, d. Jun 4, 1737) was the grandson of Benjamin and Elizabeth Pickman. Caleb was captain of the brigantine, *Abigail*, a ship owned by his brothers, Benjamin and Samuel Pickman. The cargo he carried from Salem to Jamaica was "twenty-five thousand feet of wooden boards, thirty-thousand shingles, four thousand five hundred barrel staves (handmade slats for barrels), and twenty three hogsheads (casks) of fish." He brought back "two casks of indigo (important for blue dye), a cask of pimento (a valuable spice), a cask of cocoa, a bag of cotton, three tons of logwood, and £28 cash."

You will also find his name on the Pickman Tomb in the Broad Street Cemetery, written as "Caleb Pickman Esq," and including his cause of death. It is unknown if his body was removed to the family tomb at some point, though it seems unlikely that his gravestone would still be here if that were so. He was the son of Benjamin Pickman Sr and Abigail (Lindall) Pickman. The Pickman family Bible of the time notes that Pickman was struck with lightning "while standing before his mother's door." The house stood on Essex Street midway between Sewall Street and Washington Street, and burned down in a fire in October of 1774. There is more information about the legend associated with this grave in the Lore section of this book.

Nathaniel Silsbee (b. Nov 9, 1748, d. Jun 25, 1791) and his wife **Sarah (Becket) Silsbee** (b. Feb 26, 1749, d. abt. May, 1832) have a tombstone which has an inscription indicating the stone was erected by their great grandchildren. Nathaniel Silsbee died in 1791 at the age of forty-two on a trip to New York, and was buried in the cemetery of the Old Brick Presbyterian Church in Manhattan. The church was demolished in 1856 and all occupants of the cemetery were exhumed for reburial. It would have been around this time that Nathaniel Silsbee's remains were returned to Salem and interred here. Captain Silsbee commanded the ship, *Grand Turk*, which was owned by Elias Hasket Derby (*Derby Tomb*), on voyages to the West Indies and Spain. In early 1776, as war ravaged the American colonies, Silsbee remained for a time in the Caribbean as he tried to keep Derby's business dealings from falling apart. During the war, Silsbee was part-owner of numerous privateer vessels. Nathaniel and Sarah Silsbee were the parents of Nathanial Silsbee Jr, who served as a Massachusetts congressman, state representative, and US Senator from 1817 to 1835.

Nathaniel Silsbee's grandfather, also named **Nathaniel Silsbee** (b. Oct 23, 1677, d. Jan 2, 1769) as well as his wife **Martha (Prince) Silsbee** (b. unknown, d. unknown), are buried nearby. Nathaniel was first married to Hanna Pickering on May 27, 1703, though the date of her death and place of burial is unrecorded. The date of his marriage to Martha is unknown. However, the record of the baptism of their only child, William, took place August 14, 1716. Nathaniel's occupation is listed as a housewright, and his son William was a carpenter. Bizarrely, in October of 2014, a man from Beverly attempted to dig up this grave, but was apprehended before causing much damage. The man was ordered to undergo a mental health evaluation.

Mary (Hunt) Berley (b. May 10, 1790, d. May 8, 1858) was the wife of John Berley. Her parents were Deacon Lewis Hunt and Mary (Bowditch) Hunt (*Bowditch Section*). The marble tombstone for Mary Berley is mostly faded, and it is possible the inscription may soon be completely illegible.

In Memory of
MARY
wife of
JOHN BERLEY
a daughter of
DEA. LEWIS HUNT
and Mrs. MARY
Departed
May 8 1858

William Cash (b. abt. 1625, d. abt. 1690) emigrated to Salem from Fife, Scotland, in the early days of the colony. Cash married Elizabeth Lambert in October of 1667, and had seven children, four of whom lived to adulthood and had husbands and wives of their own. The family lived on Essex Street near Gerrish Place (opposite the corner of Essex and Forrester), in a home that was torn down by 1789. Cash was the captain of the brigantine, *Good Intent*. One of his primary businesses was bringing new settlers across the Atlantic to settle in the colonies. In 1676, William brought his nephew, also named William Cash, to Salem, and the young man ended up settling down in Westmoreland County, Virginia.

It is through this nephew William Cash that the Cash family line in the American colonies begins, including one very famous Cash; genre-bending singer, Johnny Cash. After a chance encounter on an airplane with the keeper of Fife's Falkland Castle, Johnny Cash learned that his ancestral roots were in that part of Scotland, and began research into his family history. This would lead the singer to Salem's Essex Institute in August of 1979, while he was in-between playing shows at the South Shore Music Circus in Cohasset, MA. The musician visited the former site of his home and likely visited William Cash's suspected gravesite in the Old Burying Point. There was no existing tombstone for William Cash at the time. It is believed that the current stone which stands in the Old Burying Point was paid for by Johnny Cash, though it may not have been placed here until 2008, making it the newest complete stone in the cemetery. The addition of the tombstone came with little fanfare, despite the fame of his descendant, and ensures that the Cash family name will be tied to Salem for many generations to come.

William Cash

Born 1625   Fife, Scotland
Died 1690   Salem, Mass

Master Mariner

Captain & Master
of Brigantine

"Good Intent"

Here lieth the
Body of
JOHN TURNER
Aged 36 years.
who departed this life
the 9th of October.
in the year of our Lord
1680.

Turner Tomb

The Legacy of the Gabled Mansion & The Pirate Hunter

The legacy of the Turner family can be experienced today in Salem within the walls of the House of the Seven Gables. The stately home, once known as the Turner-Ingersoll Mansion, is now a house museum with beautiful gardens and a lovely view of the ocean. The mansion achieved fame as the setting of Nathaniel Hawthorne's novel, *The House of the Seven Gables*. Hawthorne's own birthplace has been relocated to the property as well. Throughout the year, guests may visit the grounds and take guided tours of the homes. In October, the museum offers "Spirits of the Gables," a dramatic experience of Hawthorne's story within the actual setting of the book. The birthplace of Nathaniel Hawthorne, a home owned by his grandfather Capt. Daniel Hathorne, was moved to the grounds of the Turner-Ingersoll Mansion in 1958. In this home, a performance called the "The Legacy of the Hanging Judge" is performed, which exhibits the author's connection to his controversial ancestor, Col. John Hathorne (*Hathorne Section*).

Capt. John Turner (b. Sep 8, 1644, d. Oct 9, 1680) was the son of Robert and Elizabeth (Freestone) Turner, and arrived in New England on board the *Blessing*, the same vessel as Richard Hollingworth's family and Richard More (*More Section*) on one of his return trips from England. While his parents remained in Boston, John Turner moved to Salem and married **Elizabeth (Roberts) Turner** (b. Apr 11, 1648, d. abt. 1691). He had his home built in 1668, which would be the early beginnings of the mansion seen today. At the time of his death in 1680 at the age of thirty-six, Captain Turner was a successful merchant, doing trade in Barbados. Elizabeth remarried to Major Charles Redford of Marblehead on June 19, 1684; he would die in Barbados in 1691.

The Honorable John Turner Jr (b. Sep 12, 1671, d. Mar 4, 1742) was the only son of John and Elizabeth Turner. His father having died when he was only nine, John Turner Jr was a young man in Salem during the chaotic years that lead to the Witch Hysteria. In 1690, Turner Jr suffered a fall from a cherry tree. On September 6, 1692, eighteen-year-old accuser (and sometime accused) Mary Warren testified to the Court of Oyer and Terminer that Ann Pudeator's spirit had caused John to fall, "to his great hurt and which amazed him in his head & almost killed him." Turner did not testify against Pudeator, who was hanged on September 22, 1692.

Turner, like many who survived the time of the Witch Hysteria, seems to have taken the lessons learned from that tragedy with him into the future. On November 10, 1696, Turner was the jury foreman for the trial of Quaker Thomas Maule (the same man who challenged William King, *Bowditch Section*), who had published his *Truth Set Forth and Maintained*, a book explaining Quaker beliefs. Sheriff George Corwin had declared the book was heretical, and had Maule's house searched and all copies burned. When the case finally came to trial, Sheriff Corwin had died, and the judges (including Samuel Sewall) chose to accept as truth the late Sheriff's claims that it slandered the church, government, and private individuals, despite never having viewed the contents of the book themselves. Maule defended himself, saying that Corwin's claims were untrue, and that without viewing the contents of the book themselves, convicting him would be similar to accepting spectral evidence in the witch trials. The jury found Maule not guilty, and Turner, as the foreman, explained that they "were not a jury of divines, which this case required," and could not convict the man with no evidence.

Turner would marry **Mary (Kitchen) Turner** (bapt. May 22, 1684, d. Aug 29, 1768), the daughter of Robert and Mary (Boardman) Kitchen. Captain Turner took to the ocean, as his father had, and purchased interests in large vessels like the brigs, *Olive Branch*, *Prosperous*, and *William*. Like many who tried to make an honest life on the sea, he was forced to contend with the greatest threat to any merchant vessel in the Caribbean, the growing numbers of pirates. In 1704, piracy hit extremely close to home, and Turner played in important role in the events that followed.

Captain John Quelch, an Englishman residing in Marblehead,

was the first mate of the *Charles*, whose original purpose was a legitimate one. However, the ship's captain, Daniel Plowman, fell ill, causing a delay in the voyage. Quelch decided to assume command, and led a mutiny, and Plowman was thrown overboard at sea. Quelch changed the ship's intent to that of privateering, and sailed to the coast of Brazil, plundering nine Portuguese vessels. The hold now packed with silver, the *Charles* returned to Salem, Quelch possibly assuming that New Englanders would be none the wiser. However, the owners of the vessel grew suspicious of Quelch's activities, and the authorities arrested Quelch, along with six of his men. However, the remaining pirates escaped and had hidden themselves away.

The fear of capture must have drawn the pirates together again, and Major Stephen Sewall was staying in Salem when he received word that the cutthroats had returned to Cape Ann. Nine of the pirates were holed up in a "lone-house" and "doub'e-arm'd," prepared to fight. Captain John Turner, Samuel Sewall, and Sheriff William Gedney (*Bowditch Section*) rode from Salem to Beverly, where they met with a company of men from Manchester and continued on to Gloucester. There, they received word that the pirates had commandeered the ship, *Larramore Galley*, belonging to local privateer, Captain Thomas Larrimore. Captain Turner requested permission to pursue the pirates, and joined with Major Sewall to chase them at sea. They managed to catch up with the pirates, who must have realized their plight was hopeless, facing forty-two men while they were only seven in number. Captain Turner and Major Sewall boarded the galley and accepted the pirates' surrender. The remaining two pirates, Peter Roach and William Jones, were discovered by the townspeople of Gloucester and taken captive. The two pirates were sent down to Salem where they were locked up in the Salem Jail; the same jail which had held the victims of the Witch Hysteria just twelve years before. Three of the pirates would be spared the hangman's noose by testifying against their fellow pirates, the rest of whom would be found guilty and hanged. It is not known if Captain Turner was present for the executions at Copp's Hill in Boston, where Captain Quelch famously uttered his last words, "Be careful how ye bring money into New England, lest they hang ye for it."

Turner would later be promoted to Major, and would again see excitement in 1708, but this time on land, and against the terrifying backdrop of Queen Anne's War. A host of eight hundred French soldiers and Native American warriors marched on Haverhill, and Major Turner led a force to meet them. The attack came more swiftly than expected, and the invading force made it to the town first. Forty townsfolk were killed or captured in the initial attack, and Major Turner's reinforcements only just arrived in time to halt the advance and force the attackers to flee. Several French officers were killed, and an Abenaki chief, Escumbuit, was wounded. It is said that Major Turner kept a collection of scalps from braves that he had killed, and displayed the scalps on the walls of a room in the Turner-Ingersoll house.

By 1750, Turner was a Colonel and had served on the Massachusetts General Court. He converted the first period Turner home into the sixteen room, seven-gabled Georgian style Turner Mansion. At some point, he purchased three enslaved African people to use as workers in the home. Recently, the House of the Seven Gables has resolved to include the story of the lives of the three enslaved persons as part of the history of the home.

John Turner III Esq. (b. May 20, 1709, d. Dec 19, 1786) was the son of John Jr and Mary Turner. What John Turner Jr gained for his family through his effort and determination, his son seemed just as determined to squander. Bad business decisions, ill-advised partnerships, and a desire to live a luxurious and opulent lifestyle caused the family fortune to slip through his fingers. He was forced to sell the family mansion to Capt. Samuel Ingersoll (*Bradstreet Tomb*) in 1782. John Turner III had commissioned an expensive portrait of himself, one of his most lavish purchases, which is still hanging in the parlor of the House of the Seven Gables today. He was married twice, first to Mary Osbourne, and then to Katherine Berry. There is presently no confirmation that either of his wives are buried with him.

At some point in the 1800s, members of the Bowditch family would gain possession of the tomb. Whether any of the Turners were removed is unconfirmed, however the tomb would still be referred to as the "Turner Tomb" in burial records. Among those interred here are **Mary (Bowditch) Upton** (b. Aug 6, 1802, d. Dec 11, 1883) and her daughter **Sarah Upton** (b. Mar 3, 1843, d. Apr 24, 1847), **Elizabeth Bowditch** (b. Aug 13, 1807, d. Mar 2, 1895), **George Bowditch** (b. abt. 1856, d. Mar 26, 1857), as well as **William Bowditch** (b. Dec 31, 1809, d. May 15, 1896) who appears to be the last individual interred in the Charter Street Cemetery.

HERE LYETH
BURIED y^e BODY
OF WILLIAM
HOLLINGWORTH

AGED 33 YEARS
DEPARTED THIS LIFE
y^e 7th OF NOVEMBER

1 6   8 8

HERE LYETH
BURIED y^e BODY
OF ELIANOR
HOLLINGWORTH

AGED 59 YEARS
DECEASED y^e 22
OF NOVEMBER

1   6   8   9

HOLLINGWORTH SECTION

The Tempestuous Alewife & The Ubiquitous Attorney

Elianor Hollingworth (b. abt. 1630, d. Nov 22, 1689) was the wife of William Hollingworth Sr. Her maiden name and origin is unknown, however, it is known that her husband's family arrived in Salem on the *Blessing* in 1635, and he began to seek out his fortune at sea. Together they had three children; Mary (Hollingworth) English, **William Hollingworth Jr** (b. abt. 1655, d. Nov 7, 1688), and Susanna Hollingworth, the latter of whom did not live to adulthood. One of the first times Elianor's name appears in Salem's history is due to an incident where a Narragansett tribe native, going by the name of John, assaulted her and "struck her dead" (i.e., knocked her unconscious). The man was given twenty lashes as punishment; ten for the assault, and ten for drunkenness.

On one of his voyages at sea, Elianor's husband William Sr appears to have been lost, though it would not be until November of 1678 that he was legally presumed dead, and Elianor was given control of the family's assets. In truth, she had been managing the home and finances the entire time William had been missing. Rather than sell off her husband's land and property, she found new ways to earn money. In 1674, she was granted a license to run a tavern; The Blue Anchor, situated near the landing of the ferry to Marblehead, where there was also a storehouse and wharf. As an alewife (an archaic term for a woman who owned an alehouse) she kept a respectable tavern, though there were reports of occasional brawling.

In 1679, Elianor got into a heated argument with Elizabeth Dicer, who cursed her as a "black-mouthed witch." This was not a formal accusation of witchcraft, merely an insult, but a weighty one, and Dicer was fined for her "railing words." It would not be the last time the word "witch" would be thrown at the Hollingworths.

William Hollingworth Jr (b. abt. 1655, d. Nov 7, 1688) followed in his father's footsteps as a mariner and travelled across Europe, however, he also seemed to inherit his father's curse of constant indebtedness and found himself running from creditors. Once, Deputy Marshal Philip Fowler attempted to arrest William at the Blue Anchor for debts owed. Fowler, who had not announced himself, ended up chasing William around the property and Elianor struck Fowler on the head four times to give William a chance to escape. She later had to pay a fine for this assault.

Soon after, Elianor conveyed the ownership of the family home to her daughter Mary, perhaps to avoid it being seized as an asset of the debt-ridden William Jr. By then, Mary Hollingworth had married a French Huguenot merchant named Philip English, and the couple were successful enough to take on the asset without worry. When William died at the age of thirty-three on November 7, 1688, succumbing to an unknown illness, he was more or less penniless. Elianor passed away on the 22nd of November the following year at the age of fifty-nine.

Mary (Hollingworth) English survived both her mother and brother and would have commissioned this intricate double headstone. It is likely the work of William Mumford, a Quaker who carved many tombstones in Salem and Boston. In the Witch Hysteria of 1692, Mary and her husband would be accused of witchcraft. Mary was the first of the couple to be accused, and when the Marshal came to arrest her, according to the family folklore, she managed to give her family time to prepare in an unusual way. The Marshall had come in the middle of the night while Philip and Mary were asleep, and Mary refused to allow the Marshall to arrest her. She agreed to cooperate in the morning once she had risen and had breakfast. Surprisingly, the Marshal agreed and posted a man outside the home until morning. Philip escaped before a warrant could be served on him, and eluded capture until he agreed to surrender. Imprisoned together in Boston, they were given better accommodations than many of the less wealthy accused. The Englishes were able to escape before they faced the Court of Oyer and Terminer, and travelled to New York and waited for the Hysteria to end.

On their return, they found Sheriff George Corwin had seized almost all of their property, including furniture, clothing, livestock, even the nails of the family home and hinges of their doors. It was customary under English law for the Sheriff to seize the property of a convicted felon, however, there had been no conviction in their case. In 1696, Philip and Mary English are named in a lawsuit against Sheriff George Corwin for the wrongful seizure of their property. The English family won their suit, and Corwin was instructed to pay restitution. Sheriff Corwin died in 1696 before the English's claim could be settled, and tradition holds that Philip English seized the Sheriff's body from his funeral and held it until the debt was repaid by his wife, Lydia (Gedney) Corwin (*Gedney Tomb*).

The date of Mary (Hollingworth) English's death and the location of her burial is unknown. It may be that she is interred here at the Old Burying Point with her mother and brother. It is also possible she was buried on the family property. Her husband, Philip English, regained his good standing in the town, and was voted a selectman. His signature is on the town selectmen meeting in 1711 ordering a wall built to protect the cemetery from erosion. He was imprisoned for a day later in life as punishment for calling the Church of Salem "the Church of Satan," and may have decided to get his own form of revenge on the Puritans. He donated his property on what is now Brown Street to the Church of England, which was met with anger from the townsfolk. This led to the construction of Saint Peter's Church in 1733, the first Anglican Church in Salem. Philip English was interred in the new cemetery behind Saint Peter's Church, and reportedly under a pseudonym, "Robert Brown," to prevent retribution like he had enacted on his rival, George Corwin. In 1833, the gravestones of Saint Peter's were removed to the front of the church when a chapel was built on top of the cemetery. Over a hundred years later, there were reports that a casket belonging to Philip English was accidentally unearthed during construction work on Brown Street.

John Nutting Esq. Sr (b. Jan 7, 1694, d. May 20, 1790) was an attorney of great respect in Salem for many decades. His name may be found on the probate records and wills of many of the people interred in this cemetery. He is interred alongside his second wife, **Elizabeth (Pickman) Nutting** (b. Jan 22, 1714, d. Jun 10, 1785). His first wife, **Ruth (Gardner) Nutting** (b. Mar 16, 1699, d. Nov 22, 1736), and their son **John Nutting Jr** (b. abt. 1718, d. Jun 28, 1729) share a tombstone that sits nearly opposite John Sr's, located in the Bowditch Section.

Mary (Touzel) Hathorne (b. abt. 1724, d. June 14, 1805) was the wife of Capt. William Hathorne, who is interred beside Col. John Hathorne (*Hathorne Section*). She died nearly ten years after her husband, and is interred by the back fence of the Old Burying Point. This may have been due to there being little room in the Hathorne plot for her, or it is possible that either her stone or her husband's were moved at some point. There is some indication that she may have had a problem with intemperance in her later years. Her daughter, also named Mary, died March 1741, and Rev. Bentley blames her death on intemperance, "of which she had too many examples around her." Mary (Touzel) Hathorne died during a particularly hot summer, and Bentley notes that this intolerable heat caused the deaths of three people that same week, claiming that age and intemperance were factors in each of those deaths.

Captain Josiah Orne Jr (b. abt 1745, d. Jun 21, 1789) was the son of Josiah Sr and Sarah (Elvins) Orne. Josiah Jr was a cousin of William Orne, who is interred in the Orne Tomb. The cousins owned a large interest in the Revolutionary War privateering vessel *Junius Brutus*. Josiah Jr would marry **Alice (Palmer) Orne** (b. abt 1747, d. Nov 16, 1776) on June 13, 1767. Their son, **Josiah Orne III** (bapt. Apr 3, 1768, d. Sep 23, 1825), would marry Alice (Allen) Orne, the daughter of Edward and Ruth (Hodges) Allen (*Allen Tomb*). Alice (Palmer) Orne died suddenly at age thirty. After Alice's death, Josiah Jr would remarry to Anne White of Charlestown, Massachusetts on August 2, 1778. Josiah Jr would die of a recurring fever, listed as "hectic," ten years later and was interred here. Josiah Jr's tombstone and footstone are on either side of the path near to the Turner Tomb, indicating the path may actually go over his grave. Alice (Palmer) Orne's tombstone appears prominently next to the path, nearby to her husband's footstone.

IN Memory of
Mrs. ALICE ORNE
Wife of Capt. JOSIAH ORNE
who Died Novr. 16th. 1776, in
the 30th Year of her Age
This Stone has Something great to teach
And what you need to learn,
For graves, my friends, most loudly preach
Man's infinite Concern

HERE LIES THE BODY OF
Mrs: MARY GARDNER
THE WIFE OF
Capt. JONATHAN GARDNER
DIED APRIL 20th 1755 IN THE
58th YEAR OF HER AGE

Gardner Section

Descendants Of The Old Planter &
The Hidden Family

This area is sometimes referred to as the "Gardner Annex," and was donated by Samuel Pickman on November 26, 1669, when he was the owner of the Pickman House and property. The first Gardner to arrive in Salem was Thomas Gardner, called "The Old Planter," as he arrived in Naumkeag with Roger Conant in 1626. Gardner had first emigrated to New England in 1623, arriving at Cape Ann (Gloucester), and helping to establish a settlement there as a member of the Dorchester Company. Gardner was Overseer of the Plantation at Cape Ann, and it has been argued that he should be called the first Governor in the Massachusetts Bay Colony. In 1625, the colony was joined by Conant, who ascertained that the soil was not suiting their purposes, and the Company permitted them to move to Naumkeag. Gardner was instrumental in the formation of the new colony, and settled in what is now part of Peabody. He was buried at Gardner's Hill, a very early cemetery, and much later the gravestones would be moved to Harmony Grove, though the fate of the bodies is uncertain.

The Gardners interred here in this part of the Old Burying Point begin with the fourth generation of Gardners in America. Gardners were part of the early makeup of the Massachusetts Bay Colony, and were connected by marriage to the Derby, Hathorne, Porter, Gedney, and Higginson families of Salem, and the Coffin family of Nantucket.

Capt. Jonathan Gardner (b. Feb 23, 1698, d. Nov 27, 1783) was the son of Lt. Abel Gardner and Sarah (Porter) Gardner. Gardner was a successful merchant and landowner who possessed land along what is now Essex Street and Brown Street in Salem. On December 2, 1725, he married his third cousin, **Elizabeth (Gardner) Gardner** (b. Oct 10, 1705, d. Apr 20, 1752), the daughter of John Gardner and Elizabeth Weld. After her death, Jonathan remarried to **Mary (Avery) Gardner** (b. abt. 1697, d. Apr 20, 1755) of Boston, on January 8, 1755. However, their marriage was very brief, as she died three months later on April 20. His third marriage was to Mary (Pickering) Gardner, on November 17, 1757, who survived him by twenty-one years, and died February 20, 1804. In Salem, he served as a constable, selectman, school committee member, and juryman. In 1741, he paid for a new bell at Saint Peter's Church. The *Salem Gazette* reported on his death and stated that he was, "for many years ... an eminent merchant in this place." He had in his service an enslaved African man named Primus (not to be confused with Primus Lynde) whom he willed to his son John upon his death.

All of Jonathan Gardner's children were by his first wife, Elizabeth. They had twin daughters born March 19, 1739, named Mary and Lydia. **Mary (Gardner) Andrew** (b. Mar 19, 1739, d. Jan 17, 1820) was married to **Jonathan Andrew** (b. Nov 23, 1745, d. May 16, 1781), and is interred with her husband nearby to the Gedney Tomb. Lydia (Gardner) Derby married Capt. Richard Derby Jr, son of Richard Derby Sr (*Derby Tomb*), on September 13, 1759. Jonathan's son, John Gardner, married Sarah (Derby) Gardner. Their son, John Gardner Jr, built the Gardner-Pingree House (129 Essex Street) in 1804. This building would eventually become the home of Captain Joseph White, and the site of White's infamous murder in 1830, which would inspire Edgar Allen Poe's "The Tell-Tale Heart." The mansion was acquired by the Essex Institute (now the Peabody Essex Museum) in 1933.

Capt. Jonathan Gardner Jr (b. May 25, 1728, d. Mar 2, 1791) was another son of Jonathan and Elizabeth Gardner. He was known as "the Commodore" amongst his acquaintances. He married **Sarah (Putnam) Gardner** (bapt. Dec 22, 1728, d. Nov 10, 1791) on January 2, 1753. Jonathan Jr was a successful businessman who was known for his interest in Salem's schools and care for the poor. He served as Overseer of the Poor for ten years, a position which is covered in more detail in the entry for Benjamin Pickman (*Pickman/Toppan Tomb*).

Capt. Gardner had fought in the French and Indian Wars as captain of the privateer *Two Brothers*, engaging in battle with French ships. He was one of the first company commanders appointed from Salem in the American Revolution, appointed as Captain of the First Company of the First Essex Regiment. Gardner was involved in civil matters relating to the American Revolution in 1775, as a member of the Committee of Minute Men, among other posts, as well as helping to procure materials to block access to Salem harbor after the burning of Falmouth, Massachusetts on October 18, 1775. He was also an early member of the Salem Marine Society. On his death, the *Salem Gazette* obituary remembered him as, "A man whose actions were governed by the most virtuous principles and whom the esteem of his fellow citizens follows to the grave." In honor of his commitment to Salem's schools, a group of schoolchildren lead his funeral procession to the burial ground.

Capt Jonathan Gardner III (bapt. Mar 16, 1755, d. Sep 27, 1821) was the only son of Jonathan Jr and Sarah Gardner. In the Revolutionary war, he served as commander of the brigs *Union, Tyrannicide,* and *Bunker Hill*. Like his father, he served on the school committee and as an Overseer of the Poor. His military record lists him as standing 5'5" with a brown complexion. He also served as treasurer of the Salem Marine Society. No tombstone remains for Jonathan III, but he is recorded as interred in the Burying Point. On November 26, 1791, he married **Sarah (Fairfield) Gardner** (b. Jan 4, 1766, d. Dec 23, 1795) of Wenham. The couple would have two sons, **Jonathan Gardner IV** (b. Aug 8, 1793, d. Dec 17, 1795), who died at the age of two, and William Fairfield Gardner, who was born in 1794 and married Elizabeth Barker. Sarah died just six days after Jonathan IV passed away. The Salem Gazette published a memorial for Sarah on December 29, 1795:

"*She was a woman of native worth, and of the most useful accomplishments. She possessed a cheerful temper, but her manners were always without offence. Her readiness of thought from her tenderness of mind, was incapable of exciting disgust, or doing an injury. From her natural disposition, her charity was equal, and constant. Her affability was directed by an uninterrupted flow of affection, towards all who approached her. Her conversation was chaste, her friendship sincere, and a uniform case and satisfaction attended her in all her domestic employments... She has left the husband she loved and one child and can never be left from the memory of her friends, who love the virtues she possessed. Her aged mother demands our most sincere condolence.*"

After Sarah's death, Jonathan III married **Lucia (Dodge) Gard-ner** (b. Jun 16, 1768, d. Mar 24, 1812) on October 27, 1799. The family homestead was on the lot where the Essex Institute (132-134 Essex Street) building stands today.

Elizabeth Gardner (b. Oct 18, 1729, d. May 6, 1818) was the daughter of Jonathan Jr and Elizabeth Gardner. She would have been referred to as a "spinster," which means she was never married and had no children. She is recorded as having died of a fever.

Catharine Andrews (b. Oct 21, 1772, d. Jul 5, 1797) was the daughter of **Capt. Nehemiah Andrews** (b. Feb 7, 1753, d. Feb 10, 1800) and **Cather-ine (Seamore) Andrews** (b. abt. 1749, d. Mar 26, 1802). Just before exiting through the Memorial, to the right, you will see a single footstone by the Liberty Street wall. The footstone reads only "Catharine Andrews." Her cause of death is unknown, and her gravestone no longer exists. The inscription on the stone was:

In Memory of

Catharine Andrews

Obt. July 5th 1797

Æt. 25 Years.

Farewell my friends, dry up your tears,
I must lie here till Christ appears,

The stone was very likely in poor condition or sunken when Derby Per-ley took down this inscription, as the last two lines are missing, but the rest of this poem can be found on the tombstone of **Mary (Ingalls) Bray** (b. Jan 28, 1737, d. Sep 28, 1805) (*Hathorne Section*)

Death is a debt to nature due,
I've paid the debt and so must you.

Sometime before 1993, Catherine's father, Capt. Nehemiah An-drews' stone was located in this same area, as was likely that of his neph-ew, also **Capt. Nehemiah Andrews** (b. Oct 21, 1779, d. ?) and unquestion-ably his nephew's wife, **Elizabeth (Ledbetter) Andrews** (b. abt. 1782/3, d. Mar 12, 1851) as her stone inscription was recorded by Derby Perley in the late 1800s or early 1900s:

Mrs. ELIZABETH LEBETTER
widow of
CAPT NEHEMIAH ANDREWS
Died March 12, 1851
Aged 68 years
& 3 mon.

Most likely because of the identical name and the location of the stones, many personal genealogical records list Capt. Nehemiah the elder as the husband of Elizabeth, a cautionary tale in taking current online records from family genealogists as fact. Capt. Nehemiah the elder was master of the brigantine *Salem* in 1780, which was recorded as a privateering vessel during the Revolutionary War. Nehemiah's enlistment records describe him as 6ft tall, with a dark complexion. He would captain the brigantine *John*, which was later lost by his successor, Captain Ebenezer Ward, on Misery Island just off of Salem Harbor. He would also captain the *Pilgrim*, and co-own the *Thomas* with his longtime employer, Nathaniel West (see *Elizabeth (Derby) West; Derby Tomb*).

Capt. Nehemiah the younger married Elizabeth on August 31, 1805 (which would have been five years after the death of his uncle), and then remarried to Mary (Thomson wd. Shepard) Andrews on February 12, 1807. He was listed as a member in the Freemasons Lodge of Salem and as captain of the ship *Mentor*, starting in 1812, likely making him a privateer like his uncle. Their daughter, **Catherine S Andrews** (b. abt. 1808, d. Jul 30, 1836), had a stone alongside the back of the Memorial wall in the Charter Street Section, but it was lost sometime between 1993 and 2007. The inscription on her tombstone read:

In Memory of
Miss CATHARINE S.
ANDREWS
who died
July 30, 1836
aged 28 years.

Both elder and younger Nehemiah Andrews had several children, and as only a few are accounted for in the Howard Street Cemetery, it is extremely likely that they would be buried here as well. A Salem undertaker, David Boyce, has a record of a Nehemiah Andrews paying for his **Child Andrews** (b. ?, bur. Nov 4, 1809) to be buried "South of your sister grave stons." While the area around the current entrance to the Old Burying Point Cemetery may seem devoid of graves, with its landscaping and newly installed accessible ramp pathway, one should be mindful that those are relatively recent additions, and the ground on which you tread may be more crowded than you imagine (See *Missing Gravestones*).

Capt. John Higginson III (b. Aug 20, 1679, d. Apr 26, 1718) has the last tombstone that may be viewed when exiting the cemetery to the Witch Trials Memorial. Captain Higginson was a merchant and selectman. His tombstone gives the name "John Higginson Jr," but he was the third John of the Higginson line in Salem. His father was Col. John Higginson, who served as a Justice of the Peace during the Salem Witch Hysteria, and his grandfather was Reverend John Higginson (*Bradstreet Tomb*). He is buried beside his first wife, **Hannah (Gardner) Higginson** (b. Apr 4, 1676, d. Jun 24, 1713), who was the daughter of Samuel and Elizabeth (Brown) Gardner. Two of their children, **Francis Higginson** (b. Nov 19, 1705, d. Nov 29, 1705) and **Henry Higginson** (b. Sep 23, 1707, d. Dec 1, 1708) are interred near the Bartlett Tomb on a double-tombstone. The twin children of John III and his second wife, Margaret (Sewell) Higginson, unnamed **Son and Daughter Higginson** (b. Jul 22, 1715, d. Jul 29, 1715) are also interred near the Bartlett Tomb, having lived only a few days.

Hannah Higginson's gravestone is overgrown with lichen and currently illegible, however, the inscription read:

HERE LYES INTER^D Y^e BODY
OF HANNAH WIFE OF JOHN
HIGGINSON JUN^R DAUG^R
OF CAP^T SAM^L GARDNER
DEC^D JUNE Y^e 24 1713 IN Y^e
38 YEAR OF HER AGE

Here Lyes Inter^d
the Body of
Mr JOHN HIGGINSON
Junr of Salem, March't
Aged 42 Years &
6 Monthes, Who Dec^d

April the 2th6 1 7 1 8

MISSING GRAVESTONES

I t is not certain exactly how many people are interred in the Old
Burying Point. There are over twelve hundred confirmed burials,
however, that number does not include the number of burials with
non-existent records, or burials occurring before records began to
be kept. Nor can this take into account the number of graves that were
washed away in the seventeenth century, the number of graves which
were re-used, or the tombs which were sold, emptied, and re-used. The
actual number may be closer to sixteen hundred interments. However,
when viewing the current Charter Street Cemetery, there are not nearly
enough gravestones to represent even the lower figure of twelve hundred.

As mentioned in the chapter on Preservation, gravestones have
been lost to many different environmental factors, and some, like the one
pictured, have no inscription at all. Locating the inscriptions for these
lost gravestones has been one of the goals of this book, and the information has been recorded for posterity where possible. In some cases, not
even the inscription for some memorials was recorded. However, records
of the lives of those people who had no tombstones often still exist. This
section is devoted to mentioning a few of those who may be forgotten.

Henry Bartholemew (b. abt. 1607, d. Nov 22, 1692) and his wife, **Elizabeth (Scudder) Bartholemew** (b. abt. 1622, d. Sep 1, 1682). A tombstone for
Elizabeth existed as late as 1885, but no longer exists. Henry was born in
London, where he became a merchant. He came to Salem on November 7, 1635, and would be married to Elizabeth sometime before 1641.
Bartholomew owned several hundred acres of land, including the area
around the body of water still known as Bartholomew Pond today. He
was a member of the General Court, representing Salem, alongside Wil-

liam Hathorne, father of Col. John Hathorne (*Hathorne Section*). Bartholomew began his term in 1646, and held his seat for nearly forty years, and was accounted as an unprejudiced lawmaker. Two of the daughters of Henry and Elizabeth are interred in the Old Burying Point; Hannah (Bartholemew) Swinnerton (*Pickman/Toppan Tomb*), and Abigail (Bartholomew) Willoughby (*Grimshawe Section*).

Mary (Bradstreet) Robie (b. abt. 1741, bur. Sep 30, 1806) was a granddaughter of Simon Bradstreet. She married **Thomas Robie** (b. abt. 1727, d. Dec 18, 1811). They were interred close by to the Bradstreet Tomb, however, by 1892 their sandstone tombstones were barely legible, and they have since disappeared.

Samuel Herron (b. abt. 1776, d. Jul 25, 1821) was a shoemaker from Ireland. He married to **Eliza (Daniels) Herron** (b. abt. 1793, d. Jun 6, 1821) on December 4, 1817. They had two daughters: Elizabeth Grant Herron on November 23, 1818, and Martha Ann Herron on June 8, 1820. Eliza Herron would die of a hernia, and the death of his wife may have driven Samuel to desperation. Just over a month after Elizabeth's passing, Samuel committed suicide by drowning. He was declared as *non compos mentis* and interred here with his wife.

Pvt. Andrew Luscomb (b. abt. 1792, d. Feb 7, 1825) served in the volunteer militia during the War of 1812 in Col. B.S. Reed's Marblehead regiment. He died of intemperance at age thirty-two.

Captain John Crowninshield (b. Jan 19, 1697, d. May 25, 1761) and his wife **Anstiss (Williams) Crowninshield** (b. abt. 1672, d. Sep 10, 1744), have tombstones which were damaged and removed from their protective brackets at some point in the last twenty years. The brackets still remain, and one bears the barely-legible inscription:

BROKEN IN GREAT SALEM FIRE JUNE 1914.
RESTORED BY DESCENDANTS 1915.

John Crowninshield was a wealthy merchant who traded in fish, and built the home that is today known as the Crowninshield-Bentley House (126 Essex Street) in 1727, where Reverend William Bentley lodged while he was the minister of the East Church in Salem, and is the location of "The Doorstep" from H.P. Lovecraft's story, *The Thing on*

The Doorstep. John and Anstiss Crowninshield had several children, each of whom who go on to live fascinating lives connected with early America. Their son, Jacob Crowninshield, was a congressman and Secretary of the Navy under Thomas Jefferson. Two of their children would marry the children of Capt. Richard Derby (*Derby Tomb*); creating an alliance that would dominate early American trade with the Far East. Elizabeth (Crowninshield) Derby married Elias Hasket Derby, and enterprising merchant George Crowninshield Sr married Mary (Derby) Crowninshield. The son of George Sr and Mary Crowninshield, Captain George Jr, commissioned the famous yacht *Cleopatra's Barge*, launched on October 21, 1816.

The inscriptions on the stones read:

This Stone Perpetuates
the Memory of
Capt. JOHN CROWNINSHIELD
Marriner Ob^t.. May 25th
ANNO Dom^i 1761
Ætatis 65

Here lies Buried
the Body of M^rs
ANSTISS CROWNINSHIELD
widow to M^r.
JOHN CROWNINSHIELD
who departed this Life
Sep^t. the 10th 1774 in y^e
73 Year of Her Age

Since the 2021 reopening of the Old Burying Point, two gravestones have been removed from the cemetery due to damage. The gravestone of **Isaac Turner** (b. abt. 1692, d. Aug 17, 1754), formerly located near the Peele Lot, was damaged in a landscaping accident and removed. The gravestone of **Samuel Hosmer** (bapt. Nov 6, 1803, d. Apr 26, 1844), formerly in the Ward Section, was damaged in a storm and removed. The gravestones are expected to be repaired and returned to their original locations, however they remain missing from the cemetery as of March 2022.

THE CROWNINSHIELD TOMBSTONES
IN THEIR PROTECTIVE BRACKETS
PHOTOGRAPH TAKEN SOME TIME AFTER 1915

THE TOMBSTONE BRACKETS IN 2020
THE STONES HAVE BEEN MISSING FROM
THEIR BRACKETS FOR OVER TEN YEARS

Black, Indigenous, and People of Color

Once the Massachusetts courts declared slavery illegal in 1783, Black Freemen would become a powerful force in Salem's communities and industry. Some of those people who were freed slaves, or people who were born free Americans, have been interred in this cemetery starting in the early 1800s. Unfortunately, if any grave markers were left at their burials, they have been lost since the late 1800s.

Christopher White Sr (b. abt. 1757, d. Jan 1, 1823) was an African American man who lived on Essex Street, and would likely have been formerly enslaved by a family with the surname White. Enslaved people were often given the last name of the family for whom they worked (see *Primus Lynde; Lynde Tomb*). It is presently unconfirmed which family gave him the name White. Captain Joseph White, who lived on Essex Street, and was murdered in 1830, was known for his involvement in human slavery. However, there was no mention of Black servants in that White home in the 1790 census. Christopher White married Hester Lindson on January 1, 1786. Their son Christopher Jr was a mariner and cook who worked on many vessels, including the brig *Rolla,* bound for India in 1842, and travelled to ports such as Marseilles, France and Cape Verde, Africa. His crew list records show his height as 5'5". Two of the daughters of Christopher Sr and Hester are interred with their father; **Lucy White** (b. abt. 1792, d. Nov 15, 1818) whose death was "sudden," and **Betsy White** (b. abt. 1802 d. Jan 30, 1828) who died of consumption. Christopher White Jr was interred in the Howard Street Cemetery, in which there was a dedicated area for burials from the African American community. The Branch Meeting House on Howard Street became a center for slavery abolitionist activism.

Dinah Ranson (b. abt. 1792 d. July 7, 1819) and **William Ranson** (b. abt. 1789 d. June 10, 1826) were the children of Cato and Remember (Freeman) Ranson. Both William and Dinah Ranson died of consumption. Cato and Remember Ranson were married on August 5, 1810 in a ceremony conducted by Rev. William Bentley. Bentley remarks in his diary that Cato was known for "diligence and frugality." The Ransons were freeholders living in South Salem. Cato Ranson was interred at Saint Peter's churchyard, while Remember was buried at the Howard Street Cemetery.

Edward Ouri (b. abt. 1826, d. Jun 9, 1840) was a fourteen-year-old boy listed as being from Patagonia; the southernmost region of South America. He is listed in the vital records as of the "family of Charles Millet," and having died of consumption. It is not known what his relationship to the Millet family was, whether he was a ward of the family, or an indentured servant.

Mary Archer (b. abt. 1731, d. Apr 1, 1809) is believed to have been an African American woman who died at the age of seventy-eight and was reportedly buried in the Old Burying Point without a marker. These dates may be entirely incorrect, as another **Mary (Pain) Archer**, was buried here, and has a stone in the Broad Street Cemetery with almost exactly these same dates. Mary (Pain) Archer is listed as the mother of Captain William Cook who died at sea (and the gravestone at Broad Street is shared with him) and the wife of John Archer. There is no Captain William Cook listed with a "Black" complexion in the ship records of Salem from this time. The Mary Archer listed here is found in the "Negroes" section of the Salem Deaths Vital Records. While it is unlikely that these two are the same person, it is reasonable to believe that there was an error in the records, which would mean that Mary (Pain) Archer's dates were accidentally listed for the Mary Archer who is also buried here.

It is confirmed that this burial ground was the final resting place of **Sally Harris** (b. abt. 1799, d. Feb 20, 1827), who died of intemperance, as well as **Simeon Peters** (b. abt. 1781, d. Jul 6, 1839) and an unnamed **Daughter Munroe** (b. abt. Apr 1824, d. Oct 26, 1825) who died at eighteen months, though her name is unknown aside from being the daughter of a Munroe family. Each of their death records identify them as "Black" or "Colored."

There are likely many more BIPOC interred in this cemetery, though details of their lives are rarely available. The early histories of those who were enslaved have most often been lost, and the town records do not always reflect fully the many people who have populated Salem throughout the years.

MARY CORRY
Yᵉ WIFE OF
GILES CORRY
AGED 63 YEARS
DYED AUGUST
Yᵉ 27 1684

LORE

"We were sitting on a dilapidated seventeenth-century tomb in the late afternoon of an autumn day at the old burying-ground in Arkham, and speculating about the unnamable."

— H.P. LOVECRAFT, "THE UNNAMABLE"

An ancient cemetery, located in the heart of a town that has woven ghosts and witchcraft into the very fabric of its identity, cannot help but inspire thoughts of the supernatural. When the sun sets, and the shadows stretch over the cemetery, so do tales of hauntings and horror. While these stories may not be rooted in proven fact, they often contain hints of plausibility that might have sprung from the seeds of truth. Whether you believe in ghosts or not, these stories have become a part of the character of this historic burial ground. Here are a few of the legends and frightening tales associated with the Old Salem Burying Point.

HP Lovecraft's story "The Unnamable" takes place in a graveyard inspired by the horror novelist's own visits to Salem. Lovecraft created the "witch-haunted" town of Arkham with settings, places, and names all connected to Salem. Lovecraft populated the mysterious New England town with the family names of Pickman, Derby, West, and others that grace the slate markers in the Old Burying Point. In "The Unnamable," the protagonists sit on a crumbling tomb nearby to an old, abandoned house. It seems likely Lovecraft was referring to the Gedney Tomb, and almost certainly the Grimshawe House. The pair muse on the great and ancient trees growing amongst the tombstones, "Looking toward the giant willow in the centre of the cemetery, whose trunk has nearly engulfed an ancient, illegible slab, I had made a fantastic remark about the spectral and unmentionable nourishment which the colossal roots must be sucking in from that hoary, charnel earth; when my friend chided me for such nonsense and told me that since no interments had occurred there in over a century, nothing could possibly exist to nourish the tree in other than an ordinary manner." As night falls, the men are shocked when an unmarked crypt bursts open, unleashing something horrible beyond their comprehension.

The home beside the cemetery is known as the "Grimshawe House," owing to the story set within its walls by Nathaniel Hawthorne, *Doctor Grimshawe's Secret*. Though the home in actuality belonged to his in-laws, the Peabodys, in this story, a mysterious doctor lives there, surrounded by spiders he breeds for use in his medicines. Much like the spiders themselves, the doctor cuts himself off from the outside world. Hawthorne writes of the young children living in the house, who often play in the cemetery, bounding over a tomb (likely the Pickman/Toppan Tomb) to play among the gravestones. While the story specifically insists that the Grimshawe House is not haunted, Hawthorne writes "it seemed hardly possible that the dead people should not get up out of their graves and steal in to warm themselves at this convenient fireside."

Certain trees in the cemetery are considered sacred to members of the Modern Witchcraft community in Salem. There is an oak tree which grows from Caleb Pickman's grave (*Cromwell Section*), which has suffered some kind of damage. A large portion of the top of the tree fell at some point, which some attribute to a lightning strike. The legend associated with this tree is that it was struck by lightning because Caleb Pickman himself died when struck with lightning, and lightning tends to strike locations (and people) it has hit before. Depending on who is telling the story of the Lightning Tree, you may hear that the tree was struck with lightning once, a few times, or up to thirty times.

The Witch Trials Memorial is open to the public all night (a reminder here, again, that the cemetery is not), and has become a favorite spot for those who are interested in the supernatural, from fun-seeking ghost photographers, to professional paranormal investigators. One of the more popular stories is that of a ghostly woman who walks the cemetery at night, thought to be Mary (Bright) Corey, seeking her lost husband, Giles. The stories say she may walk the area of the cemetery where she is buried, as well as the Salem Witch Trials Memorial, and Charter Street. The ghost of Col. John Hathorne (*Hathorne Section*) is thought to walk the grounds by his grave. The solitary figure is seen standing over his tombstone, and is thought to be reflecting on his actions as a persecuting judge in the Court of Oyer and Terminer, which earned him the nickname of "the Hanging Judge."

One of the most unusual ghostly tales comes from a legend stating that the cemetery was once used for secret meetings by the notorious pirate, Edward "Blackbeard" Teach. These legends include the story of a pirate duel which saw one of Teach's crewmen killed and buried in an unmarked grave. There is even the wild tale that one of Teach's own hands is buried there, taken after his body was retrieved, cut to pieces, and buried across the colonies, though that may be a misinterpretation of it being a member of his crew (hands). Teach was said to have had his men spread rumors of ghosts in the cemetery while drinking at the nearby taverns on the wharf in order to ward off curiosity-seekers when he held his meeting. Blackbeard himself is said to walk the cemetery at night in ghostly form; a tall, gaunt figure in a grey coat, perhaps drawn to the presence of his purported skull, which is part of the collection of the nearby Peabody Essex Museum. The skull was donated to the museum as part of the collection of New England author and historian, Edward Rowe Snow. The skull has not been displayed by the museum in over ten years, which may be due to a condition of the donation, which would not allow the skull to be viewed by anyone at night, or else the skull will come to life, its eyes glowing red.

Stories like these are what helps to weave the cemetery into Salem's current aura, that of a Halloween destination where the shops sell magic wands and Ouija boards. There are haunted houses and a monster movie museum on Essex Street, where the first homes of Salem once stood. Gone are most of the seventeenth century structures, a number of which were destroyed in a series of large fires in the 1700s, 1800s, and 1914. The Halloween tourism industry saved Salem from the fate of becoming a failed factory town, which for a time it was in grave danger of, and is one of the reasons the city can afford to maintain some historic sites, like the Old Burying Point. The mansions of the Derbys, Forresters, and Turners still stand, some are museums, and some are still private homes. One wonders if the present occupants of those homes ever come here to reflect on the men and women who lived in those homes, and built Salem into the thriving city it is today. There is much more to this cemetery than cold, grey stone and ghost stories, there are people who lived, loved, cried, and laughed as we do.

The September 22nd Benches of
The Salem Witch Trials Memorial

Salem Witch Trials Memorial

The Witch Trials Memorial was dedicated in August of 1992 on the three-hundred-year anniversary of the 1692 Witch Hysteria. The memorial was designed by Maggie Smith and James Cutler, and was selected from 246 entries. Among those in attendance for the dedication were Holocaust survivor and Nobel Laureate, Elie Wiesel, and playwright, Arthur Miller, whose 1952 play "The Crucible" inspired generations of interest in the Salem Witch Trials.

According to the artists, the design of the memorial carries symbolism of the suffering endured by those who perished during the Salem Witch Trials. The heavy stone wall, made from local granite, is meant to symbolize the silence of those who did not speak up in defense of their friends, relatives, and neighbors who were accused of witchcraft. Each of the twenty benches is engraved with the name of one of the victims, the method of their execution, and the date they died. The letters are etched in a 17th century typeface in an attempt to match the tombstones in the Old Burying Point. At the entrance to the memorial are modernized forms of the claims of innocence given by those who were accused. The words are cut off by the granite wall to symbolize the unwillingness of the judges and jurors to listen to these claims of innocence. Most of the trees that grow in the memorial are locust trees, which is believed to be the same sort of tree that would have been used for the executions by hanging. The top of Gallows Hill has always had a plentiful number of black locust trees, though none of the trees from 1692 are still there.

The victims of the Witch Hysteria are not interred in the Old Burying Point, instead, they were buried in shallow graves on Gallows Hill, and then removed by family, or other sympathetic parties for burial on private land. These graves were unmarked, and most of their locations unknown in the present day. Descendants of the victims will often come to this site to memorialize their ancestors with flowers, stones, postcards, letters, fruit, Christmas decorations, LED candles, and other items. While there is no one interred in this section, which was part of Samuel Pickman's property in 1692, it is treated as a place of respect by descendants, and is often marked as a "burial" site, so the victims of the 1692 hysteria will have entries here.

Most of what is written here about the victims involves the events surrounding their trials for witchcraft. This is due to the fact that these were, by and large, ordinary people whose lives would not otherwise have been recorded in the annals of history. If not for the records of these trials, the existence of a farmer like John Proctor, or a fisherman's wife like Wilmot Redd, would be unknown to us centuries later. We find small hints about their daily lives in the accusations made against them, but that is all we are often given.

The lives of the victims of this hysteria are intertwined with the lives of those interred in the Old Burying Point, who were their families, friends, neighbors, accusers, judges, and eventually, their descendants. Their memorial benches, which are designed to look similar to tombstones of their time, are placed nearby to the cemetery where many of them would have been buried had the tragic events of 1692 not occurred. Perhaps their fates would have been a death from old age, consumption, or accident. While there is often a great deal of reverence placed on these victims, it should be remembered that they were just ordinary people caught up in an extraordinary event, and their families grieved their unjust deaths the same as any other who lies interred in the Old Burying Point.

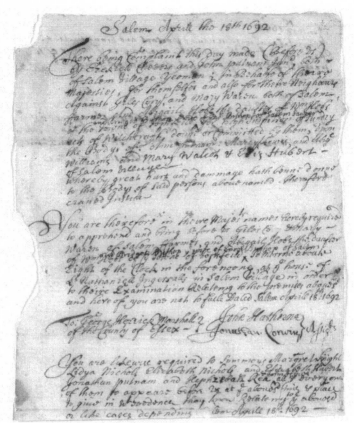

Salem. April the 18th 1692

There being Complaint this day made (Before us) by Ezekiell Chevers and John Putnam Jun'r both of Salem Village Yeomen: in Behalfe of theire Majesties, for themselfes and also for theire Neighbours Against Giles Cory, and Mary Waren both of Salem farmes And Abigaile Hobbs the daughter of Wm Hobs of Salem Sawyer for high Suspition of Sundry acts of Witchcraft donne or Committed by them, upon the Bodys of: Ann putnam. Marcy Lewis, and Abig'l Williams and Mary Walcot and Eliz/Hubert of Salem Village whereby great hurt and damage hath benne donne to the Bodys of Said persons above named. therefore craved Justice

You are therefore in their Majest's names hereby required to apprehend and bring before us Giles Cory & Mary Waren of Salem farmes, and Abigail Hobs the daugter of Wm Hobs of the Towne of Topsfeild and Bridget Bushop the wife of Edward Bushop of Salem To Morrow about Eight of the Clock in the forenoone, at the house of Lt. Nathaniell Ingersalls in Salem Village in order to theire Examination Relateing to the premises aboves'd and here of you are not to faile Dated Salem April 18th 1692

To George Herrick Marshall   John Hathorne
  of the County of Essex -   Jonathan Corwin } Assis'ts

You are likewise required to summons Margaret Knight Lydia Nichols Elizabeth Nichols and Elizabeth Hubert Jonathan Putnam and Hephzibah Rea & John Howe all & every one of them to appeare at the aboves'd time &place to give w't evedence they know Relateing to the aboves'd or like cases depending. April 18th 1692 -

234

Overview of The Salem Witch Trials

"I am afraid that ages will not wear off that reproach and those stains which these things will leave behind them upon our land."

- Thomas Brattle, October 8, 1692

The events of the Witch Hysteria in 1692 have become a defining time in Salem's history, and left an indelible mark on one of America's oldest colonies. It may be impossible for us to fully understand the experience of the people living here in the 17th century. However, it should be remembered that witch hunts were not unusual, and Salem was by no means the first community to suffer from a witchcraft hysteria. During the 16th and 17th centuries, communities in England, Germany, Norway, Sweden, and more European nations would erupt into witch hunts, caused by decades of mistrust, rumors, jealousy, and fear.

People who lived in times of war, famine, pestilence, and political upheaval, often sought an enemy whom they could blame, and fight, in order to try to take control of their lives. People might see the work of the Devil in many events which might be unexplainable in their time. A healthy cow that did not give milk, a sudden illness in a young person, a ship lost at sea that might ruin a family's fortune; all of these were a part of the everyday difficult life in colonial New England, but *could* reflect the work of witches, rather than simple misfortune. The mortality rate among children was extremely high, and there were scarce few families whose children all lived to adulthood. Nearly a quarter of all interments in the Old Burying Point were young children and infants. If a family suffered the loss of life upon life, they might feel as if they were being targeted by the forces of evil. When it was believed that witches were in a community, it was easy to assign blame on a perceived enemy, or even just an unfriendly or aloof person. As illustrated in the entry for Samuel Shattuck III (*Shattuck Section*), strange behavior or unexplained illness would most often be blamed on witchcraft, and the only way to stop an affliction would be to find the witch who was responsible.

Salem in 1692 was in the midst of a war with the Native Americans, known as King William's War. Refugees from destroyed towns and villages throughout New England streamed into more secure communities like Salem, which was surrounded by a nine-foot-tall wall of large, sharpened wooden stakes. The area beyond the town limits was known as the "howling wilderness," where fearsome beasts, or Native braves on the warpath, might be encountered. The Massachusetts Bay Colony's charter had been revoked by the new King James II, and fear of the potential loss of their colony had put tremendous strain on the Salem community. Another issue was the desire of Salem Village to break away from Salem Town. Eventually, this would happen in 1752, and Salem Village would become known as Danvers. However, by 1692, there had already been many arguments, and much bad blood festered between the communities.

Salem Village was allowed to start their own parish; however, the town did not have proper funding to pay a minister, and the parish would have trouble keeping a Teacher. Eventually, Reverend Samuel Parris would fill the role, and he presided over this most difficult time in Salem's history. Parris was a minister who had encountered failure in most of his ventures as a merchant and plantation owner, and it seems that he turned to the ministry in the hopes of finding his calling. It was in the minister's home that the first confession of witchcraft would come forth. His daughter, Betty, and her cousin, Abigail Williams, both under the age of 12, would begin to exhibit strange behaviors, and suffer from uncontrollable fits. The children would be pronounced as "under an evil hand" by Dr. William Griegs, which was an accepted medical diagnosis, and meant their suffering was the work of witches. In an attempt to seek out the witch responsible, Parris' neighbor, Mary Sibley, approached Tituba and John Indian, a Native American couple who were enslaved workers in the Parris home. Tituba was prompted by Sibley to create a 'witch cake;' a folk method in the detection of witches that involved using the urine of an afflicted person to create a cake, which would then be fed to a dog, whose bite would be felt by the supposed witch, drawing attention to him or herself.

The attempted magic did not help detect any witches, and Sibley received a strong rebuke from Reverend Parris for encouraging the use of magic. The effect on the children was that their symptoms grew even worse, and Tituba would be arrested on charges of witchcraft, as were two other women, Sarah Good and Sarah Osborne. These three women are examples of those who might be easily blamed for witchcraft in any community at risk for a witch hysteria. Tituba was a Native American, therefore already suspected of diabolical inclinations due to the fears of European colonists at the time. Sarah Osborne was a Puritan who had not been to Church in over a year, and had married her indentured servant shortly after her husband's death, an act that was considered very suspicious by many in the community. Sarah Good, a known destitute beggar, was considered a nuisance by many, and was rumored to mutter magical curses when displeased. Tituba would confess to witchcraft, though she would later state that this was a forced confession.

It would become apparent as time went by that the magistrates, John Hathorne (*Hathorne Section*) and Jonathan Corwin, would presume the guilt of the accused men and women immediately, and repeat the accusations laid on them as if they were certain fact. Tituba's confession would lay the groundwork for other members of the community to provide their own evidence against people they believed may be witches, and who they believed were responsible for their misfortunes. Examinations of those accused of witchcraft began, and the primary evidence against them would be the reactions of those afflicted by witchcraft, most notably, a group of young women, aged ten to twenty, who claimed to suffer at the hands of the witches, though later adult men and women would join the ranks of the afflicted, including Tituba Indian's husband, John.

It was a belief at the time that children could see the works of the Devil, which adults could not, because the children were free of sin. Children were used in witchcraft accusations throughout Europe. However, in Salem, the afflicted children were allowed to be physically present at the examinations, which was not commonly done in witch trials. It was considered a known fact at the time that a person afflicted by witches would have some part of the witch's spirit within them, which the supposed witch could use to manipulate or harm them. The presence of the afflicted in the examinations and courtroom trials created a chaotic atmosphere which the judges found difficult to control. The judges would assume that the disorder was caused by the accused witch, and would consider it proof of their guilt. Salem Town and Salem Village were where the hysteria began, but it quickly swept through Andover, Topsfield, Marblehead, and Ipswich.

When the new royal governor, Sir William Phips, arrived in Boston, he was presented with the requests from the Salem magistrates to form a Court which could handle the accusations of witchcraft. Phips approved of the creation of the Court of Oyer and Terminer on May 27, 1692, assigning a panel of judges to serve on the Court: Lt. Gov. William Stoughton, John Hathorne, Bartholemew Gedney, Nathaniel Saltonstall, John Richards, Peter Sergeant, Wait-Still Winthrop, and Samuel Sewall. The first session of the court was held on June 2, 1692, at the Salem Town House. After the first execution on June 10, Nathaniel Saltonstall would step down from the Court in protest, to be replaced by Jonathan Corwin.

Twenty-five accused witches would stand before the Court of Oyer and Terminer. Every one of those twenty-five persons would be convicted and sentenced to death. Nineteen of those convicted would be hanged at Gallows Hill, while the other six would escape hanging when the Court was dissolved by Governor Phips that autumn. Phips' reasons for ending the Court are expounded upon in a letter from the governor which appears the *Criticism of the Witch Hysteria* chapter.

It should be noted that none of the victims of this Witch Hysteria were, in fact, professed witches. The accused were all Christians, whether Puritan, Quaker, or Anglican, and they went to their executions praying to God for mercy, and sometimes quoting Scripture up to the moment of their death.

THE PLEAS OF REBECCA NURSE AND MARY BRADBURY
CARVED INTO THE ENTRANCE OF THE MEMORIAL

Victims of The Salem Witch Trials

"-I am innocent to a witch. I know not what a witch is."

-Bridget Bishop - April 19, 1692

Bridget (Playfer) Bishop (b. abt. 1632, d. Jun 10, 1692) lived in Salem Town, and is one of the most well-remembered victims of this 1692 hysteria due to her strong personality and affinity for wearing a red coat or skirt, which stands out to us now, but was not a taboo color in Puritan Salem, as some have suggested. She was born in England, and there married Samuel Wasselby on April 16, 1660, in Norwich, Norfolk County. The couple had no children who lived past childhood. Wasselby died after emigrating to New England, and Bridget married a widower, named Thomas Oliver, in 1666. Oliver was a calenderer; a machine worker using a calender to smooth out fabric. Their home stood on the current location of Turner's Seafood (43 Church Street), formerly known as the Lyceum Hall. Bridget was known for contentious speech, publicly insulting New Englanders as "thieves and robbers."

The couple had a difficult marriage and would often argue in public. During one of these tirades, Bridget called her husband an "old devil," which was an obscene curse at the time. Bridget was punished by the magistrates, sentenced to suffer the humiliation of standing gagged at the town pump wearing a sign that displayed her crimes. Thomas had been sentenced to stand there as well, however, his daughter, Mary (Oliver) West, paid a fee so he could avoid the penalty. Bridget had only one child with Thomas, a daughter named Christian, who later married Thomas Mason. Thomas Oliver died in 1679 and did not leave a will, so the magistrates gave his widow Bridget the home and land, while Thomas's children from his previous marriage received very little. Mary West and her siblings accused their stepmother of bewitching their father, which was dismissed by the court.

However, suspicion of witchcraft remained on her, and many neighbors would ascribe most strange events or coincidence concerning Bridget to evidence of witchcraft (see *Samuel Shattuck III; Shattock Section*). For her part, Bridget continued to publicly insult and deride any who crossed her. She remarried to woodcutter Edward Bishop in 1685, and their marriage was decidedly less turbulent than her former. Bridget was arrested for witchcraft, accused of afflicting Mercy Lewis, Abigail Williams, Ann Putnam Jr, and Elizabeth Hubbard. During her examination, she claimed her innocence, saying "I know nothing of it, I am innocent to a witch. I know not what a witch is." Her response was questioned by John Hathorne, as he says, "How can you know you are no witch and yet not know what a witch is?" She replied to the magistrate, whom she had a somewhat adversarial relationship with prior to 1692, stating, "I am clear; if I were any such person you should know it." Hathorne took this statement as a threat, and warned her that "you may threaten, but you may do no more than you are permitted," inferring that she could not harm him, perhaps believing that he himself was protected from her by God. Bishop was found guilty of witchcraft on June 2, 1692, and would be the first person to be hanged for witchcraft in Salem.

Sarah (Solart) Good (b. Jul 11, 1653, d. Jul 19, 1692) of Salem Village became destitute and homeless after her husband, William, misused the family's funds and vanished. This left Sarah with two young children to fend for themselves, often begging for alms from neighbors, including Reverend Samuel Parris. At some point, before being formally accused of witchcraft in 1692, Good had left the Parris homestead after asking for alms and, unsatisfied, allegedly muttered a curse. This occurred shortly before Betty Parris began to suffer the afflictions that would lead to accusations of witchcraft. Good was jailed in Ipswich, and according to the marshal, she fought the entire journey to escape from him. Sarah Good was convicted of witchcraft and hanged.

On the day of her execution, the presiding minister was Reverend Nicholas Noyes (*Bradstreet Tomb*), who sought confessions from the condemned before they were hanged. It was common at the time for a condemned person to deliver a speech before their execution, accepting guilt for their crimes and warning those assembled not to follow their same path. However, condemned witches were not supposed to be allowed a final speech, as it was believed that a witch could utter a curse before their death that was guaranteed to come true. In many European cases, condemned witches had their mouths bound with leather or iron. All of the condemned in Salem insisted on their innocence and did not admit guilt, which caused many tears to be shed at these executions, as well as many hearts moved to pity them. Noyes allegedly argued with Sarah Good at her execution, insisting that he knew she was guilty. "I am no more a witch than you are a wizard," Sarah told Noyes, "and if you take away my life, God will give you blood to drink." This was a reference to a verse of the biblical book of Revelations 16:6, "for they have shed the blood of saints and prophets, and Thou hast given them blood to drink," a promise by God to avenge the innocent.

It is alleged that when Reverend Noyes died years later, his mouth and throat filled with blood, perhaps due to a brain aneurysm. This has been spoken of for generations as a witch's curse, though the exchange is not recorded in any contemporary record. This statement gained more notoriety in Nathaniel Hawthorne's *The House of the Seven Gables*, uttered by the fictional accused witch, Matthew Maule, before he is hanged and his accuser mysteriously dies. Sarah Good's infant daughter, Mercy Good, died in prison. Her daughter, Dorothy Good, aged five, confessed to witchcraft. Dorothy was released from jail eventually, but suffered severe mental trauma from the experience, and died at age forty.

Elizabeth (Jackson) Howe (b. abt. 1635, d. Jul 19, 1692) was born in Rowley, Yorkshire, England, and emigrated to Rowley, Massachusetts, then to Ipswich Farms. She married John Howe, who lost his sight at age fifty. Among her primary accusers in 1692 were the Perley family of Ipswich, related to the death of Hannah Perley. At age eleven, Hannah began to suffer afflictions and claimed to her family that Howe was responsible. The Perleys worked to block Howe's admittance to the Ipswich Church. However, no formal charges of witchcraft were made at the time, and Howe may not have known that she was suspected. The Perleys would later state that Hannah and Howe were "very loving together," but that Hannah told her family she only pretended to be affectionate out of fear that Howe would kill her. Hannah Perley died soon after, and the family blamed Howe. In 1692, when she was charged with afflicting the girls of Salem Village, Hannah's parents, Samuel and Ruth Perley, testified against Howe. During her examination, Howe stated, "If it was the last moment I was to live, God knows I am innocent of any thing of this nature." Part of this statement is engraved at the entrance to the memorial.

Susannah (North) Martin (bapt. Sep 30, 1621, d. Jul 19, 1692) was born in Buckinghamshire, England, and emigrated to Salisbury, Massachusetts. She married a blacksmith, George Martin, in 1646 before moving to Amesbury. Martin was accused of witchcraft several times by neighbors, but in both cases the charges were dropped. William Sargent Jr had accused her of killing his child with witchcraft, and Susannah and her husband sued him for slander. The court granted that she was slandered in the case of murder, but not witchcraft, perhaps indicating that she was still under suspicion. During her examination with the magistrates in 1692, the afflicted claimed that she was harming them there in the courtroom. When Martin insisted she was not responsible, the magistrates asked how it could be happening and the children seeing her if it was not her doing. Martin stated that the Devil could take anyone's form, even a saint. This valid point would be disregarded in her examination, as the judges often dismissed the thought that the Devil might take the form of an innocent person, despite biblical accounts of the Devil taking the forms of saints. When asked why the children could not approach her without being afflicted, she said "It may be the Devil bears me more malice than another."

Rebecca (Towne) Nurse (b. abt. 1621, d. Jul 19, 1692) was originally from Yarmouth, England. She married Frances Nurse and they made their home in Salem Village. Nurse was an upstanding member of the community, and her accusation was a surprise to many, as the persons accused in 1692 often had prior suspicion of witchcraft upon them. Nurse's trial appears to have been the most contentious, many people arguing in Nurse's favor. A petition was signed by thirty-nine members of the community which attested to her good character.

The jury found Rebecca Nurse to be not guilty of witchcraft. However, the judges objected to the verdict, and demanded that the jury reconsider, based on a statement made by Nurse on the stand. Abigail Hobbs, a confessed witch, was brought into the court, prompting Rebecca to state that she, "used to come among us." Nurse had meant that Hobbs had been an accused witch, and now had joined the accusers, however, when asked to explain this statement, Nurse was silent. Nurse would later claim she was hard of hearing and had not heard the request, and clarified her statement about Hobbs, but her silence at that crucial time had convinced the jury to reconsider the verdict and she was convicted. The Rebecca Nurse Homestead still stands in Danvers, Massachusetts, and Rebecca Nurse is believed to be buried on the property. During her examination, she cried out "Oh Lord help me!" which is engraved here at the entrance to the memorial.

Sarah (Averhill) Wildes (b. abt. 1627, d. Jul 19, 1692) was born in Chipping North, England. Sarah Averill's family emigrated to Ipswich, Massachusetts about 1637. Sarah had several episodes with the law prior to her accusation of witchcraft. In 1649, she was whipped for "fornication out of wedlock," and in 1663 was accused of violating the colonial sumptuary laws which forbid anyone whose estate was worth less than £200 from wearing expensive clothing, i.e., "dressing above their station," by wearing a silk scarf. In 1665, she married Judge John Wildes of Topsfield, a widower, and together they had one son, Ephraim Wildes, in 1665. The family of John's deceased wife's sister, the Reddingtons, were Sarah's primary accusers in the witch trials. The Reddington family and their friends, the Symonds family, provided several testimonies about misfortune they had suffered due to witchcraft, including the deaths of cattle. Elizabeth Symonds accused Wildes of tormenting her with a spectral cat that sat on her chest and prevented her from moving or speaking. Many times, the disorder of sleep paralysis, in which the sufferers brain wakes up before their body does, and often creates fearful images, was associated with witchcraft, and may have been what Goody Symonds was afflicted by.

John and Ephraim Wildes testified in Sarah's defense, claiming that the Reddingtons were only accusing her to bring harm to their family. John spoke of a previous accusation of witchcraft made against her by the Reddingtons, which they had withdrawn when John said he would sue them for defamation. Ephraim, a Topsfield constable in 1692, testified that Elizabeth Symonds had long held a grudge against the family, and had interfered with his courtship of her daughter, Sarah Symonds. In his duties as constable, Ephraim had arrested William Hobbs on suspicion of witchcraft. Hobbs confessed, and claimed that Sarah Wildes was a witch as well, which Ephraim testified was most likely in retribution for the arrest. John's daughter from his first marriage, Sarah (Wildes) Bishop and her husband Edward, as well as his other daughter Phoebe, were arrested on witchcraft charges as well, though they would eventually be released, Sarah Wildes would not be so fortunate.

Reverend George Burroughs (b. abt. 1650, d. Aug 19, 1692) was the former minister of Salem Village. Burroughs is the only reverend executed in North America for witchcraft. Born in Suffolk, England, George Burroughs graduated from Harvard College in 1670, and became the pastor of Falmouth, Maine in 1674. Two years later, he was forced to flee from the town during a raid committed by the Abenaki tribe, who killed or kidnapped thirty-two settlers. The survivors of this raid moved to Salisbury, Massachusetts. In 1680, he became minister of Salem Village, and stayed with John and Rebecca (Prince) Putnam until a parsonage was built. During this time, ill-will was bred between the Putnams and Burroughs. As he was not paid wages by the village for over a year, Burroughs had to borrow from John Putnam to pay for his wife Hannah's funeral, and was not able to repay the debt for two years.

Burroughs took up residence in the new parsonage, a site whose foundation may still be seen today, as the Salem Village Parsonage in Danvers (67A Centre Street). He brought with him a teen-aged servant named Mercy Lewis, who was another refugee from the Falmouth massacre. In 1692, Mercy, now a servant of the family of John Putnam's brother, Thomas, would accuse Burroughs of being a wizard. In Burroughs' trial, many claims were made against him by his former neighbors in Falmouth, stating that Burroughs often spoke sharply to his first wife, Hannah, and second wife, Sarah Hathorne of Salem, both of whom died young. The afflicted claimed that Burroughs had murdered his wives. His remarkable feats of strength were mentioned, such as being able to carry a barrel of molasses with just two fingers, and using only one hand to shoot a musket with a heavy, seven-foot-long barrel.

Just before his execution, Burroughs recited the Lord's Prayer perfectly, an act which it was believed witches were incapable of doing. Burroughs' words brought many in the crowd to tears, and it seemed possible that someone might try to stop the execution. Burroughs' hanging would continue however, causing some disorder among the crowd. Reverend Cotton Mather, astride his horse, quelled the attendees by claiming that Burroughs, "was no ordained minister...the Devil has often been transformed into an Angel of the Light."

The day before Burroughs was hanged, he was approached by the granddaughter of George Jacobs Sr, Margaret Jacobs, who had confessed to witchcraft and implicated Burroughs. She begged Burroughs' forgiveness for accusing him, which he gave, and then he prayed with her, for himself, and for the sake of her soul.

Martha Ingalls (Allen) Carrier (b. abt. 1643, d. Aug 19, 1692) was married to Thomas Carrier on May 7, 1674, in Billerica, Massachusetts. A few months later, their first child, Richard, was born. Having a child conceived out of wedlock would have been a scandal to their neighbors and relatives. Due to a case of smallpox in the family, they may have been forced out of town, for they then moved to Andover. An outbreak of smallpox would occur in Andover shortly after, and the family was ordered to be quarantined and not leave their property; a constable delivering necessary supplies. Over a dozen Andover residents died of smallpox during this time. When accusations of witchcraft began in Salem, the people of Andover suspected witches in their midst as well. The afflicted claimed that Martha Carrier had killed those who died of smallpox with witchcraft, and that their ghosts appeared in the courtroom.

Martha's sons, Richard (age eighteen) and Andrew (age fifteen), were arrested on the charge of witchcraft as well. Richard confessed, and accused his mother and their aunt, Mary (Allen) Toothaker. The boys may have given these confessions under torture; John Proctor wrote "here are five persons who have lately confessed themselves to be witches, and do accuse some of us, .. two of them 5 are Carriers sons, youngmen, who would not confess any thing till they tied them neck and heels till the blood was ready to come out of their noses." On August 10, 1692, her ten-year-old son, Thomas Jr, was arrested as a witch, and confessed that his mother was a witch, as did her eight-year-old daughter, Sarah, who was arrested and examined by John Hathorne the next day. Only Martha was hanged, although Mary Toothaker confessed to witchcraft. After 1693, when the family had been released from jail, Martha's widower, Thomas, and the surviving children moved to Colchester, Connecticut.

George Jacobs Sr (b. Feb 13, 1609, d. Aug 19, 1692) is believed to be the same 'George Jacob' that was baptized February 13, 1609, at Saint Dunstan-in-the-West, London, whose parents were from Bishop's Stortford, Hertfordshire. Jacobs lived in Salem Village, and in his old age, he had difficulty walking and used a pair of canes to assist him. These canes are currently in the possession of the Peabody Essex Museum; however, they are rarely displayed to the public, recently exhibited in 2020 for the first time in several decades. Jacobs had several children from his first marriage, including his son George Jr, who was accused of witchcraft, as well as George Jr's wife, Rebecca (Fox) Jacobs, and their daughter Margaret, all of whom were acquitted in 1693.

 After his execution, Jacobs' widow, Mary Jacobs, would remarry to John Wildes, the widower of Sarah Wildes. Jacobs was accused by his servant, Sarah Churchill, a refugee of the Native American wars in Saco, Maine. Many of the afflicted had been rehomed to Salem as servants, after the wars against the natives had left them orphaned or without homes. Churchill claimed George brought her the Devil's book to sign, to which he replied that the Devil must have taken his shape, insisting "I am innocent as the child born tonight." Jacobs' most often-quoted response in his examination was the indignant exclamation, "You tax me for a wizard, you may as well tax me for a buzzard I have done no harm." A body purported to be Jacobs was recovered from his property in 1950, and reburied in the cemetery at the Rebecca Nurse Homestead.

John Proctor (b. Oct 9, 1631, d. Aug 19, 1692) was born in Assignton, Suffolk County, England. His family arrived in New England on the *Susan and Ellen* in 1635, when John was about the age of three. John Proctor may be the best known of the victims of 1692 due to Arthur Miller's 1953 stage play (and its popular 1996 movie adaptation) "The Crucible," which features the Proctor family as main characters, and centers on the fallout of an extramarital affair between Proctor and a teen-aged Abigail Williams as the cause of the accusations. This is entirely fictional and has no historical correlation; the real Abigail Williams was eleven years old in 1692, and Proctor was sixty-one. The real John Proctor worked the land at Groton farm, and had a tavern on the property which was quite successful. He married Elizabeth Bassett on April 1, 1674, which was his third marriage. Proctor and his neighbor, Giles Corey, often feuded over property lines and personal slights. Corey accused Proctor of selling hard cider to Native Americans, which was against the law of the colony. Proctor accused Corey of setting fire to his roof. Their feud seems to have been resolved after a meeting at Richard More's tavern (*More Section*).

 During the Witch Hysteria, Proctor attended the examination of Rebecca Nurse, and afterward spoke to Samuel Sibley, saying of the afflicted that "if they were let alone, we should all be Devils and witches quickly, they should rather be had to the whipping post." Proctor threatened that he would "thresh the devil out of" accuser Mary Warren, who was his household servant. When Proctor was accused of witchcraft, Sibley provided these statements as evidence against him. John Proctor's name was not brought up as a suspect until a few days before Elizabeth Proctor's examination on April 11. However, during the examination,

Abigail Williams and Ann Putnam Jr accused Proctor of sending out his spirit to harm Sarah Bibber and others in the meeting house. Proctor was immediately arrested and dragged out of the meeting house to the jail.

Thirty-one neighbors from Ipswich signed a petition in support of the Proctors. On July 23, John Proctor sent a petition from the Salem prison to Reverend Increase Mather and other clergy of Boston, claiming that the magistrates, ministers, jury, and people of Salem were, "enraged and incensed against us by the delusion of the Devil" and asked for the trials to be moved to Boston, where clearer thinking may prevail, or failing that, he hoped for a change in the magistrates handling the cases. In this letter he detailed the torture of the Carrier boys (as expanded on in Martha Carrier's entry) as well as his own son, William Proctor, who insisted on his innocence even under the same torture as the Carriers. While the Boston clergy did step in to help halt the proceedings later in 1692, Proctor's execution had already taken place.

In 1700, Proctor's letter was published in Robert Calef's *More Wonders of the Invisible World.* Calef also reported that Sheriff George Corwin seized all the goods, provisions, and cattle belonging to the Proctors, even pouring out the barrels of beer from their tavern so that he could sell the empty barrels. Before his execution, Proctor asked Reverend Noyes to pray with him and for his soul, but Noyes refused because Proctor would not admit guilt. Today, a home stands in Peabody on the Proctor's former land which is often referred to as the John Proctor House. However, the home was built by John's son, Thorndike Proctor, when he purchased the land, though it is not unlikely that this was the site of the Proctor tavern.

John Willard (b. abt. 1662, d. Aug 19, 1692) of Groton, was married to Margaret Wilkins of Salem Village. Willard served as a constable, and was ordered to arrest some who were accused of witchcraft, but refused to do so as he believed they were innocent. It is unknown who he may have been charged with arresting, as his name does not appear on any warrants, but one warrant from April 21 called for "any or all of the Constables in Salem" to arrest nine people, including Sarah Wildes and Mary Easty. Willard was even recorded as having said that he believed the afflicted themselves were all witches who would be hanged. It was in May of 1692 that his wife's family began to make accusations of witchcraft against Willard. It is believed these accusations may have risen due to jealousy within his wife's family on his success with land speculation, with which the Wilkins had bad luck. Willard travelled to Dorchester with his wife's family; his brother-in-law, Henry Wilkins Jr, and grandfather-in-law, Bray Wilkins.

According to Henry Jr, his son Daniel expressed concern that they were traveling with Willard, saying that he felt Willard should be hanged. During dinner that night in Boston with Reverend Deodat Lawson, Bray Wilkins claimed that Willard looked at him in an unusual way, and he suddenly fell ill and spent several days recovering in Boston, with symptoms that indicate he may have suffered from kidney stones, but that he believed had been caused by witchcraft. Once Bray was feeling better, the Wilkinses returned to Salem Village, Willard having already departed, and they found young Daniel had fallen terribly ill. Bray had a relapse of his illness immediately. An attending doctor claimed they were bewitched, and Mercy Lewis, Ann Putnam Jr, and Mary Walcott were brought to see if they could tell who was hurting the Wilkinses. The girls identified John Willard and Sarah Buckley. Daniel Wilkins died shortly after, and a coroner's jury found the cause of death to be witchcraft.

Willard reportedly fled to the area of modern-day Nashua, New Hampshire, where he was apprehended. In his examination, Willard tried several times to speak the Lord's Prayer and could not do so, likely due to the stress and pressure he was experiencing, at one point nervously laughing and saying, "I think I am bewitched as well as they." The afflicted accused Willard of multiple murders, and his in-laws claimed he was abusive to his wife as well, though he denied this, and his request to have Margaret testify on his behalf was not accepted.

Giles Corey (b. abt. 1621, d. Sep 19, 1692) was a farmer living in Salem Fields (Peabody). As a member of the Salem Town congregation, Corey was a frequent visitor to the Salem Meetinghouse as well as the tavern of Captain Richard More. It was at More's tavern that Corey met his second wife, Mary Bright (*Cromwell Section*). Corey was known as a cantankerous man who incessantly argued with his neighbors, frequently making claims against them. Corey was charged with murder in the death of his servant, Jacob Goodale, when Corey struck the man numerous times with a stick, then refused to bring him to a doctor, resulting in his death. Corey was not convicted of murder, but did have to pay a fine.

Corey was accused of witchcraft after having witnessed his own wife's examination, where his testimony was taken as evidence against her. Perhaps aware of the improbability that he would receive a fair trial, Corey refused to accept the authority of the court and though he proclaimed his innocence, would not enter a formal plea "before God and my [His] Country." Under English law, now in place after the revoking of the Charter of the Massachusetts Bay Colony, this meant he could be subject to the torture commonly known as "pressing" which was previously illegal under the Body of Liberties that the Puritans adhered to.

Peine forte et dure (or "forceful and hard punishment") was rarely seen in England by 1692, and was used only this one time in the American Colonies. The phrase has many different meanings, and the tortures associated with it were varied. When an accused person refused to enter a plea, a torture would be used to break down their will and force a plea from them. Witchcraft was a felony, and English law allowed for a seizure of the property of a convicted felon, so dying while under peine forte et dure would protect Corey's property from being confiscated, at the cost of his life.

The method chosen by the Court was pressing with weights; a board would be placed on Corey's chest, and heavy stone blocks added until he agreed to accept the authority of the Court. The Salem Town congregation excommunicated Corey as he was undergoing this ordeal, just one thousand feet away from the meetinghouse. Corey's friend, Capt. Thomas Gardner, pleaded with him to relent, but Corey continued to stand mute. After two days of unbearable torment, Corey's defiant final words to his torturer, Sheriff George Corwin, were reportedly "more weight," a phrase which had been uttered by previous sufferers of this torture requesting a more expedient end, due to the terrible pain and inevitable death. Sheriff George Corwin claimed that Corey's death was a suicide, and did extort money from the family for repayment of jailer's fees, but he was not entitled to seize any property. The debate afterwards over whether this torture was legal or not became part of the downfall of the Court of Oyer and Terminer.

Martha (Panon) Corey (b. abt. 1630, d. Sep 22, 1692) of Salem was a member of the Salem Village congregation. In 1677, Martha would give birth to Benjamin (sometimes listed as Ben-Oni), a biracial son whose father and history are unknown. She may have lived in a boarding house with her son until 1684, when she married Henry Rich. They had one son, Thomas, later that same year. After the death of Thomas Rich, she married Giles Corey on April 27, 1690, and moved to Salem Village.

When Ann Putnam Jr first claimed to be afflicted by the spirit of Martha Corey, Edward Putnam and Ezekiel Cheever set out to investigate, and asked Ann Jr if she could see what clothes Martha Corey was wearing that day. It was believed that the afflicted could see the spirits of the witch harming them, so their hopes were that if the child correctly identified her dress, then it could be considered proof of the affliction. This test was far from perfect, even by the standards used in the detection of witches, as most people in colonial New England did not have many suits of clothing, and might wear one set frequently, not to mention that the witch may not be bound to show their spirit in the clothes they currently wore. In this case, however, Ann Jr stated that she was blinded by Corey, and when the men advised Corey that the child claimed she was afflicting her, Corey responded asking if the child could see what clothes she wore that day. The investigators took this to mean that Corey had knowledge of the sudden blindness of Ann Jr. Martha would later say in her examination that she said this at her husband's urging, but Giles claimed that was untrue. Martha was quoted by Cheever and Putnam as saying of the prior accused, (Tituba, Sarah Good, and Sarah Osborne) "we could not blame the Devil for making witches of them for they were idle, slothful persons."

The Putnams invited Martha Corey to their home to address the complaints, which would not have been uncommon considering they were congregation members. Upon Corey's arrival, Ann Putnam Jr fell into "grievous fits of choking." Ann Jr pointed to the hearth and claimed she saw the apparition of Corey roasting a man on a spit over the fire. This disturbing image may have been a product of stories Ann Jr had heard about the Native American wars; roasting alive was said to be a method of execution some tribes had used on captured officers. With the addition of Mercy Lewis to the Putnam home, a refugee of the Abenaki raid on Falmouth, Maine, it is likely these stories were told between the children. Later that night, it would take three men to hold back Mercy from throwing herself into the fire, claiming she was dragged "by unseen hands."

A warrant was issued for Corey's arrest late in the day on March 19, which was a Saturday, and the law prevented an arrest from taking place on a Sunday, therefore Martha Corey chose to attend church in Salem Village. It was well-known that she was believed to be a witch, and according to the minister Deodat Lawson, the entire service was interrupted by constant outbursts from the afflicted, namely Abigail Williams, who claimed that Corey was sitting on a beam in the ceiling with her familiar, a yellow bird. The appearance of a yellow bird was a consistent apparition in the accusations against Corey.

During Corey's examination on the following day, the atmosphere was intense as the afflicted claimed an invisible man spoke in

Corey's ear, and Mrs. Pope threw a shoe that struck Corey on the head. The stress and helplessness Martha Corey must have felt is evident in her unusual behavior, often laughing throughout her examination. Overwhelmed by the number of people accusing her (both the children, and people her own age) Martha cried out "What can I do many rise up against me" and "Ye are all against me and I cannot help it." Giles Corey submitted testimony that his wife often stayed up late sitting by the hearth, and that he had once been unable to pray around her. Whether Giles believed his testimony would help or hurt his wife is unknown, but Giles walked alongside the cart which took his wife to the Boston ferry after she was committed to prison there. Martha Corey would have been shackled in the Salem jail while her husband was tortured to death in a nearby field. According to Robert Calef, Martha Corey "concluded her Life with an Eminent Prayer on the ladder."

Mary (Ayer) Parker (b. abt. 1637 d. Sep 22, 1692) of North Andover married Nathan Parker, and together they had nine children. Nathan died in 1685, and Mary remained in North Andover. Mary Parker was not directly related to Alice Parker. The evidence presented against her during this trial is flimsy even by the standards of the Court of Oyer and Terminer, and there is some speculation that the accusations against her by the Salem afflicted may have even been mistaken identity. There were several Mary Parkers in North Andover, and another in Salem Town who was frequently in trouble with the law. Parker herself asks if they might mean another Mary Parker in the examination. Mary Warren, an outspoken accuser, showed the judges a pin stuck in her hand and blood coming from her mouth and claimed that Parker was responsible. Several accused witches who had confessed and joined the accusers, claimed Parker had been with them at the witches' meetings, including Mercy Wardwell (daughter of Samuel Wardwell Sr) and Mary Lacy (daughter of Ann Foster), both of Andover.

Mary (Towne) Easty (bapt. Aug 24, 1634, d. Sep 22, 1692) was born in Yarmouth, Norfolk County England, and was the sister of Rebecca (Towne) Nurse and Sarah (Towne) Cloyce, both of whom were accused of witchcraft. She married Isaac Easty, and had a farm in Topsfield, Massachusetts. Easty was accused of witchcraft and jailed, however she was released on May 18, 1692. The specific reasons for her release are unknown, but Easty herself said she was "cleared by the afflicted persons." Easty was arrested again on May 20 when Mercy Lewis fell into "a dreadful fit," and seemed to fall mortally ill. Marshall George Herrick brought Elizabeth Hubbard to see if she could see the cause of the affliction, and Hubbard said it was Easty, who held a coffin and winding sheet before her (a "winding sheet" refers to the shroud placed around or on top of a corpse for burial). Herrick had Easty arrested again in an attempt to save Lewis' life. During her examination, Easty stated, "I will say it, if it was my last time, I am clear of this sin."

Mary and her sister Sarah Cloyce wrote a letter on September 9th to the judges, asking what they needed to do to prove themselves innocent (see *Criticism of the Witch Hysteria*). Their sister Rebecca Nurse had been hanged, and they sought some direction from their judges. The accused were not allowed lawyers, and had to defend themselves due to the nature of the charges, though they had little understanding of the intricacies in a case of this nature. The judges themselves did not fully comprehend those same intricacies, and would simply pressure the accused to confess. Easty and Cloyce asked for those who knew them best to be allowed to testify on their behalf, and pointed out that it was the testimony of confessed witches and afflicted being used against them, "without other Legal evidence concurring." The testimony of those who had confessed to dealing with Satan was the main evidence, and under common understanding in cases of witchcraft, even Cotton Mather concurred that accusations made by confessed witches should be disregarded, or at least considered carefully, as they might be lies to ensnare innocent people. The Court consistently disregarded this argument, likely because this method had produced subsequent confessions.

After she had been condemned to die, Mary Easty wrote a letter to Governor William Phipps in the hopes that he would investigate the actions of the Court before more lives were lost. Easty seemed to have given up hope that she would survive this ordeal, but pleaded with the Governor to step in to prevent further tragedy.

Petition of Mary Easty September 15, 1692:

The humbl petition of mary Eastick unto his Excellencyes S'r W'm Phipps to the honour'd Judge and Bench now Sitting In Judi- cature in Salem and the Reverend ministers humbly sheweth That whereas your poor and humble Petition[er] being condemned to die Doe humbly begg of you to take it into your Judicious and pious considerations that your Poor and humble petitioner knowing my own Innocencye Blised be the Lord for it and seeing plainly the wiles and subtility of my accusers by my

Selfe can not but Judg charitably of others that are going the same way of my selfe if the Lord stepps not mightily in i was confined a whole month upon the same account that I am condemned now for and then cleared by the afflicted persons as some of your honours know and in two dayes time I was cryed out upon by them and have been confined and now am condemned to die the Lord above knows my Innocencye then and Likewise does now as att the great day will be known to men and Angells -- I Petition to your honours not for my own life for I know I must die and my appointed time is sett but the Lord he knowes it is that if it be possible no more Innocentt blood may be shed which undoubtidly cannot be Avoydd In the way and course you goe in I question not but your honours does to the uttmost of your Powers in the discovery and detecting of witchcraft and witches and would not be gulty of Innocent blood for the world but by my own Innocencye I know you are in the wrong way the Lord in his infinite mercye direct you in this great work if it be his blessed will that no more Innocent blood be shed I would humbly begg of you that your honors would be plesed to examine theis Aflicted Persons strictly and keepe them apart some time and Likewise to try some of these confesing wichis I being confident there is severall of them has belyed themselves and others as will appeare if not in this wor[l]d I am sure in the world to come whither I am now agoing and I Question not but youle see an alteration of thes things they say my selfe and others having made a League with the Divel we cannot confesse I know and the Lord knowes as will shortly appeare they belye me and so I Question not but they doe others the Lord above who is the Searcher of all hearts knowes that as I shall answer it att the Tribunall seat that I know not the least thinge of witchcraft therfore I cannot I dare not belye my own soule I beg your honers not to deny this my humble petition from a poor dy ing Innocent person and I Question not but the Lord will give a blesing to yor endevers

Alice Parker (b. unknown, d. Sep 22, 1692), whose maiden name is unconfirmed, was married to John Parker, and they lived in a home on modern day Derby Street, which was rented from Philip and Mary English. She had no known relation to Mary Parker. The accusations against her consist almost entirely of the testimony of the afflicted. One man testified that she argued with him at Thomas Beadle's tavern, (63-65 Essex Street). Afterwards, he was attacked by a boar, so he concluded the boar must have either been her, or doing her bidding. Another man testified he had once found her unconscious, stiff, and unresponsive. Parker suffered from narcolepsy, a known disorder at the time, that some still attributed to witchcraft.

Parker had a history with accuser Mary Warren and her family, they being neighbors at some point. Parker and Warren's father argued about his promise to mow her lawn (mowing grass at the time would have been done with a scythe or shears) afterwards Warren's mother and sister fell ill with an unknown affliction, which lead to her mother's death and her sister's loss of hearing. What became of Warren's sister and father by 1692 is unknown. During Parker's examination on May 12, Warren began to convulse, and suffered a "dreadful fit, w'rby her tongue hungout of her mouth until it was black," and Parker responded to the sight with scorn, saying Warren's "tongue would be blacker before she dyed."

Ann (wd. Greenslit) Pudeator (b. abt. 1621, d. Sep 22, 1692) was married to Thomas Greenslit, and they lived together in Salem until his death in 1674. Her maiden name is unknown. In 1675, she assisted with the failing health of Isabel Pudeator, wife of Jacob Pudeator, a blacksmith. Isabel died the following year, and Ann married Jacob soon after. Their home was believed to be near to Salem Common, and the remains of a 17th century blacksmith's shop were discovered on the site of the current Andrew-Stafford house (270 Washington Square) by the Common. Jacob himself died in 1682 and left his estate and money to Ann and her children from her first marriage. This was viewed with suspicion by neighbors who felt that her quick marriage to Jacob after the death of his wife, and his shortly thereafter, indicated she may have had a hand in it.

During her examination, the testimony focused on oils and ointments which were found when her home was searched. She was questioned about the purpose of the oils, and Pudeator admitted to having Neatsfoot oil (an oil made from the shinbones of cattle and used for preserving leather) but no other types. A layperson creating ointments, tinctures, or other herbal remedies was looked on with suspicion, for the oils may have some nefarious intent. The constable testified that they had found close to twenty different types of ointment or greases in her home. Pudeator admitted that she did have more oils than she had said, but that they were for the purpose of making soap.

On September 15, 1692, she sent a petition to the judges asking that the evidence given against her by Jon Best Sr, Jon Best Jr, and Samuell Pickworth be thrown out. She claimed that all three men were known to be liars; Best Jr having previously been whipped for lying. Mary Warren claimed that Pudeator used magic to make John Turner Jr (*Turner*

Tomb) fall out of a cherry tree, which Pudeator denied. In her petition, Pudeator stated: "I am altogether ignorant of and know nothing in the least measure about nor nothing else concerning the crime of witchcraft for which I am condemned to die as will be known to men and angels at the great day of Judgment."

Wilmot Redd (b. unknown, d. Sep 22, 1692) was from Marblehead, and married to fisherman Samuel Reed. "Mammy Red," as she was known, was depicted as an irritable and rude old woman, and her neighbors believed that she was a witch long before 1692. She would be accused of using witchcraft to cause misfortune for those she did not like, such as turning butter to mold in the churn, and fresh milk to curdle in the pail. In 1687, Redd was confronted by Charity Pittman, and a woman known as Mrs. Syms, who claimed that Redd's servant had stolen linen from Mrs. Syms' home. Syms told Redd that if the linen wasn't returned, she would report her to John Hathorne in Salem. Redd allegedly told Syms that if she did so, she wished Syms "might never mingere [urinate] nor cacare [defecate]." Shortly afterward, Pittman said, Syms was "taken with the distemper of the dry belly-ake," which lasted until she left Marblehead. Redd's angry curse was believed to be the cause of Sym's stomach troubles.

Her examination on May 31, 1692, was brief, and it appears Redd had little to say in her defense. As the afflicted claimed she had threatened to beat them and forced the Devil's book on them, they fell into fits, which were "cured" by Redd's touch. When asked what she thought caused they afflicted to suffer, she replied, "My opinion is they are in a sad condition." Redd's Pond in Marblehead is named for her. Samuel Reed died in 1718, and was interred at the Old Burial Hill in Marblehead. A gravestone for Wilmot Redd was placed beside her husband's grave in 1998, though, like most of the victims, her true burial site is unknown.

Margaret (Stephenson) Scott (b. abt. 1615, d Sep 22, 1692) was born in England and emigrated to Braintree, Massachusetts. She and her husband, Benjamin Scott, lived in Braintree, where two of their children were born and lived to adulthood. In 1664, the Scotts were granted a small farm in Rowley. They had seven children together, but at the time of Benjamin's death in 1671, only three were still living: Benjamin Scott, John Scott, and Mary (Scott) Decker. Margaret was left with a small farm at the age of fifty-six, and lived most of her life in poverty, forced to beg assistance and money from neighbors. Her neighbors considered her begging to be a nuisance, and it would add to their suspicions that she might be a witch. Daniel Wycomb testified that once Scott had come asking for corn, and he felt she acted inappropriately by trying to rush him. The family gave Scott some corn, and when Daniel went out into his field, his oxen refused to pull the cart. A record of Margaret Scott's examination has not survived. Scott was the only person living in Rowley in 1692 that was executed in the Witch Hysteria, and a stone marker placed in the town was dedicated to her in 1992.

Samuel Wardwell Sr. (b. May 16, 1643, d. Sep 22, 1692) was a carpenter from Andover. Wardwell is the only one of the executed who confessed to witchcraft, though he later recanted. In his examination, he claimed that the Devil had come to him twenty years before, when his love was rejected by Sarah Barker of Andover. Sarah was the sister of William Barker Sr, who would be accused of witchcraft along with his son, William Jr, and nieces, Mary and Abigail Barker, all of whom would confess. Wardwell said that, in his depressed state, the Devil appeared to him as a cat, and then later as a mysterious "black man," who told Wardwell that he was a "prince and lord," and if Wardwell would worship him, he would "never want for any thing."

Wardwell's wife Sarah (Hooper) Wardwell, and daughter Mercy Wardwell, were also accused and confessed to witchcraft. Samuel was the only Quaker to be hanged as a witch in Salem (for more on the treatment of Quakers in the colonies, see *Shattuck Section*). Wardwell was said to have known how to read palms and tell fortunes. He confessed to being baptized by the Devil in the Shawsheen River in Andover, and that the witches' meetings were also attended by the sagamores of Native American tribes and by French Canadians. Wardwell claimed that Jane Lilly and Mary Taylor of Reading were witches in his company. Wardwell testified that the women were responsible for the death of William Hooper, who had died in a house fire on August 8, 1692. Wardwell later recanted his confession, and he was found guilty. At his execution, Wardwell was proclaiming his innocence to the crowd, but began to cough due to smoke from the executioner's pipe and could not finish. The afflicted shouted from the crowd that the Devil was preventing him from speaking. In 1693, Jane Lilly's case was dismissed, and Mary Taylor was found not guilty.

Victims Who Died in Prison

Several victims of the Witch Hysteria are not memorialized here, or at the Gallows Hill Memorial, but they are at the Salem Village Witchcraft Victims Memorial in Danvers (formerly Salem Village), at 176 Hobart Street. These victims were not hanged, but died in jail.

Sarah (Warren) Osbourne (b. abt. 1643, d. May 10, 1692) lived in Salem Village, and was married to Robert Prince on February 5, 1662. While she had the same last name as Mary Warren, there is no confirmation at this time that they were related, nor is their relationship addressed in any court documents. Sarah and Robert Prince had at least three children together before Robert died about 1674. Three years later, Sarah married her former indentured servant, Alexander Osbourne. This would cause the Salem Village community to whisper that perhaps she had killed her husband. These rumors only increased when Sarah and Alexander took over the management of the family's land, rather than passing it to Robert's sons, as his will had dictated. The family of Robert Princes' sister, Rebecca (Prince) Putnam and her husband John, would go to court against the Osbournes to try and keep the land for the sons. This seems to have been unsuccessful, as the sons would sue Alexander's estate after his death.

John Putnam was the brother of Thomas Putnam, who would bring charges of witchcraft against Sarah for afflicting his daughter, Ann Putnam Jr. Sarah Osbourne was one of the first to be accused of witchcraft in 1692, along with Tituba Indian and Sarah Good, facing the magistrates John Hathorne and Jonathan Corwin. She was accused of afflicting Betty Parris, Abigail Williams, Ann Putnam Jr, and Elizabeth Hubert, each of whom was present for her examination. In her defense, Sarah said that she was "more like to be bewitched than to be a witch," and explained that she had missed church services for over a year due to ill health. Her case did not go to trial, as she died in the Boston jail on May 10, 1692, after being imprisoned for over nine weeks. Her husband, Alexander, was not charged with witchcraft, and continued to live in the contested home that he had inherited from Sarah. Alexander remarried to Ruth Sibley, and the couple remained members of the Salem Village Church.

Mercy Good (b. abt. 1691, d. abt. 1692) was the infant daughter of Sarah and William Good. She died in the Boston jail, imprisoned with her mother and sister, Dorothy.

Ann Foster (b. abt. 1617, d. Dec 3, 1692) was an elderly widow living in Andover when she was accused of witchcraft. Her husband, Andrew Foster, had died in 1685, leaving her a widow at sixty-seven. Foster was no stranger to suffering, as her family had endured terrible tragedy prior to 1692. On October 15, 1667, her daughter, Hannah, married Hugh Stone. The couple was married for twelve years and had seven children before a horrific event occurred. On April 20, 1689, while Hannah was pregnant with their eighth child, the couple had an argument over the sale of some land. Hugh was drunk during this argument, and attacked Hannah with a knife. Hearing a commotion, neighbors rushed over to home and found Hannah murdered by her husband. Hugh plead guilty to the murder, and would be hanged for it, seemingly claiming that a loss of religion in his family was the cause of his actions. The details of the crime and execution were published by Rev. Cotton Mather in his work *Magnalia Christi*. Later that year, Simon Stone, the nineteen-year-old son of Hannah and Hugh Stone, was seriously wounded and mutilated in a raid by Native Americans at Exeter, New Hampshire.

Ann Foster was accused of witchcraft in July of 1692, as was her daughter Mary (Foster) Lacey Sr, and granddaughter, Mary Lacy Jr. Ann Foster confessed to witchcraft, and in her confession, she not only confessed to numerous acts of witchcraft, but implicated others who had previously claimed innocence. She stated that Martha Carrier was the witch who brought her into the Devil's fold, and that Carrier had bragged that the Devil told her she would one day be "Queen in Hell." Foster confirmed that Rev. George Burroughs was the leader of the witches, and claimed that at one of the witches' meetings, Burroughs had boasted that there were three hundred and five witches in Massachusetts. The witches, she said, intended that the Devil's Kingdom was to be established in the Massachusetts Bay Colony.

Mary Lacey Sr and Mary Jr confessed as well, and supported Ann's stories. Ann was returned to the Salem Jail, where she would complain that the spirits of Burroughs and Carrier tormented her for confessing. Ann Foster had been in jail for twenty-one weeks when she died. Her son, Abraham, was made to pay a total fee of £6 to the jail before her body would be released to him. Her burial site is unconfirmed, but may be near Foster's Pond in Andover.

Dr. Roger Toothaker (b. abt. 1634, d. Jun 16, 1692) of Billerica, Massachusetts, was the only male medical practitioner accused of witchcraft in Salem in 1692. Unlike Dr. Griegs, Toothaker did not see the diagnosis of "under an Evil hand" as an affliction that was beyond his power to cure. The doctor was familiar with "counter-magic," and had methods to combat the torments caused by witches. In 1691, he claimed to have killed a witch by putting the urine of an afflicted person in an "Earthen pott" and placing it in a hot oven overnight. While the circumstances around this claim are difficult to confirm, Toothaker was accused of witchcraft. His wife, Mary (Allen) Toothaker, (who was the sister of Martha Carrier) and their daughter, Margaret, were both accused of witchcraft and imprisoned. Roger died in the Boston jail in June, his cause of death unknown.

After his death, both Mary and Margaret confessed to witchcraft. In Mary's confession, she stated that Rev. Burroughs had been the leader of the witches, and supported Ann Foster's claim that there were three hundred and five witches in the colony. Mary also said that the Devil had appeared to her as a Native American, and promised that if she joined his side, she would not have to fear attacks by hostile tribes. Mary's confession took place on July 30, 1692, and she and Martha were committed to the Salem jail. On August 1st, a raid on Billerica was executed by Native American warriors, who slaughtered all of the inhabitants of two homesteads nearby to the Toothakers.

Lydia Dustin (b. abt. 1626, d. Mar 10, 1693), whose name is alternately spelled "Dastin," was married to Josiah Dustin in 1645. The family lived in Reading, where her husband died on January 16, 1671. Rumors had held her to be a witch for decades, as Robert Calef notes, her neighbors believed, "if there were a witch in the world, she was one." One of her accusers, Susanna Sheldon, had been found with her hands bound and hanging from a hook. The deputy cut Susanna's bonds, and she claimed it was Dustin who was responsible.

Her trial took place January 31, 1693, at the Charlestown court, before Judges William Stoughton, Wait-Still Winthrop, Thomas Danforth, and Samuel Sewall. When the Court sat, Chief Justice William Stoughton received news that seven people he had condemned to hang in Salem had been reprieved by the Governor. Stoughton stormed out of the courtroom and would refuse to judge any further cases. The cases proceeded, and as no spectral evidence was allowed in the Court, the testimony of over thirty of Dustin's neighbors consisted mainly of coincidence and accidents that they attributed to her magical power. While it was agreed among the judges that more evidence had been presented against her than perhaps any other accused, they could not convict, and Dustin was found not guilty. Danforth in particular seemed to believe that there was something to the accusations. As she left the courtroom, Danforth warned her, "Woman, woman, repent, there are shrewd things brought against you."

Dustin's daughter, Mary (Dustin) Coleson, and her granddaughter, were also acquitted that day. While Dustin was not convicted, she could not raise the money she needed to pay for her jailer's fees. Paying her fees had been a requirement of her release, and she was kept in the Cambridge jail until she could, continuing to incur more fees as she waited. Lydia Dustin would remain in jail for over a month after being declared innocent, and died in jail that March.

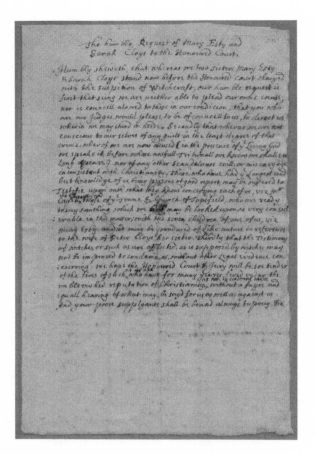

The humble Request of Mary Esty and
Sarah Cloys to the Honoured Court.

Humbly sheweth, that whereas we two Sisters Mary Esty & Sarah Cloys stand now before the Honoured court charged with the suspition of Witchcraft, our humble request is first that seing we are neither able to plead our owne cause, nor is councell alowed to those in our condicion; that you who are our Judges, would please to be of councell to us, to direct us wherein we may stand in neede. Secondly that whereas we are not conscious to ourselves of any guilt in the least degree of that crime, wherof we are now accused (in the presence of the Living God we speake it, before whose awfull Tribunall we know we shall ere Long appeare) nor of any other scandalouse evill, or miscaryage inconsistant with Christianity, Those who have had the Longest and best knowledge of us, being persons of good report, may be suffered to Testifie upon oath what they know concerning each of us, viz Mr. Capen the pastour and those of the Towne & Church of Topsfield, who are ready to say somthing which we hope may be looked upon, as very considerable in this matter; with the seven children of one of us, viz Mary Esty, and it may be produced of Like nature in reference to the wife of Peter Cloys, her sister. Thirdly that the Testimony of witches, or such as are afflicted, as is supposed, by witches may not be improved to condemn us, without other Legal evidence concurring, we hope the Honoured Court & Jury will be soe tender of the lives of such, as we are who have for many years Lived under the unblemished reputation of Christianity, as not to condemne them without a fayre and equall hearing of what may be sayd for us, as well as against us. And your poore supplyants shall be bound always to pray &c.

Criticism of The Witch Hysteria

"New England, thou hast destroyed thyself, and brought this greatest of miseries upon thyself... We cannot recall those to life again, that have suffered, supposing it were unjustly; it tends but to exposing the actors."

- ROBERT CALEF - *More Wonders of The Invisible World*

The events of the accusations, courtroom intrigue, and hangings have been written of many times over. However, as the Salem Witch Trials Memorial is considered a place to reflect on the lessons of this hysteria, we will look at the words of those who lived at the time through letters, books, and pamphlets. Often, this sorrowful episode in American history is blamed on "the ignorance of the time." However, during the time of the trials, there were many who spoke out against what was happening in Salem.

The Boston Minister

Reverend Increase Mather, who was the President of Harvard College, as well as the father of Cotton Mather and Nathaniel Mather (*Pickman/Toppan Tomb*), published his "Cases of Conscience concerning Witchcrafts," a pamphlet which rebuked the Court of Oyer and Terminer's insistence that the tormenting spirits in the visions of the afflicted had to be the same people they accused. Mather wrote:

The First Case that I am desired to express my Judgment in, is this, Whether it is not Possible for the Devil to impose on the imagination of Persons Bewitched, and cause them to Believe that an Innocent, yea that a Pious person torment them, when the Devil himself doth it; or whether Satan may not appear in the Shape of an Innocent and Pious, as well as of a Nocent and Wicked Person, to Afflict such as suffer by Diabolical Molestation? The Answer to the Question must be Affirmative.

Mather went on to point out several examples in Scripture to prove his statement, such as when the Devil appears in the likeness of the Prophet Samuel at the behest of the Witch at Endor. Another example he presents is the story of Germanus, who is shown the diabolical illusion of a large number of people at a wicked feast, when the real people are all asleep in their beds. "The particulars insisted on," Mather concludes, "so sufficiently evince the truth of what we assert, viz That the Devil may by Divine Permission appear in the shape of an Innocent and Pious person."

The Witness to Executions

Thomas Brattle of Cambridge, a merchant who was fiercely critical of the trials, appears to have attended several of the trials and executions. One of Brattle's letters regarding the trials still survives; a letter to an unnamed clergyman written the fall of 1692. In the letter, Brattle discusses what he has witnessed at the trials, as well as his observations about the afflicted, judges, and the accused.

Excerpts from Thomas Brattle's letter to an unnamed clergyman, October 8, 1692:

First, as to the method which the Salem justices do take in their examinations, it is truly this: A warrant being issued out to apprehend the persons that are charged and complained of by the afflicted children, (as they are called); said persons are brought before the Justices, (the afflicted being present.) The Justices ask the apprehended why they afflict those poor children; to which the apprehended answer, they do not afflict them. The Justices order the apprehended to look upon the said children, which accordingly they do; and at the time of that look, (I dare not say by that look, as the Salem Gentlemen do) the afflicted are cast into a fitt. The apprehended are then blinded, and ordered to touch the afflicted; and at that touch, tho' not by the touch, (as above) the afflicted ordinarily do come out of their fitts. The afflicted persons then declare and affirm, that the apprehended have afflicted them; upon which the apprehended persons, tho' of never so good repute, are forthwith committed to prison, on suspicion for witchcraft.

    One of the Salem Justices was pleased to tell Mr. Alden, (when upon his examination) that truly he had been acquainted with him these many years; and had always accounted him a good man; but indeed now he should be obliged to change his opinion. This, there are more than one or two did hear, and are ready to swear to, if not in so many words, yet as to its natural and plain meaning. He saw reason to change his opinion of Mr. Alden, because that at the time he touched the poor child, the poor child came out of her fitt. I suppose his Honour never made the experiment, whether there was not as much virtue in his own hand, as there was in Mr. Alden's, to cure by a touch. I know a man that will venture two to one with any Salemite whatever, that let the matter be duly managed, and the afflicted person shall come out of her fitt upon the touch of the most religious hand in Salem.

On the testimony of confessed witches being taken as evidence:

    These confessours, (as they are called,) do very often contradict themselves, as inconsistently as is usual for any crazed, distempered person to do. This the Salem Gentlemen do see and take notice of; and even the Judges themselves have, at some times, taken these confessours in flat lyes, or contradictions, even in the Courts; By reason of which, one would have thought, that the Judges would have frowned upon the said confessours, discarded them, and not minded one tittle of any thing that they said; but instead thereof, (as sure as we are men,) the Judges vindicate these confessours, and salve their contradictions, by proclaiming, that the Devill takes away their memory, and imposes upon their brain. If this reflects any where, I am very sorry for it: I can but assure you, that, upon the word of an honest man, it is truth, and that I can bring you many credible persons to witnesse it, who have been eye and ear wittnesses to these things.

    The great cry of many of our neighbours now is, What, will you not believe the confessours? Will you not believe men and women who confesse that they have signed to the Devill's book? that they were baptized by the Devill; and that they were at the mock-sacrament once and again? What! will you not believe that this is witchcraft, and that such and such men are witches, altho' the confessours do own and assert it?

    Thus, I say, many of our good neighbours do argue; but methinks they might soon be convinced that there is nothing at all in all these their arguings, if they would but duly consider of the premises.

Regarding the acceptance of spectral evidence:

> It is true, that over and above the evidences of the afflicted persons, there are many evidences brought in, against the prisoner at the bar; either that he was at a witch meeting, or that he performed things which could not be done by an ordinary natural power; or that she sold butter to a saylor, which proving bad at sea, and the seamen exclaiming against her, she appeared, and soon after there was a storm, or the like. But what if there were ten thousand evidences of this nature; how do they prove the matter of inditement! And if they do not reach the matter of inditement, then I think it is clear, that the prisoner at the bar is brought in guilty, and condemned, merely from the evidences of the afflicted persons.
>
> Now no man will be so much out of his witts as to make this a legal evidence; and yet this seems to be our case; and how to apply it is very easy and obvious.

Regarding the executions on August 19, 1692:

> They protested their innocency as in the presence of the great God, whom forthwith they were to appear before: they wished, and declared their wish, that their blood might be the last innocent blood shed upon that account. With great affection they intreated Mr. Cotton Mather to pray with them: they prayed that God would discover what witchcrafts were among us; they forgave their accusers; they spake without reflection on Jury and Judges, for bringing them in guilty, and condemning them: they prayed earnestly for pardon for all other sins, and for an interest in the pretious blood of our dear Redeemer; and seemed to be very sincere, upright, and sensible of their circumstances on all accounts; especially Proctor and Willard, whose whole management of themselves, from the Gaol to the Gallows, and whilst at the Gallows, was very affecting and melting to the hearts of some considerable Spectatours, whom I could mention to you: -- but they are executed, and so I leave them...

On the Court taking the word of confessed witches:

> If I believe such or such an assertion as comes immediately from the Minister of God in the pulpitt, because it is the word of the everliving God, I build my faith on God's testimony: and if I practise upon it, this my practice is properly built on the word of God: even so in the case

before us.

If I believe the afflicted persons as informed by the Devill, and act thereupon, this my act may properly be said to be grounded upon the testimony or information of the Devill. And now, if things are thus, I think it ought to be for a lamentation to you and me, and all such as would be accounted good Christians.

I am very sensible, that it is irksome and disagreeable to go back, when a man's doing so is an implication that he has been walking in a wrong path: however, nothing is more honourable than, upon due conviction, to retract and undo, (so far as may be,) what has been amiss and irregular.

What will be the issue of these troubles, God only knows; I am afraid that ages will not wear off that reproach and those stains which these things will leave behind them upon our land. I pray God pity us, Humble us, Forgive us, and appear mercifully for us in this our mount of distress: Herewith I conclude, and subscribe myself,

Reverend Sir, your real friend and humble servant,

T. B.

The Constable's Mockery

Brattle was in communication with Boston constable Robert Calef during this time, and provided much of the information Calef would use in his scathing criticism of the Court of Oyer and Terminer, and Rev. Cotton Mather in particular. Calef's book, *More Wonders of the Invisible World* (the title meant to mock Cotton Mather's own account of the Court, entitled *Wonders of the Invisible World*), would be published in 1700. Boston printers refused to publish the book for fear of angering the Mathers, so Calef had it published in London. Calef's anger at this tragic episode in Salem history in strongly expressed in his introduction to the book:

If this be the true state of the afflictions of this country, it is very deplorable, and beyond all the outward calamities miserable. But if, on the other side, the matter be, as others do understand it, that the devil has been too hard on us by his temptations, signs, and lying wonders, with the help of pernicious notions, formerly imbibed and professed; together

with the accusations of a parcel of possessed, distracted, or lying wench-
es, accusing their innocent neighbors, pretending they see spectres, i.e.
devils in their likeness, afflicting of them... and let loose the devils of
envy, hatred, pride, cruelty and malice against each other, yet still dis-
guised under the mask of zeal for God, and left them to the branding one
another with the odious name of witch; and upon the accusation of those
above mentioned, brother to accuse and prosecute brother, children their
parents, pastors and teachers their immediate flock, unto death; shep-
herds becoming wolves; wise men infatuated; people hauled to prisons;
with a bloody noise pursuing to, and insulting over the (true) suffers at,
execution; while some are fleeing from that called justice, Justice itself
fleeing before such accusations ... If this were the miserable case of this
country in the time thereof, then the devil had so far prevailed upon us...

The Governor Disbands the Court

With criticism and controversy mounting, Governor William
Phips put a hold on the Court of Oyer and Terminer in October of
1692. Phips wrote the following letter to the Earl of Nottingham, which
explains his version of the situation, and aftermath of events between
himself and the Lt. Governor William Stoughton. Stoughton had been
appointed the Chief Justice of the court by Phips when he authorized the
Court in May of 1692.

Letter from William Phips to the Earl of Nottingham, February 1693:

Boston in New England Febry 21st, 1692/3.

Sir By the Capn. of the Samuell and Henry I gave an account that att my
arrival here I found the Prisons full of people committed upon suspition of witchcraft and that continuall complaints were made to me that
many persons were grievously tormented by witches and that they cryed
out upon severall persons by name, as the cause of their torments. The
number of these complaints increasing every day, by advice of the Lieut
Govr. and the Councill I gave a Commission of Oyer and Terminer to
try the suspected witches and at that time the generality of the people
represented to me as reall witchcraft and gave very strange instances of
the same. The first in Commission was the Lieut. Govr. and the rest persons of the best prudence and figure that could then be pitched upon and

I depended upon the Court for a right method of proceeding in cases of witchcraft. At that time I went to command the army at the Eastern part of the Province, for the French and Indians had made an attack upon some of our Fronteer Towns. I continued there for some time but when I returned I found people much disatisfied at the proceedings of the Court, for about Twenty persons were condemned and executed of which number some were thought by many persons to be innocent. The Court still proceeded in the same method of trying them, which was by the evidence of the afflicted persons who when they were brought into the Court as soon as the suspected witches looked upon them instantly fell to the ground in strange agonies and grievous torments, but when touched by them upon the arme or some other part of their flesh they immediately revived and came to themselves, upon [which] they made oath that the Prisoner at the Bar did afflict them and that they saw their shape or spectre come from their bodies which put them to such paines and torments: When I enquired into the matter I was enformed by the Judges that they begun with this, but had humane testimony against such as were condemned and undoubted proof of their being witches, but at length I found that the Devill did take upon him the shape of Innocent persons and some were accused of whose innocency I was well assured and many considerable persons of unblameable life and conversation were cried out upon as witches and wizards. The Deputy Govr. notwithstanding persisted vigorously in the same method, to the great disatisfaction and disturbance of the people, untill I put an end to the Court and stopped the proceedings, which I did because I saw many innocent persons might otherwise perish and at that time I thought it my duty to give an account thereof that their Ma'ties pleasure might be signifyed, hoping that for the better ordering thereof the Judges learned in the law in England might give such rules and directions as have been practized in England for proceedings in so difficult and so nice a point; When I put an end to the Court there ware at least fifty persons in prison in great misery by reason of the extream cold and their poverty, most of them having only spectre evidence against them, and their mittimusses being defective, I caused some of them to be lett out upon bayle and put the Judges upon considering of a way to reliefe others and prevent them from perishing in prison, upon which some of them were convinced and acknowledged that their former proceedings were too violent and not grounded upon a right foundation but that if they might sit againe, they would proceed after another method, and whereas Mr. Increase Mathew and severall other Divines did give it as their Judgment that the Devill might afflict in the shape of an innocent person and that the look and touch of the suspected persons was not sufficient proofe against them, these things had not the same stress layd upon them as before, and upon this consideration I permitted a spetiall Superior Court to be held at Salem in the County of Essex on the third day of January, the Lieut Govr. being Chief Judge. Their method of proceeding being altered, all that were brought to tryall to the number of fifety two, were cleared saving three, and I was enformed by the Kings Attorny Generall that some of the cleared and the condemned were under the same circumstances or that there was the same reason to clear the three condemned as the rest according to his Judgment. The Deputy Govr. signed a Warrant for their speedy execution and also of five others who were condemned at the former Court of Oyer and terminer, but considering how the matter had been managed I sent a reprieve whereby the execucion was stopped untill their Maj. pleasure be signified and declared. The Lieut. Gov. upon this occasion was inraged and filled with passionate anger and refused to sitt upon the bench in a Superior Court then held at Charles Towne, and indeed hath from the beginning hurried on these matters with great precipitancy and by his warrant hath caused the estates, goods and chattles of the executed to be seized and disposed of without my knowledge or consent. The stop put to the first method of proceedings hath dissipated the blak cloud that threatened this Province with destruccion; for whereas this delusion of the Devill did spread and its dismall effects touched the lives and estates of many of their Ma'ties Subjects and the reputation of some of the principall persons here, and indeed unhappily clogged and interrupted their Ma'ties affaires which hath been a great vexation to me, I have no new complaints but peoples minds before divided and distracted by differing opinions concerning this matter are now well composed.

I am (&) Sr Yor. Lordships most faithfull humble Servant

William Phips

Apologies and Aftermath of The Witch Hysteria

"I did it not out of any anger, malice, or ill-will to any person, for I had no such thing against one of them-"

Anne Putnam Jr - August 25, 1706

I t was not long after the end of the Court of Oyer and Terminer that the authorities in Salem and Boston began to acknowledge that a grievous error had occurred, and that the trials had been mishandled. As monetary restitution began to be provided to the victims, apologies came forward as well.

The Judge's Apology

The Apology of Reverend Samuel Sewall came in January of 1697. Sewall was the only one of the judges to publicly apologize for his role in the trials. This apology was read by Rev. Samuel Willard at the Old South Meeting House. As this apology was read, Sewall stood before his congregation bowing in repentance:

Samuel Sewall, sensible of the reiterated strokes of God upon himself and family, and being sensible that as to guilt contracted upon the opening of the late Commission... at Salem (to which this fast day relates) he is, upon many accounts, more concerned than any that he knows of, desires to take the Name and shame of it, asking pardon of all men, and especially desiting prayers that God,who has unlimited author-

ity, would pardon that sin and his other sins, personal and relative, and according to His infinite Benignity, and Sovereignty, not visited upon himself or any of his or upon the land. But that God would powerfully defend him against all temptations for Sin, for the future and vouchsafe him the efficacious saving conduct of word and spirit.

The Jury's Apology

After Sewall's apology, the jury of the Court of Oyer and Terminer issued their own apology in 1697:

Some that had been of several juries have given forth a paper, signed with our own hands in these words. We whose names are underwritten, being in the year 1692 called to serve as jurors in court in Salem, on trial of many who were by some suspected guilty of doing acts of witchcraft upon the bodies of sundry persons.

We confess that we ourselves were not capable to understand, nor able to withstand the mysterious delusions of the powers of darkness and prince of the air, but were for want of knowledge in ourselves and better information from others, prevailed with to take up with such evidence against the accused as on further consideration and better information, we justly fear was insufficient for the touching the lives of any, Deuteronomy 17.6, whereby we fear we have been instrumental with others, though ignorantly and unwittingly, to bring upon ourselves and this people of the Lord, the guilt of innocent blood, which sin the Lord saith in Scripture, he would not pardon, 2 Kings 24.4, that is we suppose in regard of His temporal judgments. We do, therefore, hereby signify to all in general (and to the surviving sufferers in especial) our deep sense of and sorrow for our errors in acting on such evidence to the condemning of any person.

And do hereby declare that we justly fear that we were sadly deluded and mistaken, for which we are much disquieted and distressed in our minds, and do therefore humbly beg forgiveness, first of God for Christ's sake for this our error. And pray that God would not impute the guilt of it to ourselves nor others. And we also pray that we may be considered candidly and aright by the living sufferers as being then under the power of a strong and general delusion, utterly unacquainted with and not experienced in matters of that nature.

We do heartily ask forgiveness of you all, whom we have justly offended and do declare, according to our present minds, we would none of us do such things again on such grounds for the whole world, praying you to accept of this in way of satisfaction for our offense, and that you would bless the inheritance of the Lord that He may be entreated for the land.

[signed]

Foreman, Thomas Fisk
Thomas Perly, Senior
William Fiske
John Peabody
John Batcheler
Thomas Perkins
Thomas Fisk, Junior
Samuel Sather
John Dane
Andrew Elliott
Joseph Evelith
Henry Herrick, Senior

The Apology of an Afflicted Girl

Ann Putnam Jr, the daughter of Thomas and Ann Putnam Sr, was one of the principal accusers in the course of the 1692 hysteria. She was the only one of the afflicted who publicly addressed her role in the Salem Witch Trials, making this statement in 1706:

I desire to be humbled before God for that sad and humbling providence that befell my father's family in the year about '92; that I, then being in my childhood, should, by such a providence of God, be made an instrument for the accusing of several persons of a grievous crime, whereby their lives were taken away from them, whom now I have just grounds and good reason to believe they were innocent persons; and that it was a great delusion of Satan that deceived me in that sad time, whereby I justly fear I have been instrumental, with others, though ignorantly and unwittingly, to bring upon myself and this land the guilt of innocent blood; though what was said or done by me against any person I can truly and uprightly say, before God and man, I did it not out of any anger, malice, or ill-will to any person, for I had no such thing against one of them; but what I did was ignorantly, being deluded by Satan. And particularly, as I was a chief instrument of accusing of Goodwife Nurse and her two sisters, I desire to lie in the dust, and to be humbled for it, in that I was a cause, with others, of so sad a calamity to them and their families; for which cause I desire to lie in the dust, and earnestly beg forgiveness of God, and from all those unto whom I have given just cause of sorrow and offence, whose relations were taken away or accused.

[Signed]

Ann Putnam

This confession was read before the congregation, together with her relation, Aug. 25, 1706; and she acknowledged it.

J. Green Pastor

The preceding apology was read to the Salem Village congregation by the minister, Rev. Joseph Green, on the day of Ann Putnam Jr's communion. Green also convinced the congregation to revoke the excommunication of Martha Corey in 1703.

Petition of Isaac Easty

The families of victims petitioned for restitution from the colony for the suffering and financial hardships they had suffered. Below is a Petition for restitution from Isaac Easty for his wife Mary Easty:

Topsfield Septemb. 8th. 1710

Isaac Esty Sen of Topsfield in the county of Essex in N. E. having been sorely exercis'd through the holy & awful providence of God depriving him of his beloved wife Mary Esty who suffered death in the year 1692 & under the fearfull odium of one of the worst of crimes that can be laid to the charge of mankind, as if she had been guilty of witchcraft a piece of wickedness which I beleeve she did hate with perfect hatred & by all that ever I could see by her never could see any thing by her that should give me any reason in the lest to think her guilty of any thing of that nature but am firmly persuaded that she was as innocent of it as any to such a shameful death -- Upon consideration of a notification from the Honored Generall Court desiring my self & others under like circumstances to give some account of what my Estate was damnify'd by reason of such a hellish molestation do hereby declare which may also be seen by comparing papers & records that my wife was near upon 5 months imprisoned all which time I provided maintenance for her at my own cost & charge, went constantly twice aweek to provide for her what she needed 3 weeks of this 5 months she was in prison at Boston & I was constrained to be at the charge of transporting her to & fro. So that I can not but think my charge in time and mony might amount to 20 pounds besides my trouble & sorrow of heart in being deprived of her after such a manner which this world can never make me any compensation for

Isak Esty Sr
aged about 82 years

I order & appoint my son
Jacob Esty to carry this to
the Honored Committee Appointed
by the Honored Generall Court
& are to meet at Salem
Sept 12 1710

Dated this 9th of Sept. 1710

Reversal of Attainder

On October 17, 1711, an Act was introduced to reverse the attainders of those convicted and hanged as witches:

Province of the   *Anno Regni Anna Reginae Decimo-*
Massachusets Bay.

*An Act to reverse the attainders of George
Burroughs and others for Witchcraft*

Forasmuch as in the year of our Lord one Thousand Six hundred ninety two Several Towns within this Province were Infested with a horrible

Witchcraft or Possession of devils: And at a Special Court of Oyer and Terminer holden at Salem in the County of Essex in the same year 1692. George Burroughs of Wells, John Proctor, George Jacob, John Willard, Giles Core and ---- his wife, Rebecca Nurse, and Sarah Good all of Salem aforesaid. Elizabeth How of Ipswich, Mary Eastey, Sarah Wild and Abigail Hobbs all of Topsfield, Samuel Wardwell, Mary Parker, Martha Carrier, Abigail Faulkner, Anne Foster, Rebessa Eames, Mary Post and Mary Lacey all of Andover, Mary Bradbury of Salisbury, and Dorcas Hoar of Beverly Were severally Indicted convicted and attainted of Witchcraft, and some of them put to death, others lying still under the like Sentence of the said court, and liable to have [y]e same Executed upon them.~

The Influence and Energy of the Evil Spirits so great at that time acting in and upon those who were the principal accusers and Witnesses proceeding so far as to cause a Prosecution to be had of persons of known and good reputation. which caused a great Disatisfaction and a Stop to be put thereunto until their majesty's pleasure should be known therein. And upon a Representation thereof accordingly made, Her late Majesty Queen Mary the Second of blessed Memory, by Her royal Letter given at Her Court at Whitehall the fifteenth of April 1693. was Graciously pleased to approve the care and Circumspection therein; and to will and require that in all proceedings agt persons accused for Witchcraft, or being possessed by the devil, the greatest moderation and all due circumspection be used, So far as the same may be without Impediment to the ordinary cause of Justice. And Some of the principal accusers and Witnesses in those dark and severe prosecutions have since discovered themselves to be persons of profligate and vicious conversation. Upon the humble Petition and Suit of several of the sd persons and of the Children of others of them whose Parents were Executed.

Be it Declared and Enacted by his Excellency the Governor Council and Representatives in General Court assembled and by the Authority of the same That the several convictions Judgements and Attainders against the said George Burroughs, John Proctor, George Jacob, John Willard, Giles Core and --- Core, Rebecca Nurse, Sarah Good, Elizabeth How, Mary Eastey, Sarah Wild, Abigail Hobbs, Samuel Wardwell, Mary Parker, Martha Carrier, Abigail Faulkner, Anne Foster, Rebessa Eames, Mary Post, Mary Lacey, Mary Bradbury, and Dorcas Hoar and every of them Be and hereby are reversed made and de[clared] to be null and void to all Intents, Constructions and purposes wh[atso]ever, as if no such Convictions, Judgments or Attainders had ever [been] had or given. And that no penalties or fforfeitures of Goods or Chattels be by the said Judgments and attainders or either of them had or Incurr'd.

Any Law Usage or custom to the contrary notwithstanding. And that no Sheriffe, Constable Goaler or other officer shall be Liable to any prosecution in the Law for anything they then Legally did in the Execution of their respective offices.~

Made and Pass'd by the Great and General Court
of Assembly and Her Majestys Province of the
Massachusetts Bay in New England held at Boston
the 17ᵗʰ day of October 1711

The Act was Passed November 2, 1711. Over time, those who were convicted as witches would be pardoned.

1957 General Court

When interest in the Witch Hysteria renewed in the 1950s, thanks in part to the popularity of "The Crucible," Arthur Miller's allegorical tale written to draw attention to the unfair treatment of falsely accused Communists during the McCarthy Trials, the General Court of Massachusetts would take action on August 28, 1957, to condemn the Court of Oyer and Terminer:

Chap. 145
Whereas, One Ann Pudeator and certain other persons were indicted, tried, found guilty, sentenced to death and executed in the year sixteen hundred and ninety-two for "Witchcraft"; and
Whereas, Said persons may have been illegally tried, convicted and sentenced by a possibly illegal court of oyer and terminer created by the then governor of the Province without authority under the Province Charter of Massachusetts Bay; and

Chap 146
Whereas, Although there was a public repentance by Judge Sewall, one of the judges of the so-called "Witchcraft Court" and by all the members of the "Witchcraft" jury, and ~ public Fast Day proclaimed and observed in repentance for the proceedings, but no other action taken in regard to them; and

Whereas, The General Court of Massachusetts is informed that certain descendants of said Ann Pudeator and said other persons are still distressed by the record of said proceedings; therefore be it

Resolved, 'that in order to alleviate such distress and although the facts of such proceedings cannot be obliterated, the General Court of Massachusetts declares its belief that such proceedings, even if lawful under the Province Charter and the law of Massachusetts as it then was, were and are shocking, and the result of a wave of popular hysterical fear of the Devil in the community, and further declares that, as all the laws under which said proceedings, even if then legally conducted, have been long since abandoned and superseded by our more civilized laws no disgrace or cause for distress attaches to the said descendants or any of them by reason of said proceedings; and be it further

Resolved, That the passage of this resolve shall not bestow on the commonwealth or any of its subdivisions, or on any person any right which did not exist prior to said passage, shall not authorize any suit or other proceeding nor deprive any party to a suit or other proceeding of any defense which he hitherto had] shall not affect in any way whatever the title to or rights in any real or personal property, nor shall it require or permit the remission of any penalty, fine or forfeiture hitherto imposed or incurred.

Approved August 28, 1957.

THE GOULT-PICKMAN HOUSE

"Ye William Goult House"

Adjacent to the Witch Trials Memorial is the Goult-Pickman House, also known simply as "The Samuel Pickman House." This building is one of the oldest surviving homes in Salem, having been built as early as 1638. It is currently owned by the Peabody Essex Museum, and had been closed to the public for the last few decades. This home has a long and storied history, and the 2021 reopening of this historic structure has been highly anticipated by Salem historians and residents. This home is uniquely connected to the Old Burying Point, in that many who lived and died in this home are interred in the cemetery nearby.

When William Goult arrived in Salem from Bristol, Somerset, England, he was granted a plot of land to farm. A house on this property was definitely finished by 1655, as the home is mentioned in another land transfer document where Robert Britt purchased several acres of the land by what is now Central Street. In 1642, Goult was put in the stocks for "speeches against the rule of church," and subsequently whipped as well. Goult died on April 1, 1659, and his wife Mary deeded the property to Samuel Pickman. There is some dispute as to whether the actual existing house belonged to the Goults, but it certainly belonged to the Pickmans.

Samuel Pickman was the great-uncle of Caleb Pickman (*Cromwell Section*) and an ancestor of Col. Benjamin Pickman (*Toppan/Pickman Tomb*). It was Samuel who donated part of his property to expand the cemetery in 1669. Samuel Pickman died sometime before 1687, and his widow Lydia Pickman would have continued to live in the home. During the Witch Hysteria of 1692, Lydia Pickman was one of several women who were responsible for examining the bodies of accused witches for "witch marks" at the jail. The process of discovering witch marks, while often sensationalized in anachronistic interpretation, was only performed by people of the same gender as the accused. The examinations were humiliating to the accused, as the examiners would check their naked bodies for any unusual appearances, such as birthmarks as it was believed that a witch's familiar would use these to feed on the blood of the witch. The home would be purchased in 1705 by Doctor Francis Gathman of Hamburg, Germany. Three of Dr. Gathman's children died in infancy and are buried under one triple-tombstone in the Old Burying Point (*Ward Section*).

In 1744, Dr. Gathman mortgaged the home to Samuel Barnard (*Ropes Section*) who in turn sold it in 1747 to Benjamin Lynde Jr. (*Lynde Tomb*) Lynde seems to have used the home as a rental property after Dr. Gathman's death in 1751, until 1793 when it was sold to Alexander Storey. The Storey children are interred in the Hathorne section, and a photograph of their tombstone may be seen in the *Tombstones and Symbols* chapter. The Storeys then sold the home to Captain Woodbridge Grafton. Little is known of Captain Graft except that he commanded vessels involved in human slavery, and lost the home when he could not pay for damages he suffered in a lawsuit. During the time Grafton owned the home, he rented it to Michel Felice Corne, an artist from the island of Elba, in Tuscany, Italy. Corne was a well-known maritime artist, and several of his paintings are on display in the Peabody Essex Museum. Corne was also known for attempting to help introduce tomatoes into the American diet, as the fruit was commonly thought to be poisonous at the time. Folklore says Corne would sit on the porch eating tomatoes on hot, summer days, occasionally spitting the seeds at passersby.

By 1900, the Pickman House had become a tenement house, its history forgotten under a Victorian façade and new gambrel roof. In 1964, Elizabeth Reardon, a future director of Historic Salem Inc., rediscovered the 17th Century home that hid behind the newer walls of the house. In June 1964, Historic Salem Inc. voted to purchase and restore the Pickman House. Efforts to complete this restoration would begin to stall due to difficulty raising enough funds to handle the task. Not only was there the cost of restoring the home to its original appearance, but the building also needed significant structural repair. An urban renewal project scheduled the Pickman House for demolition. HSI would be unable to complete the required work before the looming deadline, and in November 1969, they voted to sell the building to Marblehead developer Philip Budrose, who agreed to restore the Pickman House to HSI's satisfaction.

The work was completed in 1972, and the Pickman House opened to the public as a historic attraction in 1973. Known as "Ye William Goult House," and operated by David Gavenda, the Pickman House became an instant favorite for tourists visiting Salem. Guests could take guided house tours and see the rooms decorated to appear as they had in centuries past. The house featured exhibits in which mannequins would be dressed as the former inhabitants, including Michele Felice Corne with his barrel of tomatoes.

After nearly ten years of operation, the Pickman House was gifted to the Peabody Museum of Salem (now the Peabody Essex Museum) in 1983. Interestingly, the gift of the home was listed in the Peabody Museum's 1983 Annual Report as being from an anonymous donor. The Museum would use the building to house administrative offices for its development and public relations departments. In 2021, the home would reopen to the public for the first time in over thirty years, serving as a Welcome Center for the Charter Street Cemetery/Old Burying Point and the Salem Witch Trials Memorial.

Related New England Cemeteries

Many people whose names appear in this book are buried in Salem, or nearby in other areas of New England. Below is a listing of people connected to the Old Burying Point who are interred elsewhere.

Bentley, Rev. William: Salem minister and diarist, Harmony Grove Cemetery, Salem, MA

Bowditch, Elizabeth: daughter of Habbakuk Bowditch, Saint Peter's Church Cemetery, Salem, MA

Bowditch, Nathaniel: husband of Elizabeth (Boardman) Bowditch, Mount Auburn Cemetery, Cambridge, MA

Bowditch, Mary Hodges (Ingersoll): wife of Nathaniel Bowditch, Mount Auburn Cemetery, Cambridge, MA

Bradstreet, Anne (Dudley): wife of Simon Bradstreet, Old North Parish Burying Ground, North Andover, MA

Corwin, Jonathan: father of Elizabeth (Corwin) Lindall, Broad Street Cemetery, Salem, MA

Corwin, Sheriff George: husband of Lydia (Gedney) Corwin, Broad Street Cemetery, Salem, MA

Crowninshield, Capt. George Jr. Captain and owner of *Cleopatra's Barge*, grandson of John and Anstiss Crowninshield, Howard Street Cemetery, Salem, MA

Crumpton, Samuel: husband of Jane (wd. Crumpton) More, Bloody Brook Mass Grave, Deerfield, MA

Derby, Gen. Elias Hasket Jr: son of Elias Hasket Derby Sr, Forest Hill Cemetery, Rockingham, NH

Derby, John: son of Capt. Richard Derby. Granary Burying Ground, Boston, MA

Hawthorne, Nathaniel: grandson of Capt. Daniel Hathorne, great grandson of Col. John Hathorne, Sleepy Hollow Cemetery, Concord, MA

Hawthorne, Sophia Amelia (Peabody): lived in Grimshawe House, Sleepy Hollow Cemetery, Concord, MA

Little, Elizabeth: daughter of Dr. Moses and Elizabeth (Williams) Little, Mount Auburn Cemetery, Cambridge, MA

Little, Francis: son of Dr. Moses and Elizabeth (Williams) Little, First Parish Burying Ground, Newbury, MA

Lovecraft, Howard Philips: author who wrote about the Old Burying Point, Swan Point Cemetery, Providence, RI

Mann, Mary Tyler (Peabody): lived in Grimshawe House, Sleepy Hollow Cemetery, Concord, MA

Mather, Rev. Cotton: brother of Nathaniel Mather, Copp's Hill Burying Ground, Boston, MA

Mathers, Rev. Increase: father of Nathaniel Mather, Copp's Hill Burying Ground, Boston, MA

Mumford, William: stone carver, Copp's Hill Burying Ground, Boston, MA

Peabody, Dr. Nathaniel: owner of the Grimshawe House, West Creek Cemetery, West Creek, NJ

Peabody, Elizabeth (Palmer): wife of Dr. Nathaniel Peabody, Howard Street Cemetery, Salem, MA

Peabody, Elizabeth Palmer: lived in Grimshawe House, Sleepy Hollow Cemetery, Concord, MA

Pickman, Col. Benjamin Sr: father of Col. Benjamin Pickman Jr, Broad Street Cemetery, Salem, MA

Pickman, Love Rawlins: daughter of Benjamin Jr and Mary (Toppan) Pickman, Harmony Grove Cemetery, Salem, MA

Pickman, Dr. Thomas: son of Benjamin Jr and Mary (Toppan) Pickman, Harmony Grove Cemetery, Salem, MA

Putnam, Ann Jr: daughter of Thomas and Ann Putnam, accuser in the Witch Hysteria. Putnam Cemetery, Danvers, MA. Unmarked grave.

Richardson, Eunice (Putnam): wife of Nathaniel Richardson, Harmony Grove Cemetery, Salem, MA

Richardson, Jesse: son of Nathaniel Richardson, Howard Street Cemetery, Salem, MA

Sewall, Rev. Samuel: friend to Simon Bradstreet and Oyer and Terminer Justice, Granary Burying Ground, Boston, MA

Trask, Daniel: husband of Louisa M. Trask, Howard Street Cemetery, Salem, MA

West, Capt. Nathaniel: estranged husband of Elizabeth (Derby) West, Broad Street Cemetery, Salem, MA

***

Gardner Hill Cemetery: Adjacent to the Harmony Grove Cemetery, the ancestors of Jonathan Gardner Jr are interred there. However, the existing tombstones were moved to Harmony Grove Cemetery.

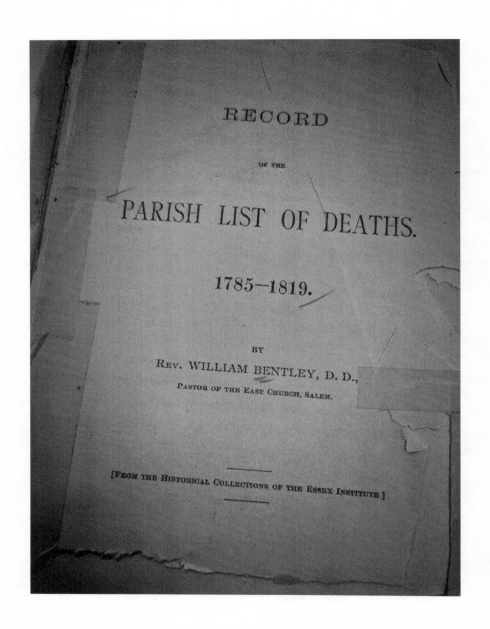

One of Many Sources for the Burial Index:
Reverend William Bentley's diary entries have been
invaluable in the confirmation of interments

Burial Index of The Salem Old Burying Point Cemetery

Compiled By Lara Fury for The Friends of the Downtown Salem Historic Cemeteries, April 2021, with Assistance from Daniel Fury and Elizabeth DuPré

For Muta, and all the unnamed children, because everyone deserves to be remembered.

This Index was made as a listing of all known burials in the Old Burying Point/Charter Street Cemetery. It was a combination of visual and Massachusetts Vital and Grave Records, cross referenced with the diaries of Reverend William Bentley of Salem's East Church and Reverend Samuel Sewall, the inscription records of David Pulsifer, Derby Perley, William Carlson, John Robert Cole, and Jeanne Stella, The Essex Antiquarian, Church Records, The Salem Press Historical and Genealogical Records, the City of Salem Death Records (1818-1907), Day book of David Boyce, undertaker, of Salem, Mass., 1804-1816, and on occasions of conflicting information, FamilySearch.org, and published personal family histories.

At the time of viewing, this list is as accurate as was possible with the given materials. This is by no means a complete list, as the cemetery was used for nearly 60 years before the records we have begin, and the human sources are fallible. In the case of discrepancies from stone to Vital Records, both will be listed, and the Vital Records are more likely accurate for genealogical purposes, though are not infallible. The list will favor Vital Records and stone carvings over family history whenever possible. Any stones with unreadable dates for which Vital Records or Grave Records could be found have been filled into the stone section.

If and when any updates are made, they will be available at:
www.SalemCemeteries.org

To Use This Index:

Names are alphabetical - Identical names are ordered chronologically by birthdate, or by maiden name if one exists

Unreadable - Does not necessarily mean that the entire stone is unreadable, but that the dates are unreadable

Information in Brackets [_] - Genealogical Records
Information in Parentheses (_) - Stone Inscriptions and Maiden Names

b. - Birth
d. - Death
bapt. - Baptized
bur. - Buried
obit. - Obituary or Death
CR - Church Record
FS - Only Footstone
NS - No Stone - Unmarked graves, lost stones, completely unreadable stones, moved bodies, or reused graves

Bold Names - Have an entry or mention in this book and will have a reference page number listed

Abbott, Mary [b. abt. 1691] (b. abt. 1693 d. October 12, 1709)

Adams, Joseph (b. abt. 1784 d. June 21, 1785)

Adams, Mary (Hilliard) [bapt. June 3, 1764] (d. June 25, 1785)

Adams, Nathan [b. abt. 1784 d. February 15, 1840] NS

Allen, Child [b. December 25, 1839 d. December 25, 1839] NS

Allen, Anna [b. abt. 1772 d. March 6, 1826] NS

Allen, Betsey [b. abt. 1788 d. September 27, 1825] (Allen Tomb) **78**

Allen, Edward [b. abt. 1737 d. July 27, 1803] (Allen Tomb) **77**

Allen, Henry [b. abt.1790 d. October 15, 1818] (Allen Tomb) **78**

Allen, Joseph (b. abt. [1643]1651 d. April 19, [1710]1718)

Allen, Margaret (Lockhart) [b. abt. 1754 d. August 13, 1808] (Allen Tomb) **78**

Allen, Mary (b. abt. 1660 d. March 10, 1703/4)

Allen, Mary (Hunt) [b. abt. 1775 d. August 26, 1842] (Moved to Harmony Grove) **79**

Allen, Mary (Saul) [bap. April 26, 1801] (d. [September 7] July 31, 1821)

Allen, William [b. abt. 1767 d. January 20, 1853] (Moved to Harmony Grove) **79**

Anderson, Deborah (Fairfield Clark) [b. abt. 1760 d. March 23, 1841] NS

Anderson, Elizabeth [Eliza] (b. May 12, 1801 d. November 27, 1801)

Andrew, Abigail [b. February 7, 1734/5] (d. February [16]25, 1734/5)

Andrew, Elizabeth (b. abt. 1685 d. January 3, 1688)

Andrew, Jonathan [b. November 23, 1745] (d. May 16, 1781) **212**

Andrew [Andrews], Jonathan [b. April 26, 1773] (d. April 18, 1844)

Andrew, Joseph [b. September 18, 1657] (d. July 28, 1732)

Andrew, Joseph [b. February 7, 1734/5] (d. February [24]16, 1734/5)

Andrew, Mary (Gardner) [b. March 19, 1739] (d. January [19]17, 1820) **212**

Andrew, Mary (Higginson) [b. October 14, 1708] (d. October 3, 1747)

Andrew, Nathaniel [b. August 10, 1705] (d. February 4, 1762)

Andrew, Nathaniel [b. June 11, 1731] (d. March 20, 1731/2)

Andrew, Nathaniel [b. December 2, 1777] (d. October [21]22, 1795)

Andrews, Child [b. ? bur. August 2, 1808] (Forrester Tomb)

Andrews, Child [b. ? bur. November 4, 1809] NS **216**

Andrews, Catharine [b. October 21, 1772 d. July 5, 1797] FS **215**

Andrews, Catharine [b. abt. 1808 d. July, 30, 1836] NS **214**

Andrews, Elizabeth (Lebeter) [b. abt. 1782/3 d. March 12, 1851] NS **214**

Andrews, Mary (Glover) [bapt. June 17, 1739 d. July 10, 1821] NS

Andrews, Nehemiah [b. February 7, 1753 d. February 10, 1800] NS **214**

Andrews, Sarah Upton [b. abt. 1838 d. April 29, 1840] NS

Appleton, Anna (Bowditch) [b. April 12, 1772] (d. June 4, 1795)

Appleton, Tamesin [Tempsin] (b. abt. 1769 d. January 27, 1850)

Appleton, William [b. April 24, 1793] (d. September 1, 1795)

Appleton, William [bapt. June 30, 1765] (d. September 23, 1822)

Archer, Abigail (Mancy) [b. abt. 1671 d. October 8, 1738] NS

Archer, Edward Jr [bapt. May 22, 1803 d. July 9[13, CR], 1826] NS

Archer, Hannah (Cook) (b. abt. 1714 d. May 21, 1767) **177**

Archer, John [bapt. March 31, 1734 d. September 20, 1819] NS

Archer, Jonathan (b. abt. 1671 d. July 16, 1746)

Archer, Jonathan [b. October 13, 1746] (d. June 1, 1800)

Archer, Judith [bapt. July 3, 1796] (d. March [13]14, 1801)

Archer, Mary [b. abt. 1731 d. April 1, 1809] NS (Dates Likely Incorrect) **225**

Archer, Mary (Beckford) (b. abt. 1777 d. October 25, 1800)
Archer, Mary (Pain) [b. abt. 1731 bur. Apr 4, 1809] NS (Also on Stone in Broad Street) **225**
Archer, Mehetable [Mehitabel] (Kimball) [b. May 6, 1749] (d. December 1, 1791)
Archer, Nathaniel [b. April 17, 1710] (d. June 10, 1772) **177**
Archer, Samuel [bapt. April 4, 1742 d. October 19, 1825] NS
Ashby, [unknown] [d. January 22, 1729] NS
Ashby, Mrs. [b. abt. 1777 d. August 26, 1821] NS
Ashby, David [bapt. April 17, 1757 d. January 18, 1822] NS
Ashby, Elizabeth [bapt. June 21, 1761 d. May 25, 1823] NS
Ashby, Jonathan (b. abt. 1746 d. November 15, 1797)
Ashby, Polly (Field) (b. abt. 1758 d. April 3, 1789)
Ashby, Robert Read [b. abt. August, 1787 d. February 9, 1828] NS
Ashby, Sally [b. March 13, 1793] (d. October 19, 1796)
Ashby, Sally (Fitch) (b. abt. 1773 d. September 24, 1807)
Ashton, Margaret (Ellison) [b. April 14, 1776 d. July 6, 1819] NS
Aylward, Elizabeth [b. abt. 1769 d. October 10, 1842] NS
Babbidge, Son [b. April 12, 1824 d. April 13, 1824] NS
Babbage, Mary [Polly] (Bateman) [b. August 19, 1786 d. November 7, 1821] NS
Babbage, Mary L. [b. abt. 1798 d. October 26, 1821] NS
Babbidge, Lydia [b. September 7, 1733] (d. July 9, 1800) **88**
Babbidge, Nancy [b. abt. January, 1817 d. October 11, 1818] NS
Babbidge, Susannah (Beckett) [b. April 14, 1714] (d. June [3]2, 1804) **88**
Bancroft, Ebenezer [b. abt. 1787 d. August 5, 1844] NS
Barlow, Henry [b. abt. 1809 d. December 28, 1849] (Tomb)
Barnard, Elizabeth (Williams) [b. January 1, 1707] (d. November 9, 1753) **175**
Barnard, Rachel (Lindall) [b. December 3, 1686] (d. August 30, 1743) **175**
Barnard, Samuel [b. December 1, 1684] (d. November 21, 1762) **175**
Barnes, Elizabeth [b. abt. 1756 d. October 24, 1828] NS
Barr, Priscilla (Symonds) [b. July 9, 1732] (d. September 28, 1794)
Barr, Robert Franklin Chase [b. February 4, 1821 d. February 10, 1826] NS
Barras, Peter [b. abt. 1750 d. February 4, 1827] NS
Bartholemew, Elizabeth (Scudder) [b. abt. 1622 d. September 1, 1682] NS **219**
Bartholemew, Henry [b. abt. 1606/7 d. November 22, 1692] NS **219**
Bartlett, Elizabeth [b. abt. 1739 d. February 18, 1819] NS
Bartlett, Walter Price [bapt. December 11, 1743 d. May 15, 1824] (Bartlett Tomb) **99**
Barstow, Child [b. abt. July, 1824 d. September 8, 1825] NS
Barton, John [bapt. Dec 5, 1711 d. Dec 30, 1774] (Pickman/Toppan Tomb) **154**
Barton, Mary (Willoughby) [b. Sept. 1, 1678 d. Jan. 7, 1758] (Pickman/Toppan Tomb) **154**
Barton, Lydia (Roberts) (b. abt. 1651 d. May 13, 1713)
Barton, Thomas [Doctor] [b. Jul. 11, 1680 d. Apr. 28, 1751] (Pickman/Toppan Tomb) **154**
Barton, Zacheus [b. April 1, 1683] (d. October 14, 1707)
Bassett, Alice Hunt [b. abt. 1840 d. May 14, 1845] NS
Batter, Edmund [Edmond] [b. January 8, 1673] (d. November 2, 1756)
Batter, Martha (Pickman) [b. June 3, 1677] (d. June 1, 1713)
Beadle, Lemman [b. July 30, 1680] (d. November 17, [1717]1716)
Beadle, Ruth [b. April 17, 1693] (d. October 5, 1716)
Beckett, Elizabeth (Ingersoll) [b. abt. 1746 d. January 23, 1790] NS
Beckett, Hannah (Waters) (b. abt. 1778 d. January 23, 1855)

Beckett, John [b. abt. 1770 d. February 15, 1822] NS
Beckett, John [b. abt. 1813 d. July 24, 1818] NS
Beckett, Mary (b. abt. 1799 d. December 12, 1846)
Becket/Beckett, Mary [b. abt. 1729 d. February 3, 1826]
Beckett, Reitier [bapt. April 23, 1704] (d. June 17, 1734)
Beckett, William [b. abt. 1668 d. November 10, 1723] FS
Bedney, Lydia (Nichols) [b. abt. 1787 d. September 30, 1849] NS
Berley [Burley], Mary (Hunt) [b. May 10, 1790] (d. May 8, 1858) **195**
Berry, Mary (Ward) [b. abt. 1768 d. September 23, 1854] NS
Best, David [b. February 20, 1694/5 d. abt. May, 1730] FS
Bethell, Hannah (Manning) [bapt. January 2, 1715] (d. December 22, 1733)
Blanchard, Aaron [b. September 2, 1751] (d. July 30, 1799)
Bowditch, Charles Ingersoll [b. December 1, 1809] (d. February [22]21, 1820) **124**
Bowditch, Deborah Marsh [b. abt 1844 d. June 1, 1847] (Turner Tomb)
Bowditch, Ebenezer [b. April 26, 1704] (d. February 2, 1768)
Bowditch, Ebenezer [b. September 28, 1729] (d. August 3, 1771)
Bowditch, Ebenezer [bapt. November 23, 1766] (d. July [17 or 24]23, 1830) **126**
Bowditch, Ebenezer [b. May 10, 1800] (d. August [21]22, 1825) **126**
Bowditch, Elizabeth [bapt. September 5, 1762 d. November 4, 1845] (Turner Tomb)
Bowditch, Elizabeth [b. August 13, 1807 d. March 2, 1895] (Turner Tomb) **202**
Bowditch, Elizabeth (Boardman) (b. abt. 1780 d. October 18, 1798) **123**
Bowditch, Elizabeth (Gilman) [b. November 30, 1732] (d. February [12]11, 1824)
Bowditch, Eunice [bapt. May 30, 1739] (d. June 11, 1765)
Bowditch, Eunice [bapt. June 15, 1760 d. December 3, 1841] (Turner Tomb)
Bowditch, George [b. abt. 1856 d. March 26, 1857] (Turner Tomb) **202**
Bowditch, Habakkuk [Habaccuc] [b. January 5, 1737] (d. July 28, 1798) **126**
Bowditch, Joseph [b. August 21, 1700] (d. October 6, 1780)
Bowditch, Joseph [bapt. November 20, 1757] (d. April 29, 1800)
Bowditch, Joseph [b. May 11, 1776 d. August 28, 1824] (Unreadable)
Bowditch, Lois (Bowditch) [b. March 29, 1781 d. July 29, 1809] NS
Bowditch, Mary (b. abt. 1742 d. April 22, 1757)
Bowditch, Mary (Appleton) (b. abt. 1772 d. May [16]17, 1819) **126**
Bowditch, Mary (Gardner) [b. February 14, 1669/70 d. December 3, 1724] FS
Bowditch, Robert [b. abt. 1830 d. July 2, 1855] (Turner Tomb)
Bowditch, Sarah [bapt. January 23, 1736] (d. October 2, 1764)
Bowditch, Sarah (Bancroft) (b. abt. 1742 d. February 26, 1808)
Bowditch, Sarah (Gardner) [b. March 25, 1734] (d. December 8, 1797)
Bowditch, Stephen [b. abt. 1773 d. August 30, 1821] NS
Bowditch, Thomas (b. abt. 1734] d. July 29, 1808)
Bowditch, Thomas [bapt. November 27, 1791 d. February 16, 1841] (Turner Tomb)
Bowditch, Thomas [b. April 5, 1824 d. November 28, 1846] (Turner Tomb)
Bowditch, William [b. September, 1663] (d. May 28, 1728) **124**
Bowditch, William [bapt. January 18, 1713] (d. November 1, 1715)
Bowditch, William [bapt. February 12, 1727] (d. June 26, 1729)
Bowditch, William (b. abt. 1734 d. December 29, 1752)
Bowditch, William [b. December 31, 1809 d. May 15, 1896] (Turner Tomb) **202**
Bradstreet, Anne (Downing) [bapt. April 13, 1633 d. April 19, 1713] (Bradstreet Tomb) **164**
Bradstreet, Simon [bapt. March 18, 1604 d. March 27, 1697] (Bradstreet Tomb) **160**

Bray, Albert [bapt. December 31, 1807] (d. January 1, 1808)
Bray, Benjamin (b. abt. 1775 d. June [3]2, 1808)
Bray, Benjamin (b. abt. 1797 d. January [19 or 20]18, [1799]1798)
Bray, Daniel (b. abt. 1731 d. June 24, 1798)
Bray, John [b. abt. 1822 d. February or December 11, 1829] NS
Bray, Mary (Ingalls) [January 28, 1737] (d. September 28, 1805) **214**
Bray, William [b. abt. 1825 d. February 15, 1839] NS
Briggs, Priscilla (Ward) [bapt. August 24, 1777 d. September, 12, 1829]NS
Brimblecomm, Elizabeth [b. abt. 1765 d. February 8, 1840] NS
Brimblecomm, Philip H. [b. abt. September, 1841 d. July 22, 1842] NS
Brimblecomm, Sarah Elizabeth [b. abt. 1830 d. June 5, 1844] NS
Brimblecomm, Susan [b. abt. 1837 d. March 14, 1840] NS
Brookhouse, Mary (Webb) [b. abt. 1759 d. March 7, 1824] NS
Brookhouse, Robert [bapt. June 20, 1719 d. July 8, 1772] FS
Brooks, Infant Daughter (b. abt. January, 1840 d. February [18]17, 1840) **84**
Brooks, Lucy (Brooks) (b. abt. 1806 d. January 23, 1840) **84**
Brown, Daughter [b. ? d. August 17, 1825] NS
Brown, Abigail (Archer) [b. August 17, 1711] (d. June 21, 1781)
Brown, Benjamin [b. abt. 1648, d. December 7, 1708] (Browne Tomb) **119**
Brown, David [bapt. December 3, 1809] (d. November 26, 1810)
Browne, Elizabeth [b. abt. 1763 d. January 21, 1843] (Browne Tomb)
Brown, Eunice [b. abt. 1740 d. March 27, 1824] NS
Brown, James [b. abt. 1759 d. May 13, 1827] NS
Brown [Browne], John [bapt. June 26, 1780] (d. December 23, 1783)
Brown, Joseph [b. abt. 1763 d. December 16, 1822] NS
Brown, Margaret (Skerry) [b. March 22, 1749 d. August 11 or 13, 1818] NS
Brown, Mary [b. abt. May, 1740 d. February 13, 1818] NS
Brown, Mary (Mansfield) (b. abt. 1780 d. November 3, 1806)
Brown, Mary [b. abt. 1793 d. July 4, 1823] NS
Brown, Mary (Ashby) [b. abt. 1788 d. December 18 or 21, 1838] (Unreadable)
Brown, Nathan [b. abt. 1742, d. August 7, 1787] NS
Brown, Rachel [b. abt. 1751 d. August 7, 1828] NS
Brown, Rebecca (White) [bapt. May 20, 1753 d. May 13, 1823] NS
Brown, Sarah (b. October 4, 1770 d. January, 20, 1854)
Brown, Sarah (Smith) [b. abt. 1614 d. February 10 or 19 1668] (Browne Tomb) **118**
Brown, Thomas (b. abt. 1747 d. June 30, 1793)
Brown, Timothy [b. October 23, 1806] (d. February 20, 1807)
Brown, Timothy (b. abt. 1778 d. March 11, 1808)
Brown, William [b. May or Mar 1, 1608] (d. January 20, 1688) (Browne Tomb) **118**
Buffington, Daniel (b. abt. 1827 d. February 23, 1832)
Buffington [Gould], Elizabeth (b. abt. March, 1827 d. July 1, 1827)
Buffington, Elizabeth (Gould) (b. abt. 1811 d. April 15, 1827)
Burbank, Eunice (Perkins) [b. March 22, 1782 d. October 5, 1865] (Forrester Tomb)
Burchmore, Mary [b. abt. 1760 d. November 13, 1821] NS
Burchmore, Zechariah [Zachariah] Sr [b. abt. 1743 bur. May 16, 1807] NS
Burnham, Elizabeth (McIntire) [b. abt. 1774 d. July 5, 1850] NS
Burns, John [b. abt. 1799 d. December 12, 1829] NS
Burrill, Anna (Breed) [b. September 17, 1746] (d. September [4]14, 1792)

Burrill, Elizabeth (Hammett) (b. abt. 1754 d. March 15, 1800)

Burrill, Ezra [b. May 10, 1746] (d. June 15, 1796)

Butman [Butnam], Elisabeth (Dewing) (b. abt. 1774 d. March 22, 1798)

Buttolph, John [bapt. September 11, 1664] (d. May 10, 1713)

Buttolph, William [bapt. September 7, 1695] (d. September 23, 1720)

Byard, Nancy (Gowan) [b. abt. 1763 d. May 1, 1849] NS

Byrne, Clifford [b. July 31, 1772 d. December 9, 1826] NS

Byrne, Margaret (Whitefoot) [b. abt. 1740 d. January 28, 1823] NS

Byrne, Mehetable [b. August 7, 1799 d. June 4, 1820] NS

Cabot, John [Doctor] [b. October 26, 1705] (d. June 3, 1749)

Cabot, William [b. October 6, 1749] (d. December [9]10, 1750)

Camball [Campbell], John (b. abt. 1797 d. April [6]4, 1840) **46**

Caldwell, Ebenezer [b. abt. 1767 d. September 28, 1823] NS

Carlin, Elizabeth (Daley) [b. abt. 1791 d. May 3, 1845] NS

Carlisle, Daughter [b. abt. April, 1720 d. August 26, 1821] NS

Carlton [Carleton], John [b. abt. November, 1811] (d. July 18, 1817)

Carnes, Jonathan [bapt. May 29, 1757 d. December 8, 1827] (Gedney Tomb) **97**

Carnes, Rebecca (Vans) [bapt. February 5, 1764 d. November 9, 1846] (Gedney Tomb) **97**

Carroll, May (b. abt 1723 d. November 18, 1728)

Carwick, Sarah [b. abt. 1740 d. September 24, 1821] NS

Cash, William (b. abt. 1625 d. abt. 1690) (Stone added in 2008) **195**

Caswell, John [b. abt. 1790 d. March 1, 1819] NS

Chandler, Elizabeth (Dean) (b. abt. 1781 d. June 5, 1837)

Chatwell [Shatswell], Nicholas (b. abt. 1644 d. October 30, 1700)

Chatwell [Shatswell], Sarah (Young) (b. abt. 1638 d. March 14, 1718)

Cheever, Elizabeth [b. July 5, 1849 d. July 6, 1849] NS

Cheever, William (b. abt. 1752 d. November 29, 1786)

Chipman, Son [b. abt. April, 1820 d. October 16, 1821] NS

Chipman, Elizabeth [b. abt. 1760 d. September 19, 1844] NS

Chipman, Elizabeth [b. abt. 1789 d. April 11, 1860] NS

Chipman, John [b. abt. 1745 d. December 26, 1819] NS

Chipman, John [b. abt. 1784 d. March 8, 1856] NS

Chipman, Mary [b. April 12, 1769 d. October 13, 1852] NS

Chipman, Mary (Carr) (b. abt. 1717 d. June 29, 1801)

Chipman, Mary Ann [b. October 3, 1834 d. February 9, 1839] NS

Chipman, Susan Poor [bapt. May 8, 1825 d. April 15, 1850] NS

Chipman, William [b. abt. 1843 d. January 5, 1844] NS

Church, Hannah [b. abt. 1815 d. February 11, 1821] NS

Clark, Francis [b. March 28, 1792 d. December 17, 1843] (Gedney Tomb)

Clark, Martha [b. abt. 1783 d. April 10, 1843] (Gedney Tomb)

Clemons, John [b. abt. 1814 d. August 29, 1818] NS

Cleveland [Cleavland], Margaret (Jeffrey) [b. Sept. 10, 1745] (d. Nov. 27, 1784)

Cleveland [Cleavland], Stephen [b. October 8, 1741] (d. October [9]8, 1801) **149**

Clough, Mary [b. abt. 1770 d. October 22, 1852] (Bradstreet Tomb)

Cloutman [Clautman], Catherine [b. abt. 1851 d. November 2, 1852] NS

Cloutman, Elizabeth [b. abt. 1759 d. August 2, 1818 bur. Aug 4, 1818] NS

Cloutman, Hannah (b. abt. 1716 d. February 28, 174[3]5)

Cloutman, Priscilla [b. abt. 1764 d. January 24, 1840] NS

Cole, Alexander (b. abt. 1653 d. June 27, 1687)
Comfort, Samuel [b. abt. 1666] (d. March 25, 1704) **44**
Conan [Conant], Christian (More) (b. abt. 1652 d. May 30, 1680) **140, 143**
Conkling, James (b. abt. 1804] (d. June 30, 1807)
Converse, Mary [b. abt. 1741 d. January 8, 1822] NS
Conway, James [b. abt. April, 1824 d. September 21, 1825] NS
Cook, Caleb (b. abt. 1771 d. June 4, 1837)
Cook, Caleb (b. abt. 1798 d. March 19, 1837)
Cook, Elizabeth (b. abt. 1748 d. August 15, 1799)
Cook, Elizabeth [b. abt. 1774 d. September 11, 1839] NS
Cook, James [b. abt. 1785 d. September 24, 1822] NS
Cook, Joseph [b. abt. November, 1825 d. March 26, 1826] NS
Cook, Rebecca (Brown) (b. abt. 1747 d. May [13 or 20]11, 1824)
Cook [Cooke], William [b. May 20, 1753] (d. September 27, 1803)
Coombs, Frederick [b. August 25, 1771 d. October 30, 1824] NS
Corry [Corey], Mary (Bright) (b. abt. 1621 d. August 27, 1684) **192**
Corwin [Curwin], Lydia (Gedney) [b. April 17, 1670 d. Dec. 23, 1700] (Gedney Tomb) **96**
Cox, Mary (Swacy) [b. abt. 1674 d. November ?, 1737] NS
Cromall [Cromwell], Mary (Lemon) (b. abt. 1611 d. November 14, 1683) **29, 189**
Cromwell, Doraty [Dorithy] (b. abt. 1606 d. September [28]27, 1673) **188**
Cromwell, John (b. abt. 1635 d. September 30, 1700) **189**
Cromwell, Phillip (b. abt. 1610 d. March 30, 1693) **188**
Crosby, Peggy [Peggey] (Smith) [bapt. June 5, 1757] (d. September 25, 1795)
Crowninshield, Anstiss (Williams) [b. abt. 1672 d. September 10, 1744] NS (Brackets) **220**
Crowninshield, Clifford (b. abt. 1761 d. June 3, 1809)
Crowininshield, John [b. January 19, 1696/7] (d. May 25, 1761) (Brackets) **220**
Crowininshield, John (b. abt. 1699 d. June 24, 1766)
Crowininshield, John (b. abt. 1728 d. June 1, 1777)
Crowninshield, Mary (Ives) (b. abt. 1728 d. June [5]4, 1794)
Crowninshield, Sarah [b. abt. 1764, d. abt. 1779] (Moved to Howard Street) **62**
Crowninshield, Sarah (Hathorne) [bapt. May 22, 1763] (d. January [18]14, 1829) **135**
Cumbs, Elizabeth (b. abt. 1767] d. April 20, 1773)
Cumbs, Elizabeth (Mansfield) [b. March 12, 1775] (d. January 24, 1800)
Cumbs, Susannah [b. December 25, 1810] (d. January 1, 1813)
Curtis, Daniel (b. abt. 1732 d. March 6, 1772)
Curwen [Curwin], Hannah [b. abt. 1815 d. October 5, 1827] NS
Dabney, John [b. abt. 1745 d. October 11, 1819] NS
Dame, Rosana (Cole) [b. abt. 1792 d. October 15, 1850] NS
Daniels, Lydia [b. abt. 1760 d. June 12, 1825] NS
Daniel [Daniels], Steven [Stephen] (b. abt. 1633 d. February 14, 1686/7)
Daniels, Stephen [b. December 2, 1667 d. March 12, 1741] NS
Daniels, Stephen [b. abt. 1717 bur. March 19, 1805] NS
Daniels, Sarah [b. abt. 1713 bur. October 12, 1805] NS
Day, Thomas [b. abt. 1784 d. February 22, 1818] NS
Dean, Benjamin [b. March 3, 1747] (d. December [8]10, 1826)
Dean, Edward [bapt. February 16, 1723] (d. September 14, [1743]1716) (Stone Incorrect)
Dean, Elizabeth [b. abt. 1747 d. January 13, 1818] NS
Dean, Hannah (Ruck) (b. abt. 1665 d. September 7, 1718)

Dean, Lydia (Waters) [b. August 2, 1763] (d. January 28, 1812)
Dean, Martha (Gillingham) [b. January 13, 1699] (d. December 24, 1729)
Dean, Mary (Daniels) [b. July 18, 1670] (d. May 7, 1701)
Dean, Susannah (b. abt. 1774 d. February 8, 1835)
Dean, Susannah (Collins) (b. abt. 1739 d. January 13, 1818)
Dean, Thomas (b. abt. 1663 d. February 10, 1705/6)
Dean, Thomas (b. abt. 1698 d. August 24, 1759)
Dean, Thomas (b. abt. 1723 d. July 8, 1802)
Deland, Horace [b. April 14, 1818 d. June 7, 1826] NS
Densmore, George Augustus [b. abt. January, 1843 d. September 3, 1843] NS
Densmore, Sarah E. [b. abt. 1823 d. December 25, 1842] NS
Derby, Caroline [b. December 24, 1805 d. August 27, 1878] (Derby Tomb) **62**
Derby, Elias Hasket Sr [b. August 16, 1739 d. September 8, 1799] (Derby Tomb) **58**
Derby, Elizabeth (Crowninshield) [b. abt. 1735 d. April 19, 1799] (Derby Tomb) **59**
Derby, Ezekiel Hersey [b. abt. 1772 d. October 31, 1852] (Derby Tomb) **61**
Derby, Ezekiel Hersey Jr [bapt. Sept. 21, 1800 d. Nov. 16, 1839] (Derby Tomb) **62**
Derby, Hannah (Fitch) [b. May 5, 1777 d. February 7, 1862] (Derby Tomb) **61**
Derby, John [b. November 14, 1792 d. July 8, 1867] (Derby Tomb) **62**
Derby, Mary (Hodges) [b. December 21, 1713 d. February 27, 1770] (Derby Tomb) **58**
Derby, Nathaniel [b. February 25 1809 d. July 9, 1830] NS
Derby, Richard [b. September 16, 1712 d. November 11, 1783] (Derby Tomb) **57**
Derby, Samuel G [b. abt. 1767 d. January 17, 1843] (Derby Tomb)
Dismore [Dinsmore], Judith (b. abt. 1691/2 d. January 2, 1716/7)
Dodge, George [b. April 10, 1726] (d. [January 18], 1808) FS or Recut **81**
Dodge, John [bapt. March, 1784 d. June 9, 1820] NS
Dodge, Lydia (Herrick) [b. March 18, 1726] (d. July 10, 1798) **81**
Dolbeare, Barnard [b. September 18, 1689] (d. February 27, 1689/90)
Driver, Elizabeth [b. April 28, 1688] (d. [September] August 25, 1690)
Driver, Elizabeth (Lawrence) [bapt. February 13, 1743 d. November 5, 1823] NS
Driver, Helena [b. abt. December, 1825 d. February 27, 1826] NS
Driver, Stephen [bapt December 20, 1741 d. Oct. 27, 1830] NS
Dutch, Barbara [bapt. December 2, 1677 d. April 10, 1678] NS (Brackets) **143**
Dyer, Elenor [b. abt. 1759 d. January 27, 1839] NS
Edwards, John [b. abt. 1768 d. December 24, 1845] (Fisk Tomb)
Edwards, Margaret (Brown) [bapt. August 7, 1774 bur. August 24, 1807] NS
Elkins, John [bapt. February 9, 1734] (d. November 29, 1736)
Elkins, Preserved (Mason) [b. abt. 1763 d. November 15, 1840] (Mason Tomb)
Elkins, Thomas [b. August 1738] (d. March 17, 1764)
Elvins, Samuel [bapt. November 2, 1718] (d. May 5, 1723)
Elvins, Sarah (Beadle) [b. September 24, 1690] (d. July 9, 1743)
Emerson, John (b. abt. 1653 d. February 24, 1711/12) **88**
Eveleth, Anna [b. abt. 1789 d. September 7, 1829] NS
Eveleth, Harriet [bapt. January 19, 1794 d. October 16, 1812] NS
Eveleth, Joseph [b. abt. 1759 d. February 3, 1847] NS
Eveleth, Mary (b. abt. 1767 d. November 17, 1798)
Eveleth, Mary [bapt. November, 1787 d. June 26, 1804] NS
Felt, Daughter [b. abt. April, 1824 d. October 1, 1824] NS
Felt, Abigail (Knapp) [b. July 1, 1707] (d. November 12, 1748)

Felt, Benjamin [bapt. July 22, 1705] (d. March 1, 1769)

Felt, Elisabeth (Ropes) (b. abt. 1711 d. December 8, 1789)

Felt, George (b. abt. 1657 d. February 24, 1729/30) **128**

Felt, Margaret (Byrne) [b. September 23, 1796 d. September 20, 1825] NS

Fessenden, Mary [b. abt. 1753 d. April 4, 1819] NS

Feveryeare, Mary (Grafton) [b. September 7, 1660] (d. November 19, 1705)

Field, Sarah [bapt. September 4, 1760] (d. September 22, 1803)

Fisk, [Infant] [b. abt. 1783 d. 1783] (Fisk Tomb)

Fisk, John [b. May 6, 1744, d. September [28]29, 1797] (Fisk Tomb) **66**

Fisk, Lydia [b. April 17, 1768 d. September 13, 1785] (Fisk Tomb) **66**

Fisk, Lydia (Phippen) [b. June 7, 1747 d. October 13, 1782] (Fisk Tomb) **66**

Fisk, Margaret [b. April 4, 1775 d. October 20, 1792] (Fisk Tomb) **66**

Fisk, Patty [b. abt. 1753 d. November 30, 1785] (Fisk Tomb) **67**

Fisk, Samuel [b. April 6, 1689 d. April 3, 1770] (Fisk Tomb) **65**

Fisk, Samuel [bapt. October 5, 1740 d. January 20, 1795] (Fisk Tomb)

Fisk, Sarah (Wendall) [b. abt. 1745 d. February 4, 1804] (Fisk Tomb) **67**

Flindar [Flinder], Richard (b. abt. 1638 d. October 19, 1707)

Fogharty, James [b. abt. 1786 d. February 13, 1818] NS

Forrester, Charles [b. abt. 1795 bur. April 13, 1816] (Forrester Tomb)

Forrester, Charles [b. January 14, 1819 d. February 7, 1864] (Forrester Tomb) **64**

Forrester, Charlotte (Story) [bapt. Oct. 19, 1788 d. Dec. 16, 1867] (Forrester Tomb) **64**

Forrester, Elizabeth [bapt. abt. May 19, 1783] (d. May 25 or 28, 1783 a. 5 Days)

Forrester, Elizabeth [b. August 14, 1820 d. May 12, 1890] (Forrester Tomb) **64**

Forrester, Henry Williams [b. January 23, 1829 d. April 3, 1830] (Forrester Tomb)

Forrester, Rachel [bapt. Dec. 28, 1778 bur. Nov. 24, 1814] (Forrester Tomb) **64**

Forrester, Rachel [b. February 6, 1817 d. April 8, 1891] (Forrester Tomb) **64**

Forrester, Rachel (Hathorne) [bapt. July 30, 1757 d. June 29, 1823] (Forrester Tomb) **63**

Forrester, Simon [b. abt. 1748 bur. July 6, 1817] (Forrester Tomb) **63**

Forrestor [Forrester], Elizabeth (b. May [19]23, 1783 d. May [25]28, 1783)

Foster, Mary (b. abt. 1713 d. March 14, 1751)

Fowlls, Zachary [b. August 2, 1668 or 1674 d. July 10, 1718] NS

Foy[e], William [b. abt. 1745 d. December 30, 1825] NS

Frye, Nabby [Knabby] (bapt. April 5, 1795 d. June 30, 1800)

Frye, Nabby [Abigail] (Gray) (b. abt. 1764 d. January 21, 1802)

Frye, Polly [bapt. June 22, 1792] (d. April 5, 1803)

Gardiner [Gardner], Elizabeth (Gardner) [b. Oct 10, 1705] (d. Apr [21 or 22]20, 1752) **212**

Gardiner [Gardner], Sarah (Bartholemew) [b. January 29, 1658] (d. September 5, 1682)

Gardner, Bartholomew [b. June 12, 1682] (d. December 20, 1684)

Gardner, Elizabeth [b. October 18, 1729] (d. May [5]6, 1818) **212**

Gardner, Hannah [b. February 23, 1742/3] (d. April 28, 1786)

Gardner [Gardiner], Jonathan Sr [b. February 23, 1697/8] (d. November 27, 1783) **211**

Gardner [Gardiner], Jonathan Jr [b. May 25, 1728] (d. March 2, 1791) **212**

Gardner, Jonathan III [bapt. March 16, 1755 d. September 27, 1821] NS **213**

Gardner, Jonathan IV [b. August 8, 1793] (d. December 17, 1795) **213**

Gardner, Lucia [Lucy] (Dodge) [b. June 16, 1768] (d. March 24, 1812) **214**

Gardner, Mary (Avery) (b. abt. 1697 d. April 20, 1755) **212**

Gardner, Sally [Sarah] (Fairfield) [b. January 4, 1766] (d. December 23, 1795) **213**

Gardner, Sarah (Putnam) [bapt. December 22, 1728] (d. November 10, 1791) **212**

Gathman, Lydia [b. July 15, 1713] (d. July 20, 1716) **183**
Gathman, Lydia [bapt. May 3, 1719] (d. August 13, 1719) **184**
Gathman, Rachel [b. February 27, 1715] (d. August 22, 1716) **184**
Gedney, Bartholomew [b. June 14, 1640 d. February 28, 1697] (Gedney Tomb) **95**
Gedney, Hannah (Clark) [b. November 11, 1643 d. January 6, 1696] (Gedney Tomb) **95**
Gedney, Hannah (Gardner) [b. April 16, 1671] (d. January 4, [1703/4]1703)
Gedney, John [b. abt. 1599 d. August 8, 1686] (Gedney Tomb) **95**
Gedney, Margaret [b. June 9, 1694] (d. December 14, 1718)
Gedney, Samuel [b. November 2, 1675 d. September 18, 1705] (Gedney Tomb) **97**
Gedney, Samuel [bapt. July 5, 1702 d. September 8, 1702] (Gedney Tomb) **97**
Gedney, Susanah [Susannah] [b. April 8, 1681] (d. December 17, 1712)
Gedney, William [b. May 28, 1668] (d. January 24, 1729/30) **127**
Gerrish, Benjamin [b. January 13, 1652] (d. April 24, 1713)
Getchel, Mary [Margaret] [b. abt. 1805 d. December 20, 1823] NS
Gibault, Sarah (Crowninshield) [b. April 30, 1730 d. October 8, 1793] NS
Gidney [Gedney], Eliezer [Eliazer] [b. March 15, 1642] (d. April 29, 1683)
Gladding, William [b. abt. 1789 d. August 20, 1819] NS
Glover, Benjamin [b. September 7, 1704] (d. May 10, 1754)
Glover, John [bapt. October 3, 1766] (d. July 29, 1758)
Glover, Mary [b. abt. 1739 d. January 21, 1825] NS
Glover, Mary [bapt. May 3, 1772] (d. February 4, 1776)
Glover, Mary [bapt. June 1, 1777] (d. September 18, 1784)
Glover, Priscilla [bapt. November 18, 1750] (d. July [7]21, 1791)
Glover, Priscilla [bapt. August 30, 1783 d. April 9, 1856] (Nathan Pierce Tomb) **188**
Glover, Susanah [Susannah] (Needham) [b. March 16, 1708] (d. December [16]10, 1761)
Glover, Susannah [bapt. December 5, 1773] (d. February 9, 1776)
Goodhue, Elizabeth [b. abt. 1745] (d. January [30]29, 1782)
Goodhue, Mercy (Gilbert) [b. abt. 1717] (d. May 22, 1772)
Goodhue, William [b. abt. 1747] (d. July 10, 1782)
Goodison, Mary [b. abt. 1794 d. October 4, 1819] NS
Gowers [Gowen], Susan [b. abt. 1755 d. February 10, 1829] NS
Grafton, Elizabeth [b. abt. 1687] (d. March 10, 1691)
Grafton, Jehodan [b. October 1, 1669] (d. December 5, 1707)
Grafton, John [b. February 28, 1639] (d. November 24, 1715)
Grafton, Joseph Sr [d. 1683]
Grafton, Joseph [b. August 17, 1658] (d. July 11, 1709)
Grafton, William (b. abt. 1695 d. June [1], 1697)
Grant, Sally [b. November 7, 1763] (d. September 16, 1789)
Gray, Child [b. ? bur. April 15, 1809] NS
Gray, Abigail [b. September 1, 1755 d. November 6, 1790] (Gray Tomb) **73**
Gray, Abraham [b. January 13, 1714 d. February 11, 1791] (Gray Tomb) **73**
Gray, Abraham [b. September 1, 1755 d. August 6, 1788] (Gray Tomb) **73**
Gray, Caroline [b. January 27, 1799] (d. December 18, 1838)
Gray, Elizabeth (Archer) [b. August 16, 1767] (d. August 17, 1814)
Gray, Francis [b. December 19, 1762 d. April 27, 1790] (Gray Tomb) **73**
Gray, Hannah [b. abt. 1763 d. September 14, 1790] (Gray Tomb) **73**
Gray, John [b. January 12, 1761] (d. December 9, 1838)
Gray, Lydia (Calley) [b. abt. 1722 d. November 27, 1788] (Gray Tomb) **73**

Gray, Mary (b. abt. 1807 d. April 15, 1836)
Gray, Mary (Holman) [b. March 11, 1768 d. October 2, 1844] NS
Gray, Mary (White) [bapt. abt. February, 1781 d. July 30, 1849] NS
Gray, Robert [b. abt. 1777 bur. November 17, 1807] NS
Gray, Sarah [b. October 25, 1784] (d. May [6]3, 1830)
Gray, William [b. ? bur. June 11, 1805] NS
Gray, William Henry [b abt. May, 1847 d. September 3, 1848] NS
Greeley, Elizabeth [b. abt. 1800 d. June 11, 1852] NS
Greeley, Mary (Porter) [b. abt. 1777 d. November 8, 1850] NS
Greely, Phillip [b. abt. 1804 d. February 5, 1830] NS
Green, Sarah [b. abt. 1755 d. September 12, 1822] NS
Grove, Mary (b. abt. 1610 d. October 14, 1683)
Hacker, Mehitable [Methitable] (Berry) (b. abt. 1767 d. October 13, 1813)
Haley, William [b. June 20, 1835 d. November 9, 1839 or February 9, 1840] NS
Hammond, Caroline [b. abt. 1824 d. June 13, 1840] NS
Haraden, Catherine [b. abt. 1808 d. September 12, 1821] NS
Hardey [Hardy], Joseph [b. September 13, 1658] (d. April [14]17, 1687)
Hardy, Martha [bapt. August 20, 1699] (d. December 23, 1707)
Hardy, Seeth [b. June 13, 1686] (d. December 21, [1712]1711)
Harraden, Mary [b. abt. 1761 d. December 29, 1846] NS
Harridan, Andrew [bapt. ? 15, 1790] (d. May 1, 1794)
Harris, Eleanor [d. November 18, 1837] (Bradstreet Tomb)
Harris [Horris], Sally [b. abt. 1799 d. February 20, 1827] NS **225**
Hart, Mary [b. abt. 1799] (d. February 15, 1800)
Hathorne, Benjamin [b. September 9, 1773 d. February 9, 1824] NS
Hathorne, Catherine (Peterson) [b. December 24, 1804 d. April 6, 1854] NS
Hathorne, Daniel [bapt. August 22, 1731] (d. April 18, 1796) **134**
Hathorne, Ebenezer [b. December 5, 1789] (d. December 5, 1858)
Hathorne, Elizabeth (Sanders) (b. abt. 1748 d. January 19, 1836)
Hathorne, Eunice [b. October 4, 1766] (d. May 10, 1827) **135**
Hathorne, John [b. September 4, 1641] (d. May 10, 1717) **131**
Hathorne, John (b. abt. 1722 d. February 6, 1750)
Hathorne, John [b. May 29, 1749 d. December 15, 1834] (Bradstreet Tomb) **168**
Hathorne, John Jr [b. July 16, 1775 d. January 21, 1829] NS
Hathorne, Joseph [b. abt. 1777 d. March 12, 1824] NS
Hathorne, Mary (Touzel) [b. abt. 1724] (d. June 14, 1805) **208**
Hathorne, Rachel (Phelps) [b. June 1, 1734] (d. April 16, 1813) **135**
Hathorne, Ruth [b. abt. 1778 d. July 21, 1847] (Forrester Tomb)
Hathorne, Susannah [b. abt. 1741 d. May 30, 1818] NS
Hathorne, William [b. February 20, 1715] (d. April 4, 1794)
Hawkins, Samuel [b. abt. 1743 d. May 23, 1828] NS
Haycock, Mary [b. abt. April, 1818 d. October 11, 1819] NS
Heard, Daniel [b. abt. 1814 d. October 4, 1818] NS
Hearsey, Henry Colman [b. abt. April, 1826 d. May 13, 1827] NS
Henderson, Mother of Benjamin [b. ? bur. September 30, 1805] NS
Henderson, Eunice (Tatum) [bapt. September 30, 1797 d. July 13, 1826] NS
Henderson, Margaret [b. abt. 1771 d. March 9, 1840] FS
Henderson, Sarah [b. abt. 1762 bur. April 4, 1811] NS

Herbeart [Herbert], Benjamin [bapt. August 21, 1709] (d. January [19]20, 1761)

Herbert, Elisabeth (Fowler) [b. May 26, 1717] (d. October 23, 1772)

Heroe, Abigail (b. abt. 1729 d. February 13, 1765)

Herrick, Lydia (Murray) [b. abt. 1738 d. August 19, 1820] NS

Herrick, Mary (Johnson) [b. abt. 1768 d. October 15, 1854] NS

Herrick, Peter [b. abt. 1769 d. January 28 [30], 1851] NS

Herrick, Sarah [bapt. April 8, 1787 d. November 28, 1849] (Unreadable)

Herron, Eliza [Elizabeth] (Daniels) [b. abt. 1793 d. June 6, 1821] NS **220**

Herron, Samuel [b. abt. 1776 d. July 25, 1821] NS **220**

Hersey, Mary Gardner. [b. abt. 1818 d. November 11, 1820] NS

Heussler [Heusler], Abigail (Russell) (b. abt. 1753 d. April 21, 1799) **144**

Heussler [Heusler], Elizabeth [bapt. January 10, 1790] (d. November 1, 1823) **144**

Heussler [Heusler], Elizabeth (Lunt) (b. abt. 1761 d. March [13]10, 1821) **145**

Heussler [Heusler], George (b. abt. 1751 d. April 3, 1817) **144**

Hicock, Daughter [b. abt. February, 1818 d. February 13, 1818] NS

Higginson, (daughter) (b. July 22, 1715 d. July [22]29, 1715) **216**

Higginson, (son) (b. July 22, 1715 d. July [22]29, 1715) **216**

Higginson, Francis (b. November 29, 1705 d. November 29, 1705) **216**

Higginson, Hannah (Gardner) [b. April 4, 1676] (d. June 24, 1713) **216**

Higginson, Henry [b. September 23, 1707] (d. December 1, [1708/9]) (Unreadable) **216**

Higginson, John [Reverend] [bapt. Aug. 6, 1616 d. Dec. 9, 1708] (Bradstreet Tomb) **162**

Higginson, John (Jr) III [b. August 20, 1679] (d. April 26, 1718) **216**

Higginson, Margaret [bapt. November 10, 1686] (d. [January]June 18, 1688)

Higginson, Mary (Blackman) (b. abt. 1637 d. March 9, [1713]1708/9) **165**

Higginson, Mehetabel [Methitable] [b. March 26, 1764] (d. July 19, 1846) **144**

Higginson, Sarah (Whitford) (b. abt. 1620 d. July 8, 1675) **99**

Higginson, Thomas [b. December 16, 1677] (d. September 18, 1678)

Hildreth, Lydia [b. June 23, 1820] (d. January 22, 1822)

Hildreth, Lydia (Luscomb) (b. abt. 1796 d. June [23]26, 1820)

Hill, [Stillborn Child] [d. January 13, 1840] NS

Hill, Bethia (b. abt. 1656 d. May 7, 1689)

Hill, Phippen [bapt. April 20, 1794] (d. October 25, 1794)

Hilliard, Margaret (Peele) [b. January 23, 1742] (d. May [7]4, 1826)

Hirst, John [bapt. August 17, 1687] (d. October 4, 1687)

Hodges, Gamaliell [Gamaliel] [b. October 13, 1716] (d. August 27, 1768)

Hodges, George [b. January 10, 1747 d. March 25, 1764] (Unreadable Stone)

Hodges, Hannah [b. January 6, 1780 d. October 9, 1792] NS

Hodges, John [b. July 8, 1787] (d. November 30, 1797)

Hodges, Joseph [b. June 10, 1757] (d. October [5]7, 1826)

Hodges, Mary (Manning) [b. July 27, 1725] (d. September 5, 1773)

Hodges, Priscilla (Webb) [bapt. March 4, 1719] (d. March 22, 1807)

Holliman, Elizabeth [b. abt. 1727 d. August ?, 1732]

Holliman, John [b. February 13, 1723] (d. July 1, 1732)

Holliman, Susannah (b. abt. 1720 or 1730 d. September 27, [1721]1731)

Holliman, Susannah (bapt. May 12, 1728 d. November 4, 1729)

Holliman, Thomas [bapt. January 17, 1725] (d. July 17, 1725)

Hollingworth, Elianor [Eleanor] (b. abt. 1630 d. November 22, 1689) **205**

Hollingworth, William (b. abt. 1655 d. November 7, 1688) **205, 206**

Holt, Esther (Varnum) [b. May 2, 1747 d. February 12, 1822] NS
Hood, Elizabeth [bapt. June 10, 1769] (d. October 24, 1788)
Hood, Joseph [bapt. June 29, 1740] (d. November 2, 1769)
Hood, Sarah (b. abt. 1762 d. September 6, 1782)
Hood, Susannah [bapt. February 26, 1764] (d. November 3, 1791)
Horton, George [b. abt. 1821 d. August 7, 1847] (Browne Tomb)
Horton, Hannah (Browne) [bapt. June 12, 1791 d. March 19, 1867] (Browne Tomb)
Hosmer, Hannah [bapt. February 10, 1793] (d. November 26, 1795)
Hosmer, Hannah (Webb) [b. abt. 1769 d. December 12, 1852] (Unreadable)
Hosmer, Mary [bapt. August 3, 1795] (d. December 1, 1795)
Hosmer, Samuel [bapt. November 6, 1803] (d. April 26, 1844) **221**
Howard, Ezekiel [b. abt. 1798 d. February 13, 1818] (Orne Tomb) **71**
Howard, Rachel [b. abt. 1749 d. April 12, 1819] NS
Hunt, Alice (Dunckley) [b. Dec 22, 1781 d. January 22, 1863] NS
Hunt, Delia [b. January 30, 1771 d. June 1, 1834] (Unreadable Stone)
Hunt, Elizabeth [bapt. November 26, 1732] (d. December 31, 1787)
Hunt, Elizabeth [bapt. July 7, 1793 d. October 15, 1819] NS
Hunt, Eunice (Bowditch) [b. March 22, 1707] (d. August 30, 1764) **127**
Hunt, Hannah [b. September, 1711] (d. November 17, 1783)
Hunt, John (b. abt. 1777 d. November 23, [1847]1817) (Stone Incorrect)
Hunt, Joseph [b. June 28, 1789] (d. August 7, 1808)
Hunt, Lewis [b. March 23, 1746] (d. October [22]23, 1797) **127**
Hunt, Lewis [b. January 23, 1783 d. July or August 25, 1800] (Unreadable)
Hunt, Lewis [b. July 16, 1805 d. April 25, 1823] NS
Hunt, Mary (Bowditch) [bapt. June 15, 1760] (d. March [21]18, 1829) **127**
Hunt, Mary Bowditch [b. abt. 1816 d. September 24, 1819] NS
Hunt, Ruth [bapt. January 14, 1706] (d. October 19, 1792)
Hunt, Sarah (b. abt. 1747 d. October 6, 1811)
Hunt, Sarah (Orne) [b. June 7, 1750] (d. November 17, 1781) **127**
Hunt, William [b. August 5, 1701] (d. September 19, 1780) **127**
Hunt, William [bapt. December 18, 1743] (d. May 29, 1769)
Hutchinson, Mary [b. abt. 1744 d. January 18, 1819] NS
Ingalls, Collins [b. abt. 1771 d. April 3, 1821] FS
Ingalls, Mary (Heikman) [bapt. June 16, 1771 d. Oct 28, 1848] FS
Ingalls, Mary Trail [Traill] [bapt. September, 1831] (d. October 1, 1833)
Ingersoll, Elizabeth (Bray) [b. October 10, 1712] (d. August 5, 1768)
Ingersoll, Hannah (Bowditch) [bapt. Dec. 13, 1761 d. Dec. 17, 1825] (Unreadable)
Ingersoll, Hannah (Townsend) (b. abt. 1760 d. March 5, 1791)
Ingersoll, Horace Lorenzo Connelly [b. abt. 1808 d. Sept. 12, 1894] (Bradstreet Tomb) [Adopted] **170**
Ingersoll, John [bapt. January 24, 1796] (d. October [5]14, 1829)
Ingersoll, John [b. June, 1824 d. December 25, 1832] (Unreadable)
Ingersoll, Judith [bapt. November 17, 1793] (d. June 28, 1794)
Ingersoll, Phillip (b. abt. 1779 d. September 8, 1781)
Ingersoll, Samuel [b. August 6, 1658 d. November 19, 1696] NS
Ingersoll, Samuel [bapt. April 14, 1760 d. July 15, 1804] (Bradstreet Tomb) **168**
Ingersoll, Samuel [b. abt. 1775 d. July 21, 1797] (Bradstreet Tomb) **168**
Ingersoll, Susannah [b. abt. 1784 d. July 13, 1858] (Bradstreet Tomb) **169**

Ingersoll, Susannah (Hathorne) [bapt. May 21, 1749 d. Dec 6, 1811] (Bradstreet Tomb) **168**
Jackman, Joseph Henry [b. abt. 1826 d. October 3, 1829] NS
Jackman, Rufus [b. December 28, 1837 d. January 2, 1840] NS
Jackman, Rufus Putnam [bapt. November 1, 1840 d. December 25, 1843] NS
Jayne, Priscilla (b. December 29, 1788 d. July 18, 1810) **106**
Jeffards, Ruth [b. after 1796, d. October 6, 1798] NS
Jeffards, Ruth [b. after 1796, d. November 30, 1800] NS
Jeffards, Samuel [b. after 1796 d. November 11, 1798] NS
Jefferds [Jeffards], Samuel (b. abt. 1774 d. February [16]15, 1805)
Jeffrey, Elizabeth (Bowditch) (b. abt. 1735 d. October 22, 1797)
Jeffrey, Lydia (Pratt) [b. May 25, 1711 d. January 13, 1756] NS
Jeffry [Jeffrey], James (b. abt. 1706 d. February 13, 1755)
Jeffry [Jeffrey], John [bapt. September 22, 1739] (d. June 6, 1812)
Jeffry [Jeffrey], William [bapt. August 21, 1737] (d. July 8, 1772)
Jennison, Abigail [b. February 10, 1731] (d. August 19, 1732)
Johnson, Israel [b. abt. 1810 d. November 15, 1845] NS
Johnson, Israel Foster [b. abt. November, 1843 d. July 11, 1844] NS
Jones, Anne B. [b. abt. 1839 d. January 5, 1842] (Browne Tomb)
Jones, Charles B. [b. abt. 1837 d. January 1, 1842] (Browne Tomb)
Jones, Emily [b. abt. February, 1841 d. March 31, 1841] (Browne Tomb)
Jones, Mary [b. abt. 1791 d. May 24, 1827] NS
Jones, Peter [b. July 26, 1741] (d. January 19, 1772)
Kehew, Lydia (b. abt. 1812 d. November 27, 1814)
Kelley, Judith (Webb) [b. abt. 1763 d. April 5, 1821] NS
Kelly [Kelley], Abigail (Gowen) [bapt. February 25, 1759] (d. August 15, 1834)
Kenny [Kenney], Sarah (Ryne) [b. January 19, 1801] (d. November 25, 1827)
Keyzer, Hannah (Davis) (b. abt. 1647 d. January 20, 1723/4)
Kimball, George Washington [b. abt. 1805 d. April 9, 1824] NS
Kimball, Moses [b. abt. 1816 d. February 4, 1822] NS
Kimball, Turner [b. September 4, 1784] (d. September 4, 1801)
King, Katherine (Shafflin) (b. abt. 1626 d. December [17]15, 1718) **128**
Knapp, Mary (Jenkins) [b. abt. 1740 d. July 25, 1830] NS
Knowlton, Hannah (Fitz) [bapt. June 3, 1764] (d. September 28, 1787)
Ladd, Daniel [b. abt. 1810 d. January 22, 1840] NS
Lamb, Elizabeth (Mugford) [bapt. March 10, 1771 d. August 6, 1849] NS
Lamb, Simon [bapt. January 17, 1771 d. February 4, 1851] NS
Lambert, Joseph (b. abt. 1731 d. August 17, 1790) **88**
Lane, [Anna] Nancy (Bezoill) (b. abt. 1751 d. February 16, 1800)
Lang, Hannah (Simes) [b. August 27, 1707] (d. October [13]3, 1748)
Lang, Nathaniel (b. abt. June, 1774 d. October 6, 1774)
Lawrence, Henry [bapt. December 20, 1789] (d. August 13, 1798) **84**
Lawrence, Mary [bapt. May 5, 1788] (d. October 29, 1796) **84**
Lawrence, Moses (b. abt. 1807 d. October 7, 1826)
Lawrence, Polly (b. abt. 1782 d. October 14, 1785) **84**
Leach, Lydia [bapt. August 10, 1800 d. November 4, 1848] NS
Leach, Mary [bapt. April 8, 1809 d. October 26, 1818] NS
Leech, Samuel (b. abt. 1769 d. October 20, 1846)
Lefavour [Lafavour], Betsy [bapt. September 13, 1789] (d. May 20, 1795)

Lefavour [Lafavour], Polly (b. November 9, 1773 d. October 1, 1793)
Lefavour [Lafavour], Robert [b. October 25, 1751] (d. April 15, 1795)
Lefavour, Sarah [b. abt. 1780 d. September 8, 1820] NS
Lemon, Jane [b. February 6, 1800 d. November 26, 1802] NS
Lindall, (daughter) (b. June 23, 1720 d. June 23, 1720 - A Few Hours)
Lindall (son) (b. April 25, [1709]1714 d. April 25, [1709]1714) **50, 149**
Lindall (son) (b. abt. January 2, 1704 d. January 12, 1704)
Lindall, Bethia [b. November 17, 1717] (d. November [23]28, 1717)
Lindall, Caleb [b. February 5, 1684] (d. November 13, 1751)
Lindall, James [b. February 1, 1676] (d. May 10, 1753) **148**
Lindall, James [b. May 21, 1710] (d. August 19, 1754)
Lindall, Mary [b. December 14, 1705] (d. July 22, 1776)
Lindall, Mary (Veren) (b. abt. 1648 d. January [6]7, 1731/2) **148**
Lindall, Rachell (b. August 9, 1714 d. September [9]6, 1714) **50, 149**
Lindall, Sarah (Butler) (b. abt. 1694 d. June 27, 1754)
Lindall, Timothy [b. June 3, 1642] (d. January 6, 1698/9) **48, 148**
Lindall, Veren (b. May 14, 1711 d. April 29, 1712) **50, 149**
Little, Elizabeth (Williams) [b. April 25, 1774] (d. May [28]29, 1808) **175**
Little, Moses [Doctor] [b. July 7, 1766] (d. October 13, 1811) **38, 40, 175**
Logan, George [Doctor] [b. abt. 1751 d. July 16, 1793] (Mason Tomb) **75**
Lord, Mary (Moulton) [b. June 15, 1661 d. June 2, 1693] (Unreadable)
Lovering, Lydia (Herrick) [bapt. March 1, 1789 d. May 25, 1873] NS
Low, Emily [b. abt. 1838 d. March 19 or 20, 1840] NS
Lufkin, Charles H. [b. abt. November, 1842 d. January 24, 1843] NS
Lufkin, Mary [b. January 18, 1840 d. January 21, 1840] NS
Luscomb, Son [b. abt. 1817 d. November 2, 1821] NS
Luscomb, Andrew [b. abt. 1793 d. February 7, 1825] NS **220**
Luscomb, Bailey [b. abt. 1822 d. August 8, 1824] NS
Luscomb, Betsey [Elizabeth] [bapt. January 16, 1800 d. July 28, 1818] NS
Luscomb, Caroline (b. abt. 1837/8] d. October 1, [1838]1833)
Luscomb, Clara W. [b. April 10, 1849 d. October 7, 1850] NS
Luscomb, Henry [b. April 23, 1781] (d. August 18, 1837)
Luscomb, Methitable (Mansfield) [b. 1773 d. July 24, 1825] NS
Luscomb, Sarah [bapt. May 17, 1829] (d. May 7, 1835)
Luscomb, Susan [b. abt. 1761 d. March 1, 1824] NS
Luscomb, William [b. abt. 1747 d. April 12, 1827] NS
Luscomb, William [b. April 17, 1774 d. February 4, 1820] NS
Lynde, Benjamin [b. September 22, 1666 d. January 28, 1744/5] (Lynde Tomb) **114**
Lynde, Benjamin [bapt. October 5, 1700 d. October 5, 1781] (Lynde Tomb) **114**
Lynde, Hannah [b. August 17, 1735 d. December 21, 1792] (Lynde Tomb) **115**
Lynde, Mary (Browne) [b. abt. 1679 d. July 12, 1753] (Lynde Tomb) **114**
Lynde, Mary (Goodridge) [b. abt. 1709 d. May 31, 1790] (Lynde Tomb) **114**
Lynde, Primus [Primis] [b. after. 1722 bur. June 14, 1787] (Lynde Tomb) **115**
Lynde, William [b. October 27, 1714 d. May 10, 1752] (Lynde Tomb) **115**
Mackmilling, Wife of Mr. [b. ? bur. August 12, 1807] NS
Manning, Anstiss (Chipman) [b. abt. 1752, d. April 27, 1821] **83**
Manning, Hannah [b. abt. 1828 d. January 2, 1854] NS
Manning, Joseph Henry [b. abt. 1824 d. July 25, 1826] NS

Manning, Thomas (b. abt. 1778 d. April 1, 1798) **83**

Mansfield, Benbrim [bapt. March 19, 1758 d. December 12, 1839] NS

Mansfield, Elizabeth (Burchstead) [b. June 29, 1730] (d. June 20, 1785)

Mansfield, Hannah [bapt. June 5, 1774] (d. December 16, 1788)

Mansfield, Hannah (b. abt. 1744 d. September 3, 1789)

Mansfield, Hannah (Proctor) [b. October 22, 1730] (d. February 11, 1799)

Mansfield, Jonathan [b. April 29, 1717] (d. March 9, 1791)

Mansfield, Joseph [b. April 17, 1743] (d. February [20]16, 1820)

Mansfield, Joseph [bapt. June 29, 1777] (d. January [10]9, 1798)

Mansfield, Lydia [bapt. March 17, 1775] (d. September [13 or 30]31. 1794)

Mansfield, Matthew [b. November 22, 1726] (d. October 29, 1800)

Marston, John (b. abt. 1615 d. December 19, 1681)

Marston, Mary (Chichester) [b. abt. 1643 d. May 25, 1686] NS

Marston, Methetable (b. abt. 1759 d. December 20, 1784)

Mason, Abigail [b. abt. May, 1795 d. May 1, 1869] (Mason Tomb) **76**

Mason, Ann [b. February 10, 1805 d. August 14, 1869] (Mason Tomb) **76**

Mason, Thomas [b. July 9, 1723 d. July, 1801] (Mason Tomb) **75**

Masury, Anna (Browne) [b. June 22, 1770 d. May 17, 1850] (Browne Tomb)

Masury, Mary (Dike) (b. abt. 1722 d. May 17, 1748) **36**

Masury, Richard [b. abt. 1798 d. June 18, 1818] NS

Mather, Nathaniel [b. July 6, 1669] (d. October 17, 1688) **155**

McIntier, Sarah [b. abt. 1749 d. June 5, 1821] NS

McIntire [MacIntire], Elizabeth (Field) [bapt. Oct. 13, 1754] (d. Oct. 16, 1815) **109**

McIntire, Hannah (Hammonds) [b. June 2, 1780] (d. January 14, 1862) **110**

McIntire, Hannah [b. abt. 1813 d. February 8, 1850] NS

McIntire, Joseph [b. abt. 1748 d. June 10, 1825] NS

McIntire, Joseph [b. abt. 1779 d. September 21, 1852] NS

McIntire, Joseph (b. abt. 1771 d. April 17, 1788)

McIntire [MacIntire], Nancy [b. ? bur. September 5, 1813] NS

McIntire [MacIntire], Samuel [bapt. January 16, 1757] (d. February 6, 1811) **109**

McIntire, Samuel F [b. January 26. 1784 d. September 27, 1819] NS **110**

McMillan, Mary [b. abt. 1747 d. March 28, 1820] NS

McPherson, Christian [b. abt. October, 1791 d. September 16, 1793] NS

McPherson, John [b. abt. 1752 d. February 24, 1826] NS

Millet, Son [b. abt. July, 1820 d. December 14, 1821] NS

Millet, Carrie [b. December 28, 1787 d. October 17, 1863] NS

Millet, Elizabeth (Phillips) [b. abt. 1773 d. August 18, 1798] (Unreadable)

Millet, Harriet [bapt. May 30, 1807 d. September 4, 1825] NS

Millet, Jonathan [b. December 25, 1735] (d. June 4, 1795)

Millet, John [bapt. July 10, 1768 d. February 15, 1819 bur. February 16, 1819] NS

Millet, Margaret [b. abt. 1767 d. February 13, 1823] NS

Millet, Mary [b. April 10, 1836 d. June 4, 1836] NS

Millet, Nathan [b. May 17, 1772] (d. September 23, 1804)

Millet, Rebecca (Beckford) [b. October 2, 1770] (d. November 3, 1798)

Millet, Sally (b. abt. 1835 d. June 4, 1836)

Millet, Sally (Leonard) [b. March 11, 1785] (d. February [23]25, 1830)

Millet, Sarah (Mansfield) [b. May 21, 1736] (d. January [31]29, 1811)

Millet, William [b. June 2, 1781] (d. August 14, 1836)

Molloy [Malloy], Mary (Crowninshield) (b. abt. 1748 d. June 6, 1832)
More, Caleb [bapt. January 31, 1645] (d. January [10]4, [1678/9]1674) **140, 143**
More, Christian (Hunt) (b. abt. 1616 d. March 18, 1676) **ii, 140**
More, Jane (Crumpton) (b. abt. 1631 d. October, [5]8, 1686) **141**
More, Richard [bapt. November 13, 1614] (d. [1696]1692) **139**
More, Samuel [b. November 2 or 16, 1673 d. November 11 or 24, 1673] NS (Brackets) **143**
Morong, Martha [b. abt. 1742 d. March 8, 1827] NS
Morris, Thomas [b. abt. 1820 d. May 31, 1829] NS
Morse, William [b. abt. September, 1818 d. October 6, 1818] NS
Morshead [Marshead], Sarah (Lindall) [b. April 4, 1682] (d. December 25, 1750)
Moses, Mary (b. abt. 1780 d. August 2, 1838)
Moses, Samuel [b. abt. 1809 d July 15, 1825] NS
Mottey, John [bapt. May 24, 1772 d. February 27, 1860] NS
Mottey, Mehetable [Methitable] (b. abt. 1741. d. May 24, 1801)
Mould, Edward [Doctor] (b. abt. 1630 d. November [9]5, 1688)
Mould, Elizabeth [b. May 1678 d. February 6, 1680] (Unreadable) **26**
Mould, Elizabeth [b. April, 1683] (d. August 20, 1684) **26**
Mould, Thomas [b. April, 1680] (d. August 1, 1681) **26**
Mould, Willmet (b. abt. 1626 d. July 1684)
Muckford [Mugford], Ebenezer (b. abt. 1801 d. August 13, 1802)
Muckford [Mugford], George (b. March, 1799 d. September 2, 1801)
Mudge, Nancy (Bickford) [bapt. November 22, 1778] (d. January 9, 1801) **136**
Mugford, Mary (Peele) (b. abt. 1763 d. May 29, 1804)
Mundey [Munday], Granddaughter [bur. December 11, 1808 - Stillborn] NS
Mundy, Hannah [b. abt. 1742 d. September 1, 1818] NS
Munroe, Daughter [b. abt. April, 1824 d. October [26]31, 1825] NS
Neale, Judath (b. abt. 1683 d. February 20, 1697/8)
Neale, Judath (Croade) [b. abt. 1655 d. October 10, 1690] (Unreadable)
Neal, Sally [b. abt. July 1822 d. December 3, 1823] NS
Newhall, Ezra [b. May 1, 1733] (d. April [5]7, 1798) **88**
Newhall, Joseph [b. abt. 1768 d. December 14, 1827] NS
Newhall, Mary [b. abt. 1811 d. April 2, 1829] NS
Nichols, Hero [b. abt. 1778 d. August 5, 1822] NS
Nichols, Mary (Luscomb) [b. abt. 1787 d. February 9, 1828] NS
Nourse, Abigail (Cumbs) (b. abt. 1744 d. March 1, 1814)
Nourse, John (b. abt. 1762 d. January, 1790) **2**
Noyes, Edmund [b. abt. 1817 d. February 23, 1823] NS
Nutting, Elizabeth (Pickman) [b. January 22, 1714] (d. June 10, 1785) **207**
Nutting, John [b. January 7, 1694] (d. May 20, 1790) **207**
Nutting, John [b. abt. 1716 d. June 20, 1720] NS
Nutting, John [b. abt. 1718] (d. June 28, [1729]) (Unreadable) **207**
Nutting, Ruth (Gardner) [b. March 16, 1699] (d. November 22, 1736) **207**
Oliver, Child [b. October 14, 1818 d. October 14, 1818] NS
Oliver, William [b. abt. 1808 d. March 31, 1829] NS
Orne, Abigail (Ropes) [b. abt. 1761, d. May 24, 1813] (Orne Tomb) **70**
Orne, Alice (Palmer) (b. abt. 1747 d. [March]November 16, 1776) **208**
Orne, Benjamin [b. December 31, 1735] (d. September 7, 1736)
Orne, Charles [b. Apr 1, 1786, d. Dec 15, 1816] (Orne Tomb) **70**

Orne, Joseph [b. Jan 31, 1795, d. Sept 3, 1818] (Orne Tomb) **70**
Orne, Josiah (b. abt. 1745 d. June [21], 1789) **208**
Orne, Josiah [bapt. April 3, 1768 d. September 23, 1825] NS **208**
Orne, Naomi (b. abt. 1661 d. October 2, 1718)
Orne, William [b. abt. 1751 d. October 14, 1815] (Orne Tomb) **69**
Orrington, George [b. abt. 1806 d. February 21, 1829] NS
Osgood, Hannah (Buttolph) [b. December 9, 1689] (d. March 4, 1774)
Osgood, Martha (Ayre) [b. March 1, 1668] (d. September 10, 1760)
Osgood, Peter [b. August 30, 1663 d. September 24, 1753] (Unreadable)
Ouri, Edward [b. abt. 1826 d. June 9, 1840] NS **225**
Packer, Hephzibah (Drake) [b. July 4, 1659] (d. January 22, 1684/5)
Packer, Susana [Susannah] (b. abt. 1682 d. October 21, 1683)
Page, Elizabeth [Betsey] (b. abt. 1776 d. January 5, 1799) **82**
Page, Lois (Lee) [b. April 22, 1753] (d. June 6, 1779) **82**
Page, Samuel [b. December 3, 1749] (d. June 24, 1785) **82**
Page, Sarah (Porter) (b. abt. 1752 d. October 6, 1791)
Paine, Dinah [b. abt. 1728 d. November 2, 1828] NS
Palfray, Benjamin [b. November 8, 1767] (d. December 11, 1793)
Palfray, Warwick [bapt. October 23, 1715] (d. October 10, 1797)
Palmer, Child [b. August 3, 1818, d. August 3, 1818] NS
Parshley, [daughter] [b. abt. 1834 d. April 1, 1839] NS
Parshley, Albert [b. abt. 1837 d. August [16]10, 1839] NS
Parshley, Charles H. [b. abt. August, 1849 d. February 25, 1852] NS
Parshley, David Augustus [b. abt. February , 1842 d. August 18, 1843] NS
Parshley, Emily A. [b. abt. 1848 d. April 1, 1851] NS
Parshley, Lydia Ann [b. abt. 1840 d. June 20, 1846] NS
Parkman, Deliverance [b. June 3, 1651] (d. November 15, 1715) **111**
Parkman, Deliverance (b. abt. 1685 d. March 19, 1688)
Parkman, Margaret (Gardner) [b. July 14, 1664] (d. March 25, 1689) **111**
Parkman, Mehitabel (Waite) [b. September 15, 1658] (d. December [17]7, 1684) **111**
Parkman, Samuel [b. June 24, 1687] (d. September 20, 1688)
Parkman, Susannah (Clark) [bapt. March, 1643] (d. February 19, 1727/8) **111**
Patterson, William (b. abt. 1746 d. September 6, 1793)
Peeas, Daniel (b. abt. 1754 d. November 18, 1774)
Peele, Betsy (Smith) [b. August 21, 1768] (d. December [17 or 18], 1828) **148**
Peele, Elizabeth (Ropes) (b. abt. 1743 d. August 6, 1770) **148**
Peele, Elizabeth R [bapt. March 10, 1816] (d. October [21 or 24]27, 1882) **148**
Peele, Eunice (Sterns) (b. abt. 1733 d. June 20, 1780) **148**
Peele, Jonathan [b. December 16, 1702] (d. January 1, 1782)
Peele, Josiah [b. February, 1765] (d. June 20, 1784) **148**
Peele, Josiah [b. November, 1796] (d. [August]July 3, 1822) **148**
Peele, Margaret (Bartoll) [b. Feb. 11, 1682 d. Aug. 1728] (No Dates on Stone) **147**
Peele, Mary (Bartlett) [b. May 10, 1730] (d. May 4, 1771) **147**
Peele, Robert [b. August 12, 1712] (d. April 29, 1773) **147**
Peele, Robert [b. January 4, 1737] (d. June 12, 1792) **148**
Peele, Robert [b. April 19, 1767] (d. [March 21], 1842) **148**
Peele, Robert (b. March ?, 1794, d. April 4 or 7, 1874]) (Unreadable) **148**
Peele, Roger [b. January 25, 1676] (d. 1728) **147**

Peele, Sarah [b. abt. 1726 d. March 15, 1819] NS
Peele, Sarah (Brown) [b. October 4, 1770] (d. January 20, 1854) **148**
Peele, William [b. December 17, 1738] (d. March 4, 1817) **148**
Peele, William [b. April 30, 1799] (d. July 20, 1801)
Perkins, Eunice [b. abt. 1772 d. April 21, 1827] NS
Perkins, Peggy (Cheever) [b. October 1, 1777] (d. September 24, 1795)
Peters, Simeon [b. abt. 1781 d. July 6, 1830] NS **225**
Phelps, Rachel (b. January 12, 1741 d. September 5, 1776) **84**
Phillips, Christopher [d. July 24, 1699] NS
Phillips, Elizabeth (Lambert) (b. abt. 1747 d. August 12, 1798)
Phippen, David [b. July 27, 1775] (d. January 14, 1849)
Phippen, Joseph (b. abt. 1759 d. May 11, 1783)
Phippen, Lois (Hutchings) (b. abt. 1754 d. March 11, 1794)
Phippen, Margaret [b. abt. 1752 d. April 23, 1842] (Fisk Tomb)
Phippen, Mary (Lindall) [b. April 4, 1674] (d. March 19, 1722/3)
Phippen, Rachel (Guppy) (b. abt. 1658 d. February 1, 1710/11)
Phippen, Samuel [b. April 30, 1649] (d. February [11]1, 1717/8)
Phippen, Samuel (b. abt. 1744 d. February 22, 1797)
Phippen, Samuel [b. April 13, 1785] (d. October 2, 1804)
Phippen, Sarah (Hathorne) [b. abt. 1774 d. January 21, 1847] NS
Phippen, Ursula (Knapp) [b. abt. 1748 d. December 20, 1818] NS
Phippen, William [bapt. March 1, 1753] (d. May 28, 1796)
Pickman, Abigail (Lindall) [b. September 15, 1681] (d. March 24, 1737/8)
Pickman, Abigail (Willoughby) [b. April 4, 1679] (d. August 24, 1710)
Pickman, Benjamin (b. abt. 1625 d. December 31, 1708) **193**
Pickman, Benjamin (b. abt. 1673 d. April 26, 1719)
Pickman, Benjamin [b. November 7, 1740 d. May 12, 1819] (Pickman/Toppan Tomb) **151**
Pickman, Caleb [b. June 16, 1715] (d. June 4, 1737) **194**
Pickman, Elizabeth (Hardy) [bapt. February 28, 1650] (d. October 19, 1727) **193**
Pickman, Haskett Derby [b. Mar. 12, 1796 d. Oct. 22, 1815] (Pickman/Toppan Tomb) **155**
Pickman, Joshua [b. August 28, 1681] (d. January 24, 1750)
Pickman, Mary/Polly (Haraden/Harrenden) [bapt. Oct. 15, 1775 bur. Sep. 21, 1806] (Pickman/Toppan Tomb)
Pickman, Mary (Toppan) [b. Aug. 29, 1744 d. Apr 28, 1817] (Pickman/Toppan Tomb) **151**
Pickman, Mary Anne/Anna [b. Dec. 9, 1800 d. Jan. 2, 1809] (Pickman/Toppan Tomb] **155**
Pickman, Thomas Dr [b. abt. 1774 bur. January 5, 1817] (Has Tombstone in Harmony Grove) **153**
Pierce, Aaron [b. abt. 1817 d. December 10. 1819] NS
Pierce, Anna (Mansfield) [b. April 28, 1765 d. April 29, 1842] (Asa Pierce Tomb) **187**
Pierce, Asa [b. March 21, 1754 d. May 1, 1820] (Asa Pierce Tomb) **187**
Pierce, Betsey (Glover) [b. abt. 1778 d. July 8, 1835] (Nathan Pierce Tomb) **188**
Pierce, Ellen [b. December 9, 1806 d. March 11, 1875] (Nathan Pierce Tomb) **188**
Pierce, Mary [bapt. December 25, 1803 d. December 7, 1871] (Nathan Pierce Tomb) **188**
Pierce, Nathan [b. abt. 1749 d. May 22, 1812] (Nathan Pierce Tomb) **187**
Pierce, Nathan [b. November 12, 1775 d. July 6, 1848] (Nathan Pierce Tomb) **188**
Pierce, Nathan [b. abt. 1839 d. June 19, 1888] (Nathan Pierce Tomb)
Pierce, Rebecca (Allen) [b. June 12, 1743 d. July, 1815] (Nathan Pierce Tomb) **187**
Piniham, Samuel [b. abt. 1791 d. August 25, 1821] NS

Pitman, Mary [bapt. August 31, 1760] (d. May 31, 1802)

Pitman, Thomas [b. October ?, 1791] (d. January 17, 1792)

Porter, Anne Marie [b. abt. 1839 d. March 4, 1840] NS

Porter, Edward [b. April 19, 1721] (d. August 20, 1722)

Porter, Edward A. [b. abt. 1787, d. December 30, 1819] (Allen Tomb) **78**

Porter, Sarah (Chipman) [bapt. September 26, 1813 d. June 22, 1840] NS

Pousland, Richard [b. abt. 1802 d. May 2, 1826] NS

Pratt, Elias [b. August 23, 1702] (d. November 17, [1707]1706)

Pratt, Hannah [b. January 25, 1707] (d. February 9, 1765)

Pratt, John [b. ?, 1665] (d. March 12, 1729/30)

Pratt, Margaret (Maverick) [b. ?, 1672] (d. March 22, 1759)

Pratt, Maverick [b. July 30, 1713] (d. January 23, 1763)

Preble, Elizabeth (Derby) [b. March 1, 1769 d. February 1, 1799] (Possibly in Derby Tomb - Conflicting Information)

Prescott, Mary [bapt. March 17, 1771 d. September 1, 1825] (Unreadable)

Prescott, Mary [b. abt. 1783 d. September 15, 1823] NS

Prince, Louise [Loisa] (Lander) [b. February 20, 1785 d. November 14, 1839] NS

Prince, Martha (Derby) [bapt. April 29, 1744 d. June 26, 1802] (Derby Tomb) **58**

Proctor, Elizabeth (Hathorne) [bapt. July 15, 1773] (d. December 15, 1834)

Pulling, Edward [b. October 30, 1755] (d. December 1, 1799)

Pulling, Lois [b. November 29, 1764] (d. November 4, 1818)

Purchas, John [b. August 22, 1695] (d. September 17, 1712)

Putnam, [Boy] [b. February 5, 1794 d. November 22, 1794] (Fisk Tomb)

Putnam, Charles [b. October 19, 1802 d. January 1, 1863] (Fisk Tomb)

Putnam, Ebenezer [bapt. October 20, 1717] (d. August [12]10, 1788)

Putnam, Ebenezer [b. September 22, 1769 d. February 20, 1826] NS

Putnam, George [b. June 10, 1804 d. December 4, 1860] (Fisk Tomb)

Putnam, Harriet [b. February 5, 1794 d. November ?, 1794] (Fisk Tomb)

Putnam, Sarah [Sally] (Fiske) [b. June 30, 1772 d. January 8, 1795] (Fisk Tomb)

Putnam, Sarah (Sage) [b. October 9, 1809 d. March 11, 1896] (Fisk Tomb)

Ramsdall, Allen [b. January ?, 1799] (d. May 25, 1800)

Ramsdall, George [b. abt. 1799] (d. October 23, 1802)

Ramsdall, George [b. January ?, 1799] (d. July 6, 1800)

Ramsdall, Huldah (b. abt. 1766 d. June [8]5, 18[01])

Ramsdall, William (b. abt. 1792 d. May 14, 1801)

Rand, Mary (b. abt. 1734 d. September [4]3, 1819)

Ranson, Dinah [b. abt. 1792 d. July 7, 1819] NS **224**

Ranson, William [b. abt. 1789 d. June 10, 1826] NS **224**

Rantoul, Mary [b. September 17, 1755] (d. July 17, 1816) **90**

Rantoul, William (b. abt. 1794 d. July 7, 1816) **90**

Read, Elizabeth Holyoke [b. July 7, 1791] (d. July 22, 1793)

Read, Henry [b. September 30, 1809] (d. October 11, 1810)

Reed, Mary [Polly] (Archer) [b. April 1, 1776] (d. September 29, 1796) **183**

Reed, Paul (b. abt. 1735 d. January 21, 1799)

Remon, John [b. abt. 1788 d. April 4, 1851] NS

Remmon, John [b. abt. 1788 d. April 1, 1851] NS

Richardson, Betsey [b. December 24, 1788] (d. December 5, 1789)

Richardson, Joshua [b. February 14, 1745] (d. February 26, 1774) **34, 83**

Richardson, Mary [b. abt. 1743 d. August 18, 1821] NS
Richardson, Nathaniel [b. March 20, 1742] (d. January 25, 1796) **82**
Roach, Mercy (Brown) [b. February 25, 1765 d. May 26, 1830] NS
Robens, Mary [b. abt. 1783 d. November 8, 1839] NS
Robie, Mary (Bradstreet) [b. abt. 1741 bur. September 30, 1806] NS **220**
Robie, Thomas [b. abt. 1727 d. December 18, 1811] NS **220**
Robinson, Hannah [b. abt. 1745 or 1748 d. October 12 or 13, 1825 or 1828] NS
Robinson, Samuel [b. December 19, 1665] (d. [December]October 8, 1699)
Rogers, Elizabeth [b. July ?, 1644] (d. February 11, 1713/4)
Rogers, Sarah Knight [b. abt. April, 1838 d. October 2, 1842] NS
Rogers, John (b. abt. 1647 d. November 30, 1715)
Ropes, Daughter [b. abt. September 1824 d. February 27, 1826] NS
Ropes, Mrs. [b. abt. 1721 bur. November 5, 1807] NS
Ropes, Abigail [b. abt. 1785 d. January 5, 1846] (Orne Tomb)
Ropes, Benjamin [b. March 6, 1836 d. June 11, 1840] NS
Ropes, Daniel [b. June 13, 1737] (d. October 8, 1821) **173**
Ropes, Edward [b. November 9, 1838 d. May 19, 1840] NS
Ropes, George [b. October 17, 1727] (d. October 30, 1755) **174**
Ropes, George [b. September 18, 1755] (d. March 28, 1756) **174**
Ropes, Hannah [b. October 2, 791 d. July 16, 1862] (Orne Tomb)
Ropes, Hannah (Harraden) [b. September 1, 1768 d. June 29, 1845] (Orne Tomb)
Ropes, John [b. abt. 1763 d. July 9, 1828] NS
Ropes, John [b. abt. 1783 d. July 29, 1825]
Ropes, Mary (Brown) [b. abt. 1761 d. August 3, 1818] NS
Ropes, Priscilla (Lambert) (b. abt. 1739 d. September 22, 1808) **173**
Ropes, Rachel [b. abt. 1797 d. April 27, 1839] NS
Ropes, Ruth [b. December 20, 1768] (d. July 25, 1797) **174**
Ropes, Ruth [b. abt. 1800 d. November 20, 1826] NS
Ropes, William [b. May 6, 1758 d. March 25, 1828] NS
Rose, Anna (b. abt. 1715 d. January 17, 1796)
Rose, Brackley [Blackler] [b. abt. 1767 d. October 4, 1823] NS
Rose, Brackley (b. abt. 1795 d. April 18, 1796)
Rose, Eliza (b. abt. 1800 d. September [19]18, 1801)
Ross, Hannah (b. abt. 1749 d. October 31, 1812)
Ruck, Stephen (b. abt. 1663 d. March 17, 1741)
Russell, Abigail [bapt. June 12, 1737] (d. June 15, 1790)
Russell, Edward [b. 1739] (d. January 14, 1815)
Ryne, William [bapt. October 13, 1804] (d. October 3, 1826)
Sampson, Eunice [b. abt. 1754 d. January 20, 1789]
Sampson, Joseph (b. abt. 1755 d. December [3]6, 1793)
Sanders, Elizabeth [b. August 28, 1678] (d. June 25, 1708) **120**
Sanders, John [b. November 1, 1640] (d. June 9, 1694) **120**
Saul, Joseph (b. abt. 1751 d. August 13, 1825)
Saul, Joseph [b. abt. 1821 d. September 9, 1825] NS
Saul, Mary (b. abt. 1762 d. February [23]28, 1845)
Saul, Sarah [b. July 24, 1813] (d. January 30, 1816)
Saunder, Jonathan [bapt. July 10, 1785 d. February 22, 1844] (Mason Tomb)
Saunders, Hannah (Pickman) (b. abt. 1640 d. March 18, 1706/7) **120**

Saunders, Sarah (Gill) [b. abt. 1770 d. February 5, 1843] (Fisk Tomb)
Sawyer, Hannah (Mansfield) (b. abt. 1751 d. October 9, 1810)
Scobie, John [b. abt. 1764 d. July 26, 1823] (Mason Tomb) **76**
Scobie, Mary [b. August 27, 1804 d. October 15, 1890] (Mason Tomb) **76**
Scollay, Robert [b. May 17, 1732 d. March 7, 1732/3] NS
Seldon, Richard (b. abt. 1753 d. January 29, 1801)
Seldon, Robert (b. abt. 1760 d. September 4, 1797)
Shattock, Hannah [b. abt. 1624 d. September 14, 1701] (Unreadable) **101**
Shattock, Retire [b. March 28, 1664] (d. September 9, 1691)
Shattock, Samuel [b. September 7, 1668] (d. December 14, 1695) **104**
Shattock, Samuel (b. abt. 1630 d. June 6, 1689) **101**
Shepard, Elizabeth [b. abt. 1747 d. September 26, 1830] NS
Shepard, Eliza (Rea) [b. October 14, 1792 d. February 6, 1819]NS
Shillaber, Lemon [b. abt. 1777 d. September 26, 1825] NS
Short, Elizabeth (Parnal) [b. abt. 1772 d. May 3, 1840] NS
Short, James [b. abt. 1809 d. August 29, 1818] NS
Short, Joseph [b. February 7, 1835 d. November 16, 1844] NS
Silsbee, Martha (Prince) (No Information on Stone) **195**
Silsbee, Nathaniel [b. October 23, 1677] (d. January [2], 1769) **195**
Silsbee, Nathaniel (b. November 9, 1748 d. June 25, 1791) **194**
Silsbee, Rebecca (Reed) [b. abt. 1763 d. July 9, 1857] NS
Silsbee, Samuel [b. abt. 1763 d. June 7, 1822] NS
Silsbee, Sarah (Beckett) (b. February [15]26, 1749 d. [April 30]May, 1832) **194**
Silver, Clarrisa [Caroline] [b. abt. 1831 d. January 6, 1840] NS
Silver, William Augustus [b. abt. 1842 d. February 5, 1847] NS
Simmons, Elizabeth [bapt. September 6, 1741] (d. September 5, 1804)
Sims, Hannah [b. August 27, 1707 d. ?, 1744] (Unreadable Stone)
Sims, Richard [bapt. June 17, 1715 d. October 7, 1720] FS
Sims, Sarah (Norris) [bapt. November 29, 1730] (d. July [8]18, 1767)
Skery [Skerry], Daughter [b. ? bur. December 31, 1806] NS
Skery [Skerry], Francis [b. ? bur. January 20, 1805] NS
Skinner, Betsey [b. abt. 1792 d. July 7, 1845] NS
Sleuman, Margaret [b. abt. 1754 d. December 9, 1827] NS
Sleuman, Thomas [bapt. April 7, 1751 d. September 25, 1820] NS
Slocumb, William [b. September 14, 1820 d. September 20, 1820] NS
Sluman, Franklin (b. abt. 1824 d. October 18, 1825)
Smith, George [b. abt. 1819 d. September 11, 1821] NS
Smith, Jonathan [bapt. August 8, 1824 d. June 5, 1865] (Fisk Tomb)
Smith, Sarah (Leach) [b. abt. 1779 d. May 17, 1842] (Fisk Tomb)
Smith, Patience (Shattock) [b. November 18, 1666] (d. April 7, 1690) **32**
Smith, Stephen (b. abt. 1796 d. April 3, 1815)
Smith, Thomas (b. abt. 1767 d. April 11, 1771)
Smothers, Hannah (Mugford) [bapt. July 19, 1761] (d. March 11, 1844)
Smothers, Peter (b. abt. 1761 d. March 1, 1821)
Smothers, Peter [b. 1755 d. March 3, 1819] NS
Sparhawk, Eliza [b. abt. 1770 d. July 25, 1843][4] (Orne Tomb)
Sparhawk, John [b. September 1, 1713] (d. April 30, 1755) (Bradstreet Tomb) **166**
Stacey, Sarah (Miles) [b. abt. 1758 d. October 17, 1849] (Fisk Tomb)

Staniford, Judith [b. September 11, 1829 d. September 12, 1829] NS
Staniford, Sarah [b. September 11, 1829 d. September 12, 1829] NS
Stetson, Emeline [b. Sept 26, 1824 or abt. 1815 d. Jul 27, 1817] NS (Conflicting Information)
Stetson, Mary [b. abt. April, 1820 d. November 6, 1821] NS
Stetson, Nancy [b. abt. September 1817 d. October 4,1818] NS
Stevens, Mary [b. abt. 1763 d. January 22, 1820] NS
Still, Child [b. ? bur. April 25, 1807] NS
Stivers, Sarah (Fisk) [bapt. October 24, 1742 d. June 3, 1819] (Fisk Tomb)
Stocker, Mary [b. abt. 1797 d. January 26, 1802] (Unreadable)
Stocker, Mary (Herrick) (b. abt. 1773 d. October 22, 1799)
Stocker, William B. [b. abt. December, 1822 d. January 6, 1823] NS
Stone, Adeline [b. abt. 1820 d. December 1, 1823] NS
Stone, Elizabeth (Hardy) (b. abt. 1688 d. July 14, 1763)
Stone, Hannah [b. July 27, 1662] (d. April [17]14, 1691)
Stone, Robert [b. June 24, 1662 d. June 16, 1688] NS
Stone, Robert [b. March 4, 1687] (d. May 20, 1764)
Stone, Sarah [b. abt. 1682 d. August 22, 1708] NS
Stoone [Stone], Benjamin [b. February 28, 1665] (d. November 30, 1703)
Storey [Story], Alexander (b. abt. 1791 d. December 31, 1795) **42**
Storey [Story], Elinor (b. abt. 1792 d. September 13, 1794) **42**
Storey [Story], Sally (b. 1779 d. June 17, 1782) **42**
Strafford, Benjamin [b. abt. June 1818 d. September 9, 1819] NS
Sumner, Laura [Lora] P. [b. July 30, 1851 d. January 13, 1852] NS
Sumner, Margaret [b. abt. June, 1843 d. December 15, 1843] NS
Sumner, Sarah (Tufts) (b. abt. 1813 d. February [24]22, 1839)
Swan, Benjamin [b. abt. 1781 bur. September 9, 1808] NS
Swan, Mehitable [b. abt. 1786 bur. October 16, 1808] NS
Swasey, David (b. abt. 1783 d. August 26, 1807)
Swasey, Rachel [b. abt. 1761 d. May 11, 1845] NS
Sweetser, Polly [b. March 2, 1779] (d. October 5, 1800)
Swinnerton, Hannah (Bartholemew) [b. February 13, 1642] (d. December [13]23, 1713) **155**
Swinnerton, John (b. abt. 1633 d. January 6, 1690) **155**
Swinnerton, Mercy [b. December 24, 1684] (d. November [3]30, 1727)
Symonds, Child [b. ? bur. January 7, 1805] NS
Symonds, Child [bur. August 4, 1806 - Stillborn] NS
Symonds, Daughter [b. abt. 1820 d. September 8, 1821] NS
Symonds, Elizabeth [bapt. December 26, 1731] (d. October [13]15, 1814)
Symonds, Elizabeth (Masury) [bapt. May 30, 1807] (obit. July 22, 1837)
Symonds, Hannah (Skerry) [b. March 28, 1714] (d. March 1, 1736/7)
Symonds, Samuel [bapt. December 29, 1776 bur. June 14, 1808] NS
Symonds, Sarah (Hunt) [b. October 16, 1772] (d. October 29, 1832)
Symonds, Sally (Clarke) [b. abt. 1790 d. August 26, 1825] NS
Tayan, Michael [b. abt. 1805 d. May 24, 1840] NS
Taylor, Jonathan [b. abt. 1820 d. September 12, 1823] NS
Taylor, Mary [b. abt. 1787 d. June 2, 1828] NS
Teague, Caroline A. [b. abt. January, 1840 d. July 16, 1842] NS
Teague, George A.K. [b. abt. January, 1845 d. January 22, 1846] NS
Teague, George Augustus [b. abt. January, 1848 d. February 29, 1848] NS

Wakefield, Susana [b. February 20, 1680/1 d. August 14, 1682] (Unreadable)
Wakefield, Susana [b. January 26, 1682] (d. February 7, 1682/3)
Ward, Abigail [b. April 16, 1731] (d. May 22, 1731) **180**
Ward, Alicia (Burill) [b. abt. 1773 d. September 15, 1825] NS
Ward, Anne [b. March 22, 1735] (d. May 2, 1737) **180**
Ward, Benjamin [b. April 8, 1725] (d. August 11, 1806)
Ward, Deborah [b. July 28, 1700] (d. April 6, 1736)
Ward, Ebenezer [b. April 9, 1710] (d. March 3, 1791)
Ward, Ebenezer (b. April 13, 1737 d. April 13, 1737) **180**
Ward, Elisabeth [b. February 7, 1729] (d. April 11, 1737) **180**
Ward, Elisabeth (Webb) [b. December 27, 1709] (d. April 13, 1737) **179**
Ward, Elizabeth (Babbage) [b. February 22, 1738] (d. October 17, 1797)
Ward, Hannah (b. abt. 1777 d. December [31]30, 1795)
Ward, John [b. June 6, 1818] (d. January 16, 1822)
Ward, John (b. abt. 1653 d. October 7, 1732)
Ward, Jonathan [John] [b. abt. July, 1818 d. January 16, 1822] NS
Ward, Joshua [b. August 15, 1699] (d. December 2, 1779)
Ward, Joshua [bapt. October 29, 1752 d. September 14, 1825] NS
Ward, Joshua III [b. abt. 1758 d. May 2, 1827] NS
Ward, Mary (Farmer) (b. abt. 1749 d. December 29, 1810)
Ward, Mary (Osgood) [b. December 9, 1722] (d. April 30, 1796)
Ward, Miles [b. March 11, 1672] (d. August [29]30, 1764) **179**
Ward, Nathaniel [b. July 29, 1746 bapt. August 3, 1746] (d. October 12, 1768) **180**
Ward, Nathaniel [b. abt. 1778 d. March 29, 1825] NS
Ward, Priscilla (Hodges) [February 11, 1749 d. June 2, 1822] NS **183**
Ward, Rachel (Pickman) [b. July 25, 1717] (d. January 7, 1789)
Ward, Ruth (Woodward) (b. abt. 1714 d. June 5, 1787)
Ward, Samuel [b. April 30, 1740 d. July 21, 1812] NS **183**
Ward, Sarah [b. October 19, 1728] (d. August 10, 1729) **179**
Ward, Sarah (Massey) [b. July 25, 1669] (d. November 20, 1728) **179**
Watkins, Daughter [b. abt. 1833 d. March 8, 1839] NS
Watson, Abraham [b. August 20, 1712] (d. July 6, 1790)
Watson, Elizabeth (Pickering) [b. January 5, 1712] (d. October 11, 1797)
Webb, Joseph MacKey [b. May 26, 1827 d. March 22, 1828] NS
Webb, Peter (b. abt. 1658 d. February 12, 1717/8)
Webb, Priscilla [b. abt. 1175 d. March 8, 1856] NS
Webb, Ruth (Putnam) [b. June 27, 1768] (d. June 24, 1790)
Webber, Cornelius [b. abt. January, 1822 d. February 27, 1822] NS
Webber, George [b. abt. 1795 d. January 13, 1822] NS
Wellcome, Elizabeth (Lambert) (b. abt. 1765 d. October 20, 1793)
Wellman, Margaret (Brown) [d. January 6, 1849] NS
Wellman, Deborah [b. abt. May, 1820 d. June 5, 1820] NS
Wellman, John S [b. abt. April, 1852 d. September 10, 1852] (Browne Tomb)
Wellman, Mary (Browne) [b. January 3, 1824 d. September 9, 1858] (Browne Tomb)
Wellman, Sarah [Sally] (Browne) [b. June 15, 1774 d. April 24, 1853] (Browne Tomb)
Wells, Mehitable (Andrews) [b. April 18, 1816 d. March 1, 1864] NS
Wells, Nathaniel [b. abt. 1774 d. April 24[26, CR], 1826] NS
Wertman [Child] [b. January 1840 d. January 1840] NS

West, Edward Augustus [b. abt. December, 1827 d. August 23, 1828] NS
West, Elizabeth (Derby) [b. abt. 1762 bur. Mar. 11, 1814] (Derby Tomb) **60**
White, Abigail (Blaney) (b. abt. 1726 d. August 2, 1776) **30**
White, Betsy [b. abt. 1802 d. January 30, 1828] NS **224**
White, Eliza (Orne) [b. May 10, 1784, d. Mar 26, 1821] (Orne Tomb) **70**
White, Christopher [b. abt. 1757 d. January 1, 1823] NS **224**
White, Henry (b. abt. 1777 d. September 16, 1778)
White, John (b. abt. 1722 d. October [10]26, 1792)
White, Lucy [b. abt. 1792 d. November 15, 1818] NS **224**
Whitford, Rebekah [Rebecca] (b. abt. 1737 d. April 14, 1744) **145**
Whitford, Samuel [b. abt. 1759 bur. October 2, 1805] NS
Whittemore, Elizabeth [b. abt. 1747 d. October 23, 1799] NS
Wicks, Child [b. ? bur. April 1, 1808] NS
Wiggin, Thomas [bapt. October 29, 1795 d. November 2, 1849] NS
Wiggins, James [b. abt. 1789 d. June 18, 1822] NS
Wiggins, John [b. abt. 1789 d. April 4, 1819] NS
Wigings, Son [b. abt. 1819 d. November 13, 1821] NS
Wigings, Joseph (b. abt. 1744 d. November [3]4, 1821)
Wigings, Mary (b. abt. 1754 d. August [12]11, 1821)
Wigings, Richard (b. April 1, 1784 d. September 16, 1816)   .
Wilds, Joshua Jr [bapt. December 15, 1800 d. February 25, 1826] NS
Willard, Jane (Jacob) [b. September 8, 1681] (d. April 25, 1726)
Willard, Josiah [b. May 24, 1682 d. April 7, 1731] (Unreadable)
Willard, Martha (Jacobs) (b. abt. 1649 d. October [14], 1721)
Williams, Abigail (Russell) (b. abt. 1750 d. May 4, 1822)
Williams, George [b. February 10, 1731] (d. June 12, 1797)
Williams, Hannah (Hathorne) [b. May 30, 1730] (d. October 30, 1756)
Williams, Henrey [b. February 2, 1703] (d. June [11]14, 1750)
Williams, Henry [bapt. July 22, 1744] (d. August [14]17, 1814)
Williams, Samuel (b. abt. 1733 d. October 11, 1801)
Williams, Sarah (Porter) [bapt. August 26, 1739] (d. January 14, 1814)
Williams, Sophia [b. abt. 1786 d. October 21, 1825] NS
Williamson, Elizabeth [b. abt. April, 1822 d. September 7, 1822] NS
Willoughby, Abigail (Bartholemew) [b. August 6, 1650] (d. September 3, 1702) **89**
Willoughby, Bethia (Gedney) [b. May 27, 1672 d. November 24, 1713] (Gedney Tomb) **96**
Willoughby, Nehemiah [b. abt. 1647 d. November 6, 1702] NS **89**
Wilson, William [b. May 31, 1836] (d. July 4, 1839)
Wind, John [b. abt. 1653 d. October 7, 1732] NS
Winn, Marcia (b. abt. 1765 d. October 2, 1805)
Woodbridge, Dorcas [b. abt. 1776 d. March 6, 1820] NS
Woodbridge, Dudley [b. March 3, 1733] (d. October 21, 1799)
Woodbridge Dudley [b. January 1, 1764] (d. August 11, 1771)
Woodbridge, Martha [b. August 23, 1719] (d. February 10, 1726[/7])
Woodbury, Ruth A. (b. abt. 1832 d. June 11, 1843] NS
Woodbury, Sarah Cole [b. abt. September, 1827 d. March 29, 1844]
Wright, Male Child [b. August 9, 1854 d. August 10, 1854] NS
Wright, Mary (b. abt. 1752 d. July [26]27, 1819)
Wright, Mary [b. abt. 1851 d. September 29, 1852] NS

Wright, Mary (Remon) [b. abt. 1829 d. September 10, 1854] NS
Wyatt, Sarah [b. December 6, 1725 d. November 18, 1796] (Unreadable)
Wyatt, William (b. abt. 1725 d. December [10]9, 1796)
Yell, Rebecca [Rebeckah] [bapt. January 15, 1748/9 d. January 29, 1825] NS
Young, Child [b. abt. May, 1821 d. August 25, 1821] NS
Young, Eliza [b. abt. November, 1817 d. September 15, 1818] NS
Young, Widow [b. abt. 1749 d. February 8, 1826] NS

UNCONFIRMED

Allen, Ruth (Hodges) (b. October 24, 1727, bur. October 10, 1774) **78**
Andrews, Catherine (Seamore) [b. abt. 1749 d. March 26, 1802] NS **214**
Andrews, Nehemiah [b. October 21, 1779, d. ?] NS **214**
Burley, Mary (Upton) [b. abt. 1822 d. July 21, 1851] (Turner Tomb)
Diman, James [b. November 29, 1707 d. October 8, 1788] (Bradstreet Tomb) **170**
Fisk, John Jr [b. Feb 20, 1780, d. Feb. 7, 1801] (Fisk Tomb) **66**
Noyes, Nicholas (b. December 22, 1647, d. December 13, 1717) (Bradstreet Tomb) **166**

Bibliography and Further Reading

Bartholomew, George Wells. *Record of the Bartholomew family*. United States, n.p, (1885)

Bentley, William., Waters, A. G., Dalrymple, M., Waters, J. Gilbert., Essex Institute. *The Diary of William Bentley, D. D..* Salem, Mass.: The Essex institute

Burr, George Lincoln. *Narratives of the Witchcraft Cases, 1648-1706.* (1914)

Berry, Robert E. *Yankee Stargazer: the life of Nathaniel Bowditch.* New York: Whittlesey House. (1941)

Bouchard, Betty. *Our Silent Neighbors A Study of Gravestones in the Old Salem Area,* 2nd Ed. Gangi Printing, Salem (2000)

Campbell, Helen. *Anne Bradstreet and her time.* Boston: D Lothrop company, (1891)

Carlson, William. "Charter Street Cemetery Burial Records Salem, Massachusetts", Higginson Book Company (1993, rev 2009)

Cole, J.R. *The Visual Cemetery Guide to the Charter Street Cemetery* vol. 1-5, (2007)

Cousins, F., Riley, P. M. *The wood-carver of Salem: Samuel McIntire, his life and work.* Boston: Little, Brown, and Company. (1916)

Essex Institute historical collections. Salem, Mass.: Essex Institute.

Felt, Joseph B. *Annals of Salem.* 2d ed. Salem: W. & S. B. Ives. (1789-1869)

Forbes, Harriet M. *Gravestones of Early New England and the Men Who Made Them.* The Pyne Press, Princeton. (1927, 1955)

Gardner, F. Augustine. *Thomas Gardner: planter (Cape Ann 1623-1626; Salem, 1626 1674) and some of his descendants...* Salem, Mass.: Essex Institute. (1907)

Gavenda, David T., "The Goult-Pickman House in Salem, Massachusetts." Salem, MA. (1973)

Hawthorne, Nathaniel. *Passages from the American note-books.* Boston. (1867)

Lindsay, David. *Mayflower Bastard: A Stranger Among the Pilgrims,* Thomas Dunne Books, St. Martin's Press, New York (2002)

Lynde, Benjamin, Oliver, F. E. (Fitch Edward)., Lynde, B. *The diaries of Benjamin Lynde and of Benjamin Lynde, Jr..* Boston: Priv. print. [Cambridge, Riverside Press] (1880)

Mather, Cotton. *Magnalia Christi Americana* vol. 2, London, 1702.

McAllister, Jim. "A Brief History of Historic Salem, Inc" Salem, Massachusetts. (1994)

Morse, Alice. M. *Customs and Fashions in Old New England.* Charles Scribner's Sons, NY. (1893)

Norton, Mary Beth. *In the Devil's Snare,* Vintage Books, New York, (2003)

Paine, R. Delahaye. *The ships and sailors of old Salem: the record of a brilliant era of American achievement.* Chicago: A. C. McClurg. (1912)

Perley, Sidney. *The history of Salem, Massachusetts* vols 1-3. Salem, Mass. S. Perley

Pestana, Carla Gardina. "The Social World of Salem: William King's 1681 Blasphemy Trial." American Quarterly, vol. 41, no. 2, 1989, pp. 308-327. JSTOR, www.jstor.org/stable/2713027.

Philips, James D. *Salem in the Eighteenth Century,* Houghton Mifflin, New York (1937)

Philips, James D. *Salem in the Seventeenth Century*, Riverside Press, Cambridge, MA (1933)

Phillips, James D. "William Orne: A Distinguished but Forgotten Merchant." Proceedings of the Massachusetts Historical Society, vol. 67, 1941, pp. 168-177. JSTOR, www.jstor.org/stable/25080353.

Pulsifer, David. "Inscriptions from the Burying-Grounds of Salem, Massachusetts", James Loring, Boston, MA. (1837)

Roach, Marilynne K. *The Salem Witch Trials: A Day-by-Day Chronicle of a Community Under Siege*, Taylor Trade Publishing, (2004)

Roach, Marilynne K. *Six Women of Salem*, MJF Books, New York, (2013)

Roads, Samuel Jr. *The history and traditions of Marblehead*. Boston: Houghton, Osgood, (1880)

Salem Press Historical and Genealogical Records, Vols I & II, The Salem Press Printing and Publishing Co., Salem, MA. 1890-1892

Schwartz, D.K. (1942) "Peele's Pepper," Master's Thesis, New York University, Auraria Library Digital Collections

Sewall, Samuel. *Diary of Samuel Sewall: 1674-1729.* v. 1 [-3]. Boston: Massachusetts Historical Society

White, William Orne 1821-1911, and Eliza Orne White. *William Orne White, a Record of Ninety Years*. Boston: Houghton Mifflin, (1917)

Websites:

Ancestry.com

FamilySearch.org

HistoryofMassachusetts.org

Ma-vitalrecords.org

PICTURE CREDITS

All photographs, except those listed below, are the work of Daniel Fury and Lara Fury.

Bowman, George Ernest, "The Only Mayflower Gravestone," Photograph of Captain Richard More gravestone, undated. Public domain.

Eldridge, Hayley, "Henry Lawrence grave". Used with permission.

The following historical photographs are courtesy of the Phillips Library Collection, Peabody Essex Museum. Used with permission:

Cousins, Frank, "Nathaniel Ward gravestone (Librarian of Harvard College), Charter Street Burying Point, Salem, MA," undated, Frank Cousins Collection of Glass Plate Negatives, 1325. Digital Commonwealth, https://ark.digitalcommonwealth.org/ark:/50959/2b88rq12m (accessed April 16, 2021).

Cousins, Frank, "Doraty, wife of Phillip Cromwell, gravestone, Charter Street Burying Point, Salem, MA," undated, Frank Cousins Collection of Glass Plate Negatives, 312. Digital Commonwealth, https://ark.digitalcommonwealth.org/ark:/50959/2b88r256r (accessed April 16, 2021).

Cousins, Frank, "John and Anstis Crowninshield gravestones, Charter Street Burying Point, Salem, MA," undated, Frank Cousins Collection of Glass Plate Negatives, 3421. Courtesy of Phillips Library, Peabody Essex Museum, Rowley, MA. Digital Commonwealth, https://ark.digitalcommonwealth.org/ark:/50959/2b88sk98j (accessed April 13, 2021).

Cousins, Frank, "Judge Benjamin Lynde tomb, Charter Street Burying Point, Salem, MA," Photograph, undated, Frank Cousins Collection of Glass Plate Negatives, 668. Courtesy of Phillips Library, Peabody Essex Museum, Rowley, MA. Digital Commonwealth, https://ark.digitalcommonwealth.org/ark:/50959/2b88r964w (accessed April 13, 2021).

Cousins, Frank, "Monuments, Salem, Charter Street Cemetery", [ca. 1865-1914], Frank Cousins Collection of Glass Plate Negatives, Negative 465. Courtesy of Phillips Library, Peabody Essex Museum, Salem, MA.

Documents:

"Warrant for Apprehension of Giles Corey, Mary Warren, Abigail Hobbs & Bridget Bishop with Summons for Witnesses v. Corey and Others" and "Petition of Mary Esty and Sarah Cloyce" appear courtesy of Salem Witch Trials Documentary Archive, University of Virginia, Project Director: Benjamin Ray. Used with permission.

"Grants at Burying Point" and "Location of Wharves" illustrations originally from *The History of Salem Massachusetts, Volume 2* by Sydney Perley. Public domain.

About The Author

Daniel Fury is an author, historian, playwright, and tour guide in Salem, Massachusetts. He was born in Braintree, Massachusetts, and has been a resident of Salem for fifteen years. He previously co-wrote *Black Cat Tales: History and Hauntings of Old Salem* with his wife, Lara Fury. His fascination with the lives of Salem's former residents began over a decade ago, and started the process of research which led to the creation of this book; a collection of those Salem stories. He is a founding member of The Friends of the Downtown Salem Historic Cemeteries. He graduated from the University of Massachusetts: Boston in 2001.

Further Reading by Black Cat Tours Press:

Black Cat Tales: History and Hauntings of Old Salem

Take a Tour of Salem With Us!

www.BlackCatSalem.com